Praise for *The Hands*

"Fernandez is scathing on the co
about equity and diversity, ant⎽   ⎽ ⎽⎽⎽ ⎽⎽⎽⎽ ⎽⎽⎽⎽⎽⎽ ⎽⎽⎽ can't
deal with people actually defending themselves or challenging
authority. What he offers instead isn't heroics or militant slogans
or even measured analysis—it's the messy story of a 'fucked-up
person' trying to 'channel rage into something less destructive,' a
guy who tends to run face-first into danger but also has the good
sense to run away screaming when confronted with a knife-wielding
racist. Fernandez's account of violence, trauma, and loneliness is
hard to read in places, but there's an underlying sweetness here, a
hopefulness about flawed people helping each other out, a sense
that if we can get past the lies, we can remake this world together."
—Matthew N. Lyons, author of *Insurgent Supremacists: The
U.S. Far Right's Challenge to State and Empire*

"'I had a keen sense of right and wrong from an early age and simply
preferred to do the wrong thing,' says Josh Fernandez, who debuts
with a force, rigor, and candor that punches you in the gut. As a
trenchant critique of neoliberalism's facade, which pays lip service
to diversity and equity in academia, this memoir fights fire with fire,
rage with rage. Fernandez holds an unflinching mirror to people and
institutions who think good intentions are enough and arms a reader
with a language 'to defend themselves as the world turns in the last
gasp of white supremacy.' This book disrupts with the incandescent
lyricism of a poet's eye and unearths beauty in the darkest moments
of solitude, longing, and loss. 'Some see me as a good man,' says
Fernandez, 'so I remind them I am not. Some see me as evil, so I
show them why they are wrong. I am the sum of my life, little hands
tinkering away to make me better, my own hands fixing their work as I
go.' Put simply, this book is a verb, kindling to burn the house down."
—Marcelo Hernandez Castillo, author of *Children of the Land* and *Cenzontle*

THE HANDS THAT CRAFTED THE BOMB

Josh Fernandez

Portions of this book appear in *We Are Antifa: Expressions against Fascism, Racism, and Political Violence in the United States and Beyond*; *Hobo Camp Review*; *Sacramento News & Review*; *From Sac*; and the *Dominic J. Bazzanella Literary Journal*.

ISBN: 979–888–744–023–1 (paperback)
ISBN: 979–888–744–026–2 (ebook)
Library of Congress Control Number: 2023936719
Cover by John Yates / www.stealworks.com
Interior design by briandesign

10 9 8 7 6 5 4 3 2 1

PM Press
PO Box 23912
Oakland, CA 94623
www.pmpress.org

Printed in the USA.

CONTENTS

AUTHOR'S NOTE

This memoir is based on experiences over a forty-five-year period. Names have been changed, characters combined, and events compressed.

ACKNOWLEDGMENTS

I would like to acknowledge the writers and artists who have inspired, mentored, given advice, spoken with my students, given me a shot, and helped along the way: Art Luna, Jan Lee, Jenn De La Vega, Nick Brewer, Joey Garcia, Matt Saincome, Jon Kiefer, Skid Jones, Melinda Welsh, Kel Munger, Matt Bell, and Doug Rice. And to the LRCFT, Local 2279: Let's do it again.

I couldn't have been half as coherent without my fierce and tenacious editors, Amy Bee and Charles Allison, and all the good folks at PM Press.

For giving me strength, standing by my side, and repeatedly punching me in the face, I'd like to thank all the fighters at the Sacramento Community Self-Defense Collective.

To my sisters, Rebecca and Lauren, my sun and stars.

To my parents, John and Sylvia, whose love I feel, even through the static.

To my father, Bobby Fernandez, who taught me the art of chaos.

And, of course, Crystal, Ezra, and Luna, who are always by my side, playing, loving, dreaming, and conducting this silly orchestra of madness.

In memory of Randy Murray, aka Rasar Amani, whose art is forever with us.

To all the SHARP, RASH, and 161 crews: Stay dangerous.

HOW TO GET FIRED

I am a Mexican, but not dark like my ancestors tucked in Mexico's hills or the dry Sonoran Desert. My skin is the color of the strip malls that line Highway 50, a route from Sacramento, where I live, to Maryland—the loneliest road in America. Because of my racial ambiguity, I see the school administrators eyeing me, wondering if I'm easier to tame.

My dean is sitting at the table with the vice president. And there's another person at the table, a confused-looking white man in a suit. He's smiling at me but not saying anything.

"Who's he?" I say.

"That's the athletics dean," my dean says with no further explanation, as if it's perfectly natural for the athletics dean to be at all disciplinary meetings, like I'm taking part in some freak show where all the rubber-neckers crowd around to gawk.

Because I understand the severity of being called before the college administration, I bring with me two union reps: James, our campus president, and the executive director, Robert, a surly old man who still goes to the gym. They're both angry they're here; the ridiculousness of the administrators dragging us into this shitshow carves a frown on both their faces. I love that their anger is visible. If you're representing me, I want you to be angry. I want you to have skin in the game. I want Johnnie Cochran. Or the guy who represented Ted Bundy. I want them to throw all morals and ethics out the window and defend me by any means necessary. I want them to enter the room, set fire to it, and then walk away in slow motion, leaving a pile of glowing embers in the distance. They sit next to me stewing at the conference table, large yellow paper pads resting on the table like shields before a battle.

James and Robert can't stand what the administration is doing to me, and they give me their word that nothing will happen, that the district will waste all its money trying to get rid of me, but it won't. I'll get my tenure, if it's the last thing they do. Still, I'm scared. I have a family. A wife and two beautiful kids who have gotten used to the plush Macy's couch I bought with the salary that I'm certain will be taken away.

My dean slides three pieces of paper toward me like a detective on a *CSI* show.

It's their evidence.

The first piece of evidence is a flyer for a community self-defense class that I posted to the Queer Straight Alliance Facebook page. It says *Antifascist Fighting Club* and has a picture of a person with a bandanna over his face. Next is another flyer for the class, with a picture of a group of people in pink masks with *Bash Back!* scrawled at the top. Their last piece of evidence is a printout of a Gmail account. It's the password to our campus club, the Campus Antifascist Network. The password is: k1llnazis.

I look at the two administrators quizzically. "This is it?"

They look back at me like I just got caught standing over the freshly butchered corpse of JonBenét Ramsey.

I give them the Seinfeld: "Okay ... and?!" It's a look I've perfected in the classroom when my students try to pull some bullshit.

My dean clears his throat. "I know you might think this is superficial, but—"

"Those are pictures," I interrupt.

"Yes, but he has a mask on," he says, pointing to a drawing of a person in a mask. "And it says 'Bash Back.'"

"Queer people are getting beaten in the streets," I say. "This is a response to that."

I try to explain that Bash Back! was a movement born out of necessity in 2007 to solidify a radical queer base, to literally save the lives of queers from right-wing terror. They bash us, and we bash back, was the basic idea. Seems pretty fair to me.

The vice president smiles like a madwoman and nods in agreement, as if to say, *Yes, we get it. Don't worry; this is all just a formality.*

There's true rage behind her fake smiles and wild eyes. I still remember her enthusiasm when she hired me and her giddy tone when she told me I got the job. Her eagerness probably wore away as soon as she understood the person I am: a thorn in the side of everything I think is unfair—even the institution she's pledged her allegiance to. She hates me and wants more than anything for me not to work here anymore.

They think I don't know that the wheels are in motion to get rid of me at any cost, but I can see the blood dripping from their fangs. Their little jokes, their dumb smiles, their tiny brains filled with neoliberal buzzwords, like *Night of the Living Dead* zombies, lurching across the campus growling, "Equity and diversityyyyyy." It's all bullshit. They know it. I know it. But nobody's supposed to say anything, like some unwritten pact of professionalism we're all presumed to follow.

I learned much sitting through countless meetings when I joined the Equity and Diversity Committee. People who have dedicated their lives to education with little break in their paths from high school to college to graduate school—the liberals or progressives or whatever fashionable name they use—are, on paper, for all the right things: decolonization, gay rights, Black and Brown liberation. But it's just on paper. It's stuff they read about in books. It's stuff they vote for. They want gay rights but can't feel the brick in their hands before it's lofted into a line of cops at the Stonewall Inn. They want equity but don't understand what it's like to be called a wetback while wiping the spit of a whiteboy out of your eye. They don't understand that equity doesn't come from books. It doesn't come from ticking a box on a ballot. It comes from discomfort. From struggle. Somebody's got to get hurt.

"But you said your club wasn't violent," the dean says.

"We're not," I say.

It's the truth. Our campus is affluent and mostly white, a demographic that brings with it a conservative, often dangerous ideology, especially for queer and Brown students. I helped our students start a chapter of the Campus Antifascist Network to get together to talk about politics, create flyers and zines, and occasionally attend protests.

My dean points to the flyer for the self-defense class, which has nothing to do with the school or our club. It's a separate entity altogether. But they love this piece of evidence, the drawing of the masked fighter standing with his fists up in front of a black flag with the text *Antifascist Fighting Club* in bold letters above. I can tell by how they're eyeing the flyer—like demons about to feast upon a young soul.

"This flyer is for a self-defense class. Self-defense is . . . self-defense," I say. "We're not teaching people to go out and punch people. We're teaching people from marginalized communities how to defend themselves."

They're unmoved. Their evidence has locked them into one narrative: I've been leading students to commit violence at political protests. The thought of that is too ridiculous to entertain. I can't even get my students to turn in their fucking assignments on time.

The vice president can't contain herself. "But can't you see how if someone went to a protest and got hurt, this could come back on us?" she says. "We could be liable."

"Okay, sure," I say. "But this has nothing to do with the school. I posted this flyer on the Queer Straight Alliance Facebook page because I thought people would be interested."

It turns out they *were* interested. I hosted the class in my backyard. Two students came over early on the first night to paint banners for an upcoming protest and eat dinner with my family. Some people from the community came. My son, Ezra, who was four then, ran around the house and helped paint the lettering while sixteen-month-old Luna pointed at stuff and ate strawberries in the backyard. As more people arrived for the class, we shared food and gathered in the yard, doing stretches and some core exercises, then practicing jabs and hooks. I put on some pads and sparred with a skinhead who punched me so hard in the face that I closed my eyes and discovered a new galaxy behind my eyelids. We kept sparring until it got dark, the moon barely lighting my backyard. By the night's end, we were all out of breath. We sat in a circle in the dark and talked for another hour or so. We couldn't wait until the next Saturday rolled around. I'm not sure exactly what happens in church, but these self-defense classes became something like our church: a ceremony of physical exertion and human connection that can't be taught in a classroom. What is education if not an awakening of the senses? Or is education simply a script read by a tired old man that doesn't end until the bell rings?

By the end of the meeting, the forced smiles on the administrators' faces tell me everything I need to know about how the meeting just went: I'm fucked.

"We'll be in touch," my dean says, excusing me from the room.

I get up from my chair shaking my head, unable to hide my rage. James and Robert follow me out, and we shoot each other glances but don't know what to say. We're all confused, but mostly pissed. "It's okay, buddy," James says. "This is bullshit."

"Yeah," I agree. "Fucking bullshit."

I walk back to my office through the quad, where a class of students is outside with rulers and they all seem to be measuring random shit. One student kneels on the concrete, measuring a plant stem. Another is measuring a stone wall. Another student digs cautiously through a trash can. Community college is often a confusing place.

A week after the meeting with the administrators, I get a letter in the mail from the district lawyer informing me that the district has opened an investigation into whether I am "soliciting students for potentially dangerous activities," which sounds so fucked up when I say it to myself, like I'm teaching a bomb-making class out of the back of my van.

When I get to work on Monday, my Outlook is full of messages from deans and administrators. I shut off my computer and walk out to the quad to get a bit of sun before my class starts. Our campus sits atop a hill that overlooks other hills peppered with multimillion-dollar homes. Some of my students live in those homes, their unfinished, unintelligible essays turned in on their parents' expensively thick monogrammed printer paper.

My colleagues pass by but don't say anything. I see one who pulled me aside once to warn me: *You shouldn't say anything bad about cops. After all, what if one of your students has a dad that's a cop?* If I went through every day trying not to offend my students, I wouldn't be able to say anything. I don't worry about that kind of shit. Some of my colleagues put their heads down when they get close. I'm wondering how the news travels so fast, but then I remember that my colleagues love this kind of thing—the punitive culture, the discipline, the gossip—as long as it's not happening to them. I say hi to one of the math professors, but she pretends not to hear me and walks past. I get it. Nobody wants to be associated with a professor who solicits students for possibly dangerous activities.

In the quad, I watch two military men in fatigues approaching students as they walk to class. One of the soldiers is burly and white, and the other is a skinny Mexican. They stop a Black kid, talk to him for a second, then hand him a brochure. I think about the letter I got in the mail—*soliciting students for potentially dangerous activities*. The military men continue passing out pamphlets to students as they head to class. Everyone takes one. Some smile and talk to the men in fatigues, enthusiastically nodding their heads. I walk up to one of the recruiters, and he gives me a glossy pamphlet. On the cover is the silhouette of two soldiers jumping out of a helicopter with machine guns. It seems pretty dangerous to me.

The more I think about it, the more I understand how I got here. I hated teachers for my whole life. I couldn't stand sitting in those uncomfortable desks at the back of the room, some hungover old lady or sourpuss old man wagging their finger in my direction, any lesson to be learned overshadowed by their overblown sense of importance. As if it wouldn't be easier to sit in front of a book at home, without all the distractions of girls and bullies and giant cafeteria cookies, and learn to divide fractions by ourselves. Especially now, with YouTube. I don't know why anyone goes to school at all.

When I interviewed for this job, I talked about how I was perfectly fit to teach. All my flaws, my struggle to maintain sanity in a world whose premise I reject, gave me insight. The interview panel nodded their heads at the idea of a good teacher but a flawed man, until the reality of a flawed man entered their institution. Their idea of *good* was probably some intangible academic theory they learned in a contemporary issues course while getting their doctorates in education. Maybe a paragraph of an entire book. Most people like the idea of a fucked-up person redeeming himself until they're put face-to-face with the fucked-up person. The textbooks go out the window. Words are easier to digest than the reality of a fucked-up man working in their institution.

So many times, I've thought, *This job isn't for me*. Which is probably why I took it, part of a sick obsession with making the wrong choices. Maybe my stepdad is right about me. Maybe my mom is right about me. And the administrators. I'm no good. A perpetual maker of bad choices. An eternal self-destructor.

It is me. I am the fucked-up man.

I remember reading about another fucked-up man, this old Mexican priest called Blessed Miguel Pro. He was a Jesuit. And a charmer. Everyone seemed to love the lightness of his presence, his wit, and his way with words. On his first assignment as a priest, he went to Belgium to preach the Gospel to the miners, who were mostly a ragtag bunch of communists and anarchists. But Pro was able to convert many of them using the likability he had come to rely on time after time. When he returned to Mexico, it was under the presidency of the extremely anti-Catholic Plutarco Elías Calles, who instituted the Calles Law, which punished priests who spoke out against the government. Pro went underground, conducting church business under a shadow of secrecy. He probably knew it was a bad idea, that he'd be punished, but he was just trying to do something good. He was eventually arrested and released but kept under a watchful eye by the government. When the incoming president, Álvaro Obregón, was wounded by an assassination attempt, Pro was arrested and charged for the crime without a trial, and he was eventually lined against a wall and executed.

Not that I'm some sort of preacher. Or renegade. It's not that I'm even courageous. I'm actually the opposite. I don't give a shit about much, and I'm a coward with no skills other than teaching. But I'm always misunderstood by those in power. I don't necessarily want to kill them or destroy them. I mostly just want them to leave me alone.

I spend a lot of time in my office now with the door closed, staring into my computer screen, mimicking a regular man who is working, unable to do much but read historical texts about all the dead people of the world, playing my life before me as a prisoner might as he sweats in the executioner's chair. Dramatic, I know. But I imagine the executioner standing behind the mirrored glass, waiting for his cue to flip the switch. The wires are tucked neatly into the machinery of the chair to maintain the appearance of safety, to show the condemned this is all humane. Sit down. It's just a fucking chair. There will be no pain. This is a just punishment for the crime committed. This is fair. The damned prisoner pleads his innocence one last time, to no avail. He understands exactly what is happening. He is going to die. All that's left is to replay the entirety of his life, like an uncut film, trying to figure out where it all went wrong and how much pain will be involved when the current finally runs through his system.

Sunshine

To understand how I ended up here, a middle-aged man about to get fired from his job for starting an antifascist club with his students, we have to go back to the first thing I remember, which is my sister.

Her name was Sunshine.

Seriously.

We didn't know it then, but my dad was in the early stages of psychosis and named her Sunshine before he lost his mind and left his family in Sacramento. He wanted to name me Bear, but my mom drew the line and named me something normal, maybe so I wouldn't get teased, but more likely so she wouldn't get teased. She wanted everything to be regular and didn't want to draw any extra attention to herself. She went with Joshua. It's almost like she found the name on a discount rack at Sears. Cheap enough. Not offensive to anybody. It's fine. We'll take it.

The name Sunshine fit my sister. She was happy and energetic, and people basked in her presence. I could see the entire world reflected in her big, bright eyes. My eyes were matte black, like an unfinished automobile, glossless and utilitarian. She was eight. I was five. She was happy. I wasn't.

While our parents worked, a woman named Eva babysat us. She spoke mostly in Spanish. She sat us in front of the TV and turned on PBS— *Sesame Street*, *Mister Rogers' Neighborhood*, Bob Ross, and nature shows where insects ripped the heads from other insects. Everything was interesting to my sister. The sky. The street. My mom's face. The little bees that buzzed through the flower patch. All of it. I was so bored with everything that I decided to watch TV sitting on my head while Eva sat on the couch right side up. I know *Sesame Street* was supposed to be fascinating to children with the little colorful monsters and the Brown guy with the guitar, but I didn't care about the spectacle. It was just something to do while I was upside down, my brown velour shirt with yellow stripes bunched over my chin, belly button out like a third eye. I practiced sitting on my head for extended periods. I got good at it too. So good that I eventually preferred living that way: everything upside down. I could sit forever with my head and back resting against the wall, blood rushing from my toes to my brain, while upside-down polar bears fucked on the upside-down tundra. Sometimes I'd fall asleep, then wake up still upside down. Other times I'd fall asleep, topple over mid-dream, and wake up with my face smashed against the wall. If that happened, I'd slide my head against the wall, invert my body again, and continue watching TV. I imagined that my upside-downness was a nuisance to everyone, that they gathered in rooms together to speak in hushed tones about my upside-down problem. *Did you see him today, that boy? His face was blood-red like some kind of demon!* But I don't think anyone noticed or cared.

"Bye," Sunshine said, her bright eyes beaming toward the sidewalk where our neighbors skidded around the block on their Big Wheels. They'd call my name, and I'd pretend not to hear. They couldn't compete with upside-down Oscar the Grouch, upside-down Mister Rogers, the upside-down man painting happy upside-down clouds, upside-down cannibalistic insects, and naked upside-down islanders swinging their upside-down tits in ritual. I'd rather stay indoors.

Sunshine had more friends than I. Friends seemed too hard to manage. They always wanted to take my things. Or play with my toys. I didn't know how I was supposed to act around them. One time I went to a birthday party where the little boy unwrapped his Star Wars X-wing starfighter and set it aside to unwrap more presents. I played with it while they ate cake, and when I tried to adjust its wing, it snapped. I placed the pieces back together, hastily left the party, and never talked to any of them again. They never spoke to me either—an unwritten contract to which we all agreed.

Sunshine played and played and played, and everyone loved her. "Sunshine!" they'd say. "Oh, you *are* a sunshine." I felt like a little tombstone—an inverted tombstone with etchings too worn to read. Nobody bent down, pinched my cheeks, and said, "Oh, look at how Josh he is! He is so Josh-like!"

When I wasn't upside down, I wanted to be upside down. In the grocery store, I'd tilt my head around and down until I could finally read the flipped-over packages—Fruit Loops and Morton salt and canned peaches all looked more delicious in my overturned world. I pretended that I couldn't do anything until I was upside down. My mom showed me a cereal box and I stared straight ahead like I was in a coma, unable to communicate in this right-side-up world, and my mom's eyebrows raised. She was so beautiful in her long dress with flowers of every color moving with the fabric. I wonder now if my mother hated me for being an upside-down boy. If she wanted a regular boy who wanted to be right side up. If she did, she didn't show it.

At night she sat on the edge of the bed, ran her soft fingers against my back—"feelies," she called them—and read fables of the origins of things, like how the zebra got his stripes or how elephants got their tusks, until my eyelids heavied and I fell asleep, lying horizontally, like a regular boy.

I wish she had told me the story of when she met my father. It was at a march against the Los Angeles police after they killed the Chicano journalist Ruben Salazar with a tear gas projectile. Hundreds of Brown people flooded the streets, shouting with rage, so furious that they all fell in love with each other, even if they weren't meant to be.

But she never told that story. I only heard it secondhand. She only told normal stories, the ones that couldn't hurt me.

It was night. A sliver of moon peeked through the blinds. I sprawled across my mom's legs on the couch while she ran her fingers across my back.

"I love you," she said.

I couldn't say anything back. I didn't know what to say. Love embarrassed me. The thought of it turned my cheeks red.

Matte black absorbs but doesn't reflect.

Sunshine is my sister who shares my blood but is so different from me. She is the light and I am the dark. That's what I thought. But we share the blood of our mother. We share the blood of our father. She is strong when she needs to be. She can appear normal sometimes. Like me, she is an antiauthoritarian. She is a rebel. She is flawed. She is broken. She is whole. She is my mother. She is my father. None of us are normal. We are so fucked up in so many ways that it forms a sort of beauty. Like an alleyway in the corner of the city, filled with graffiti and trash, the colors are an abstract painting, so gross that you can't help but notice its magnificence.

Robert Villalobos Fernandez

My dad walked through the kitchen, chest out, ponytail swinging from side to side, holding a glass of lemonade, ice cubes clinking with each step.

"Hey, maaaan!" he said like a Mexican surfer, slow and drawn out. "We're going to the flea market. Get your sister."

I jumped up and scrambled to find Sunshine, who was in her room making ballerina poses in front of a mirror.

"Come. On," I said, annoyed.

"Fine," she shrugged, finishing a half-assed grand plié.

I loved when our dad took us places. The store. The park. Anywhere.

We drove to the market through our neighborhood in Sacramento, the part with playgrounds every few blocks and lush trees hanging over the sidewalks, and pulled into the lot full of cars. My dad tapped out the drums to Earth, Wind & Fire's "Let's Groove" on the steering wheel until we pulled into the flea market parking lot, full of beat-up cars just like ours.

We wandered around the market looking at the toys, the colorful dresses on sales racks, the wobbly tables full of old memorabilia. Old men sitting in chairs eyed us carefully so we wouldn't slip something into our pockets. Dad skipped over to a booth and came back with a maniacal grin and a bag of weird persimmon candy coated in coconut. He looked like a little kid with his bag of orange candy. Sunshine and I glanced at each other with exaggerated frowns. It looked so disgusting that I didn't want any, and neither did Sunshine.

"Time to go," our dad said, and we skipped back to the car.

He buckled us in and opened his bag of candy, pulling out an orange glob covered in white flakes. He held one of the pieces up to the light and smiled.

"You sure?" he asked.

My sister and I held our noses.

"Your loss," he said, and he stuffed one of the nuggets into his mouth. He chewed, then started the car, setting the bag on the floor. Before he could pull out of the parking lot, a weird look contorted his face, which began to redden and went completely flush. His eyes scrunched up and his mouth puckered under his beard. "Oh shit."

And then he heaved—hurled a massive stream of vomit that spewed onto the steering wheel, the dashboard, everywhere.

"Fuck!" he screamed. "Shit!"

He balled his fist and punched the steering wheel until his hand slipped on the barf and hit the dashboard, slicing his knuckle wide open. He beat the steering wheel again and again, the blood mixing with vomit, and I gagged in disgust. My sister found a shirt in the back seat and gave it to my father, who clumsily sopped up all the barf while sulking in the front seat.

We rolled the windows down for the ride home, but it was still rancid in the car. My dad muttered curse words all the way back, and when we got home, he slammed the car door and stormed into the house.

I looked at Sunshine for a bit of light, but she looked just as sullen as I did. That incredible joy of our father that turned to violent anger, like an unseen hand flipping a switch in his brain. More often I would catch him with a faraway glazed look, the muscles in his face too relaxed to be human, as if he was wearing a cheaply made mask of himself. I didn't really know what was happening with my dad, but I knew that I didn't want to be like him. He was too weird. Too mad. Too scary.

My parents began arguing all the time, and dad started ranting about God. I'd only heard about God from friends. A kid in my class had parents who listened to heavy metal. They blasted Dio's "Heaven and Hell," and I'd never heard anything so amazing: the loud, crunchy guitars and Ronnie James Dio screaming about the devil.

One day, I asked Dad about the devil while we were driving to the grocery store.

"Don't talk about the devil."

I asked him if I could have a new name.

"You already have a name," he said.

"But my name is stupid."

"Your mom says it's strong."

"I'm not strong."

"Your name is in the Bible, you know."

"The devil is in the Bible," I said.

"Fucking hell," he cried, slamming his feet on the brakes. His shit-orange station wagon skidded into a bush, and it took all my strength not to laugh. Something changed in his eyes. A glow. A scary energy, like an electric current that ran through his body and shot out through his eyes. He scowled around the house with that look until he finally split for good. He pulled up all the marijuana plants in the backyard and took off, and my mother wouldn't tell me where. All I know is that he went crazy. His last day, he looked at me the way someone looks at their glass when they're expecting water but they get milk. He didn't say a word. I mouthed the word *devil* under my breath to see what he would do. He pretended not to hear.

Maybe that's why he went crazy. No son of his would mention the devil's name. No son of his would pervert his Bible. The Old Testament, the New Testament, the hand-cutting, the slave-checking, the sin, the penance, all of it. It all was real for him. Realer than anything. Realer than his family. Realer than the Chicanos, his people, our people, who he used to believe in and march for in the streets. In a sense, I admired his compulsion to desire something—in his case, a higher power, and more specifically, God—so unconditionally that it would tear the heart from his own child.

He took off to Samoa, where he was going to practice law. He hadn't passed the bar exam and didn't have any job prospects, so it wasn't exactly a solid plan, but he did it anyway, another trait he passed on to me—the great Fernandez clan, known for poverty and fistfights in the street. We run face-first into trouble, if only to make a grand, dramatic statement to the world.

A Place Where the Snails Can Kill You

Not long after he split, Dad somehow convinced my mom to let us visit him on the island of Samoa. She never told us why, but I imagine she had yet to develop a complete distrust of the world, so she reluctantly packed up my sister and me and sent us to Samoa, where we were only supposed to visit for a week.

Samoa's damp air clung to my body like a wet layer of clothing. Everything was dark brown and gray. When I first arrived on the island, a gigantic snail parked itself right in the middle of our walkway, and I reached out to touch its shell.

"Don't!" My dad grabbed my arm and yanked me back. "That thing will kill you!"

I didn't know if he was serious. It was hard to imagine the snail, so fat and slow, as a child murderer, but I didn't want to take any chances, so I left it alone.

Our house was a *fale*, a little hut without windows, not far from the beach. Our neighbor, a humongous man named Tamatoa, took us spearfishing in the ocean on a raft with a glass window to watch the slithering creatures beneath us. We hiked through the wet mountains and sucked on sugarcane, careful not to step on the gigantic poisonous snails. We rode on an old wooden boat to see the grave of Robert Louis Stevenson and watched my father shoot a bat out of the foggy sky with a shotgun. Our neighbor's daughter took me on a secret path in the jungle to a little store where the owner gave us candies that we sucked on underneath a giant palm tree. And there was Maggie, a white lady with glasses, who wasn't my mom. She stormed off one day, yelling "Fuck you" at my dad, and we never saw her again.

We didn't go to school. We ran through the jungle with our neighbors. We looked under rocks for moving insects. We listened to the waves crashing back and forth, waiting for our dad to return home from town.

We played and played in the breezy openness of the island. Sunshine made some friends. She wore colorful dresses and put flowers in her hair. I wore a *lavalava* with no shoes, and my feet hardened from running barefoot on the rocks.

Sometimes I wonder what my life would have been if I had stayed there, if I'd have been an islander, a simpler version of myself who didn't have to unfurl his twisted wires every few years to avoid a short circuit. Or would I have found a way to ruin myself in the same ways, only in a more tropical setting?

I hardly noticed that I had been gone past the week I was supposed to be there. Two weeks. Three. A month.

The day my mom and grandma would come to get us, my dad told Sunshine and me to come to him. He kneeled to our level, and took our hands in his. He spoke softly, like he was about to tell us a wonderful secret.

"If they come," he said, "get on my shoulders and kick them."

It was a simple plan. An exciting one.

They came. First the police, then my grandma and my mom, and behind them, rows of combatants moved through the thick, salty air.

I got on my dad's shoulders just like we planned. Sunshine strode next to us, marching like a little soldier in a floral dress. Dad charged at the first cop, and I kicked his gloved hand away victoriously. But more cops swarmed, and my little legs couldn't kick anymore.

There was no crying. No anger. Nothing. The only evidence I have of the aftermath is a faded old photograph I found in a box at my mom's house. It's of my sister, my grandma, and me sitting on a bench, the gray ocean shining behind us. We're eating ice cream cones. I'm looking at my sister with a huge grin as if nothing has happened. As if my entire life hasn't just been forcibly rearranged, my family structure dissipated into the atmosphere like smoke after a car wreck.

I'd just kicked my grandma in the face and physically fought the FBI, and there I was, sitting on a bench, smiling because I was eating an ice cream cone. If nothing else, I am easy to bribe.

From the ice cream shop to the airport, then from the airplane to the mainland, and on to the suburb of Boston called Brookline, where a little rental house with a backyard full of vines good for swinging waited for us.

We entered our new life sometime around Christmas. It was snowing then in Brookline. Blankets of snow covered the streets and the trees and the mailboxes. It looked like a holiday card. It was the opposite of Samoa, where poisonous creatures lurked in every corner.

Nothing could kill you in Brookline.

And there I was, fancy-free on the other side of the planet, standing like Santa's little helper next to my new stepdad. John was one of my mom's friends from Sacramento, an Irish man with a mustache. He had a hyper dog named Tar who once jumped through John's living room window.

I loved John when he was my mom's friend. I wasn't so sure about this new situation.

They got married when I was in Samoa.

I was supposed to call him Dad.

There was a Christmas tree.

And gifts.

It was warm, and it smelled good.

I had no choice but to bask in it. We had everything. A house. A car. Food. All the love we could ever want. But I wanted something else. I wanted to know what was going on. I wanted to know the answers. I wanted my mom to sit me down and cry and hug me and tell me that my father was a fucking psychopath and she'd had to marry her friend John out of survival. Instead I was presented with a new, beautiful life to wrap myself up in like a warm blanket designed to help me forget the cold of the world.

That Christmas I got more presents than I'd ever seen, one of them an electric race car set. My new dad and I spent the day putting it together, and we took turns with the controller, pressing the trigger, watching the cars speed around the track so fast that they barely hung on, as the snow fell all day over the little suburb. Everything looked like a dream, like we lived inside a globe that you shake around violently, then stop to let the fake snow fall. Later, I woke up in the middle of the night. I heard the cars going around the track, so I tiptoed into the living room. My new dad, my stepdad, was stretched out on his side with the trigger in his hand, watching the cars race around and around and around again. I watched for a minute before quietly padding back to my bed, but I couldn't get the image out of my head: my stepdad alone on the floor, playing with a present that wasn't even his. I cried myself to sleep.

Maybe I cried because we weren't blood, because he was an outsider in our little family, an Irishman from Philadelphia in a family of Mexicans from Los Angeles. It was the loneliest thing I'd ever seen. In all these years, I never brought it up to him, never told him how I was sad for him, how I didn't want him to feel like he didn't belong. Maybe one day I will.

HOW TO TALK TO ASSHOLES

I'm in my living room, admiring the shadows, the sinister kind with bent angles that stretch across the room and creep around the corner until they're out of sight. My department dean's name pops up on my cell phone. *Why would this fool be calling my cell phone on the weekend?* I wonder.

Then I realize: *Oh, right. He's about to pull some bullshit.*

Up until recently, I've gotten along with my dean. He's something of a slick talker in an expensive suit, someone who acts like he's never bothered by anything. He's quick to bring up his street cred in the proper situations—a calculated piece of slang during equity meetings to show everyone he hasn't forgotten his roots. I imagine he listens to Jay-Z at the gym and thinks of himself as a down-to-earth man of the people, but he's an average, middle-aged opportunist—a doughy suburb-dweller who shaves his head to hide the bald spot. As one of the few Black people on our campus, he's lauded as a hero, a symbol of what can happen if you follow all the rules and don't upset the system. He mentioned to me once that he has cop friends, and I've kept my distance ever since.

Our school district is a perpetual campaign of superficial wokeness, where the administration and staff repeat the words *diversity* and *equity* repeatedly, their meanings marinated and cut against the grain like a flank of carne asada by administrators and then overcooked and unseasoned on the grill until their very idea of justice is a mess of smoking charcoal. The administrators view Brown people with the eyes of wolves, salivating, waiting to ravage us for our meaty demographic data, leaving the bones of our savage cultures for the lesser animals to devour.

I move from the living room through the kitchen and slide the back door open so I can talk in the backyard. My wife, Crystal, and I bought our house in 2016. Neither of us figured we'd be able to afford something like this. Rooms. Toilets. Running water. When I saw pictures of it online, I told Crystal, "It looks like a real fucking house." And she agreed. A real house we bought with her salary from working in public relations. And my teaching gig that I'm probably about to lose.

I answer the phone.

"Professor ... Fernandez," my dean says, his voice booming through the phone and pausing between words as if my middle name is an elongated blank space.

"Yeah," I say. "Hi."

"I just wanted to have a conversation about your club," he says, like he's about to sell me a dream cruise package to Tahiti.

Here we fucking go, I think.

Everything's a "conversation" with this guy, a strategy he learned in some institutional effectiveness class. He's a proud practitioner of Rogerian argument, a communication style with no clear winner because everyone's caught in a perpetual cycle of bullshit; they're too busy being polite to get anything done. It's the model ideology of people who trust the greatness of civilization and its institutions with all their hearts.

The club he's referring to is the chapter of the Campus Antifascist Network my students started as a response to the fascist creep seen across college campuses. Originally, the club was founded in 2017 by a couple of activist professors, one from Stanford and the other from Purdue. Since then, it's grown exponentially, with chapters across the country, but ours was the first community college to start a chapter—something of which the students were so proud.

Ever since I started teaching at this college, I've had students filing into my office to tell me how they've been attacked or bothered by students or staff at the school because of their race or gender.

One girl told me that she was walking to her car and a kid from a neighboring school called her the n-word. A transgender student told me one of her professors refused to call her by her correct pronouns. Another girl said she got panic attacks in her class because of the frat-bro, date-rapist vibe that permeates our institution. Our school is mostly white and affluent. For marginalized people, that combination can make the daily act of going to college like walking across a highway blindfolded.

"The club is making people nervous," my dean says.

"How so?"

"Antifascist. Antifa. It's—"

He stops before he finishes the sentence, but I hear it anyway: *too radical*.

"It's not like that," I say. "It's a club. We don't run around burning down buildings or punching people in the face. We talk about fascism. Don't worry."

"Well, the name," he says.

"What about it?"

"You might need to change it."

"We can't."

"Why not?"

"It's the Campus Antifascist Network. It's part of a network. They're all called that."

"What's the idea?"

"The idea is that we're in Folsom, and our school is mostly white. I have white nationalists in my class. People post death threats on my office door. My students don't feel safe." I walk over to the part of my backyard our cats use as a bathroom, but I don't find any shit, which is rare. It's usually a wasteland of cat turds. But not today. Maybe I've tamed them. Whatever the reason, I declare it a cat-parenting victory. I'll take any victory I can get. It's been a hard road, lately. Or maybe it's been a hard road for my entire life, a minefield of never-ending failures. It seems that I've been stepping on the same mine, time after time, blowing off chunks of my leg, but still managing to live on my stumps. *Look at me! I can still walk on these fucking things!* I know I'm in trouble again because these administrators usually stay out of the way. They don't want any drama. They don't want to deal with professors as much as we don't want to deal with them. Separation of church and state. That kind of thing. Unless they're getting pressure from the higher-ups. If someone at the district office tells them to light the fuse, then they're the first ones with a book of matches. Then it's all-out war.

Suburbs That Smell a Certain Way

I loved it in Brookline. I didn't want to, but I couldn't help it. The house was small, and the landlords lived upstairs, but everything was easy there. Sunshine was in charge of walking me about ten blocks to school in the morning. We'd take the same path every time, and she held my hand as we walked. We passed by Zeke and Zeba's house—the one with the crooked driveway and huge brown fence. We'd go by the sick-looking dog. And then we'd pass the house where the bearded guy lived. He said hello to me, always with a green beer bottle in his hand, even in the morning. His wife was angry, and whenever I passed by, she'd get a sour look on her face and go inside.

Next to their place was a plain brown house where the window shades were always drawn shut. I never saw anyone come out, and I'd have sworn the house was vacant had it not been for its brilliantly decorated front yard, a garden of small, wild plants and hundreds of yellow, red, and orange tulips. There wasn't much flair in suburban Massachusetts, so I had to stop when I saw the patch of tulips crowded with thick green stems and colorful heads reaching toward the sun. Looking at them, I felt big, like watching another world from above. I sniffed each flower, starting from the left side and moving to the right. I sniffed hundreds of them. I'd sniff a flower, wiggle my nose around a bit, and then sniff another one. My sister was nice about it, mostly. She held my hand until the nagging tingle of responsibility rang in her head like a rusty bell.

"We're late," she'd say, squirming around and pulling my hand toward school.

It didn't matter to me how late we were to class. I hated Mrs. Clark, and school was nothing compared to flowers. Every bloom smelled different, each one with a unique personality. The red one on the middle left was joyful because he smelled sweet and loud. The angry yellow one to the right made me sneeze with his bitter, poisonous stench.

After another ten minutes of waiting, my sister would finally let go of my hand, finger by finger. Then she'd leave me there. She didn't yell; she just went to school. I wouldn't leave until each flower was properly sniffed. It wasn't a good recipe for academic success. But it did teach me other things, like what's important and what's not.

Time Out

I was convinced Mrs. Clark was a witch. She hated kids. Especially when we talked. On the first day of kindergarten, we faced her in rows as she sat perched on her stool like a crow, the lights hitting her wet, glowing skin, like she woke up every morning in the dumpster behind an Italian restaurant. She was the greasiest woman I'd ever seen. Whenever a kid talked, Mrs. Clark would yell at the top of her lungs, "Be quiet!" She did this so often that when she asked a question, nobody would say anything, enraging her even more. I found it hilarious. I couldn't stop laughing at her.

Mrs. Clark was my first teacher, my first oppressor; she showed me how she hated me with the squint of her eyes. She sat far away from the class like we were a bunch of lepers, leaving a huge gap between herself and her students. We were six-year-olds, not dumb. We noticed everything.

She hated me so much that halfway through the year she constructed a wooden time-out box at the back of the classroom. She draped it with silk sheets and put pillows inside like it was a little castle. But it was more like a colorful prison for the kids who acted out in Willy Wonka's chocolate factory, who would all die tragic but hilarious deaths. Sometimes I'd yell out in the middle of class just so I could sit in that thing. It didn't take much, just a little outburst, and she'd stop what she was doing and point to the back of the room.

There was another kid in the class, Joey, who wore huge glasses and a shiny NASA jacket. I could tell he wasn't a fan of Mrs. Clark either. One day when I was in the time-out box, I heard Joey yell out right in the middle of a story. I peeked out of the velvet curtain just in time to see Mrs. Clark's frown glistening under the lights. She raised her crooked finger, slowly, like an evil witch, and Joey walked from the front of the room to me in the time-out box.

He sat on one of the pillows.

"You got in trouble?" I asked.

"Yup," he said.

We smiled at each other. Not the nice smiles. The smiles six-year-olds give when they know they're going to start some shit together for the rest of their lives.

This Is My Dad on Drugs

Nobody knows how my dad found us in Brookline. The last we knew, he moved from Samoa and was now in California. There was no internet then. Plus, he was crazy. And on drugs. According to my mom, his schizophrenia was in full bloom. Maybe his psychosis gave him some sixth sense, like a deranged superhero. Whatever it was, he wasn't the same man she married. But there he was one day, sitting on the sidewalk with a scraggly beard in front of our house, strumming a guitar and singing songs. Probably not Slayer or Dio, but something more mellow. He liked Cat Stevens. Bullshit like that. I kept trying to peek my head through the blinds, but my mom pulled me away. She and my stepdad were silently freaking out. I could tell my mom was stressed because she'd constantly clear her throat.

"*Ahem*, we're going to leave the house, *ahem*," she said.

"Yeah," my stepdad agreed. "Get your coat."

"*Ahem*."

When the garage door opened, my mom shoved my head down so my dad wouldn't see us.

"Sunshine, stay down."

My sister ducked and we pulled away.

It was like a secret operation and I loved every second of it.

I caught a glimpse as the car passed and drove down the road toward the city. My dad strummed his guitar with one hand and drank a beer with the other. He was singing, but I couldn't hear the words. He looked all alone out there, alone and crazy. Part of me wanted to be out there with him, sitting on the patch of grass with a beer and a guitar, saying "Fuck you" to my mom and stepdad, Mrs. Clark, and the rest of the world. The other part of me felt the excitement of a new and dramatic scenario, a little fire of drama raging in my belly provided a bit of familiar warmth. I started to get this feeling lately deep inside my belly, like a little bit of electricity that buzzed through my body. It only happened when I sensed danger. It was such a unique feeling that I began to seek it out. Anything but the regular, monotonous feeling of life.

We never discussed my dad's musical return, and when we came home hours later, Dad was gone. It was as if the second our car pulled out of the driveway and drove into the distance, the memory had been erased, overwritten by whatever new memory we created, like when you record over a used cassette tape and the old recording still shines through and you can hear both, but they both sound shitty and it's impossible to understand either one. That's how everything felt. There was too much going on. I didn't know what to listen for. So I tuned out, waiting for that little electric buzz in my belly to return.

The Russian War

I started hanging out with Tatiana, the most beautiful girl in the world, a Russian with bright orange hair like a matchstick that was constantly aflame. She listened to me talk about everything—my dad, my strict parents, and my new sister, Lauren, the cutest little baby on earth, half my stepdad and half my mom, a little Mexican potato.

"You really love her?" Tatiana said.

"Yup," I said, trying to kick a rock into the sewer grate but missing extraordinarily.

"I wish I had a sister to love," Tatiana said.

"You have a brother," I said. "You love him, right?"

Tatiana didn't say anything back, so I didn't push the question.

We walked together up Beaconsfield Road under a canopy of trees with branches turned inward, like two birds in a birdcage. A tacky carpet of fallen yellow, orange, and red leaves covered the streets. In the gutter nearby, a moving thing caught my eye. I pointed and Tatiana shrieked.

Before us, a pigeon writhed on the ground, its left wing bent back and turned upward. A thick crust of blood glistened on its belly.

"It's hurting," Tatiana said. Her smile was gone. She kneeled like a concerned mother to inspect the wounded bird.

I found a stick and kneeled next to Tatiana.

"Are you crazy?" she snapped, grabbing the stick from me. "Would you want a stick in your side if you broke your wing?"

What a dumb question, I thought, but before I could dwell on it, a car pulled up.

An older Russian kid named Sasha jumped out of the driver's seat. Sasha was a bully who stood a good foot and a half taller than every other sixth grader. He could have been fifteen. He sported a little peach fuzz mustache on his upper lip like a badge of honor and drove his *babushka*'s car everywhere.

"Hey, you little fuckers!" he called out. His car was still running, but he was kneeling next to us in the street. The bird became aware of its new audience and started to struggle with more ferocity.

Rumor had it that Sasha had spent a whole night in the park once, curled up in a ball under the jungle gym, crying because nobody had come to his birthday party. Whenever he passed me in the hallway pointing his fat sausage finger in my direction, yelling "bitch" or "faggot" loud enough for everyone in the hallway to hear, I'd think of him lonely and weeping in the playground under the moonlight and it would soften my rage a little. But many nights I dreamed that I was big enough to smash Sasha under my foot, squirting his blood in all directions, while a field full of my classmates filled the city with cheers.

"So, what do we have here, doctor?" said Sasha. "Looks serious."

We all crouched, watching the bird squirm around on the leaves in pain until it stopped to catch its breath and continue its futile attempt to flip over.

Sasha reached out to poke it.

"Leave it alone, Sasha," Tatiana said.

"So, who's going to stomp it?" Sasha yelled, pointing at me.

Sasha's face was too round, and his eyes always seemed to be squinting. And he smelled like steak all the time, even in the morning, which made everyone want to vomit during class.

"Shut up, Sasha," Tatiana said.

"You shut up, you prissy bitch. Your boyfriend is going to stomp him. He said so."

I looked at Sasha and wondered what it would be like to be him. He must have felt light, even in that big, oafish body, with no hefty thoughts weighing him down.

Sasha stood up and grabbed my neck with his gigantic hands. They felt like vise clamps, cutting off the circulation to my brain. I laughed, trying to hide my fear. But Sasha kept choking me, and I started to struggle. The more I struggled, the more aggressive Sasha became and the more lightheaded I got. I wiggled and finally shook myself free, but not before Sasha's knee made contact with my nose, jerking my head backward. My face went numb. Tears welled up in my eyes, and I leaped at Sasha, who moved away and pushed me to the ground. Tatiana stood on the sidewalk while I cried.

"Fuck you, you big fat fucking Russian fucker," I yelled at Sasha with my head folded into my arms. I peeked from behind my fingers. Sasha and Tatiana stared back at me stupidly. I could have punched them both, but I was so angry that I couldn't breathe. The fact that Sasha and Tatiana were united at the moment and waiting for me to do something made me furious. They were probably thinking the same thoughts.

Look at the crying Mexican, they thought. *Let him cry, the Russian-hating asshole.*

The bird had nearly stopped moving, its energy exertion reduced to a slight twitch. I looked at Tatiana's face and saw that she was angry, mostly at me, and just as thoughtless and ignorant as everyone else.

It was a split-second decision to leap in the air and land square on the bird's belly. Its body flattened like a giant marshmallow underneath my feet. Guts, brain, blood, and other innards sprayed out of its beak and asshole. Sasha burst into hysterical laughter and fell against his car in a big melodramatic show of joy.

"He did it! That stupid fuck! He did it!" he said, holding his sides. A spray of pinkish innards dotted the street.

I was so flustered that I couldn't see. A sharp pain shot through my brain. My nose felt like it was too dry and also bleeding, my face swollen with adrenaline.

Tatiana was most likely horrified, and I didn't want to look at her face, which I knew was covered in tears and hatred. When she ran up the street toward her grandmother's house, I watched her, too angry to speak or run after her, while Sasha got in his car and sped off. I tried to follow Tatiana with my eyes, but all I could see was a trail of red and orange leaves smashed against the concrete with no real discernible pattern.

I walked home slowly, thinking about Samoa. I should have stayed there all those years ago in the jungle, sucking on sugarcane, leaping over poisonous snails, sleeping on those hard pillows, the ocean breeze blowing freezing air into our windowless dwelling. There were no Russians there. Or sidewalks. There was only the beach. And the ocean that stretched as far as the eye could see. And those gigantic snails with poison in their shiny skin that I'd leap over to avoid a certain death.

HOW TO EXPLODE

"What will the club do?" my dean says.

At this moment, I can't help but hate everything about him. His voice sounds the same over the phone as in person, as if before every conversation he spends a few minutes adjusting his institutional equalizer. He used to be a communications professor before joining the dark ranks of the school administration. Before he made a blood pact with Satan. Only the greediest and most evil professors move into administration.

"The club is a form of unity and solidarity," I say. "The students feel better when we're together. We put zines together, set up a table, talk to students and staff."

"Well, maybe you can put together some statistics about how a club like this might help."

"Sure," I say, lying. Clubs don't have to prove their value to administrators. It says so in the employee handbook.

After a few vague niceties, we end the call and I head back into the house, turning on the TV as I pass by. A CNN host is talking about Trump's Twitter page. The president is going on another rampage against Mexicans. The tweet goes:

> *Congress must immediately pass Border Legislation, use Nuclear Option if necessary, to stop the massive inflow of Drugs and People. Border Patrol Agents (and ICE) are GREAT, but the weak Dem laws don't allow them to do their job. Act now Congress, our country is being stolen!*

I briefly imagine my mother and father being dragged by a cowboy across the US-Mexico border.

These days, I'm constantly reminded of the Brown struggle to not be slaughtered in the streets, to be treated once and for all as human beings, as well as the other struggle—to maintain the status quo of white supremacy, to keep the Brown people in check in case they get any funny ideas. Our institutions, even the academic institutions known for their progressive rhetoric, are on the precipice, riding the fence between the two struggles. They vocally support the Brown struggle but will never give up their allegiance to white supremacy, their testing standards, their undying love of professionalism and business, their constant worship of the military and capitalism. It's only a matter of time until colleges implode under their own contradictions.

I think about Ruben Salazar, a hero among Chicanos, the first Mexican to cover the struggle. He went to work one day to cover the Chicano Moratorium march, a protest of the disproportionate number of Latinos killed in the Vietnam War. When the rally became violent, he slipped into a bar to gather his thoughts and sip a cool beer, and then a cop shot a projectile into the bar, hitting Salazar and killing him instantly.

A State Farm commercial blares on the TV. The sunlight in the living room has moved over a pile of toys in the corner, shining on a doll's head, casting a grotesque open-mouthed shadow over the entirety of the back wall of the house.

This world has always been a time bomb, and I know my little world, the one made from scraps, a little here and a little there, leftover wires and rusted circuit boards, is in its last seconds. So a few days after my call with the dean, I'm not exactly surprised when I'm called into an emergency meeting with him and the vice president of instruction. This is the explosion I've been waiting for.

The vice president of instruction is a tiny lady with an abundance of nervous energy. If she stuck a lightbulb in her mouth, it would illuminate her entire head. Then it would explode. She is sitting at the conference table, smiling so hard it could double as a frown.

"Welcome!" she says, like a hospitality clerk at a fancy hotel.

When I was first hired, she told me she was a slam poet and suggested we do a reading together, and I nodded along because I wanted the job. Secretly I hoped she'd get transferred to the district office before she tried to make that a reality.

Before I sit down, I think about shaking her hand, but I don't. I'm sweaty. She's sweaty. Everyone is sweaty. I try not to make any sudden movements or act suspicious, so I glance at my watch, but I'm not wearing a watch. I take a seat and stretch my arms on the table, but it seems too much like an alpha male maneuver, so I retract them, hoping she doesn't notice. The series of events that led me here flash like snapshots before my eyes: Donald Trump. Distressed students. The antifascist club. The phone call from the dean. This meeting.

Or maybe it goes back further. To the day I was born. To my family. To my trouble in school. To drugs. To chaos. To love. To my wife.

I don't know.

I'm fairly certain that, whatever the origin, it brought about the end of my career.

Boom.

Alley Cat

The neighbor girl was incredibly ugly, and kids called her Alley, as in *alley-way*, which is pretty messed up now that I think about it. Her face was dirty and freckled, and she always smelled of cat piss. She lived in the place behind us with her younger sister, her mom, who rarely emerged from the house, and her dad, who had a horrible temper. He was a massive man who reminded me of the lumberjack on the paper towel wrapper.

We'd run around together on the weekends playing hide-and-seek, lurking around in storage sheds. Sometimes I could feel her chapped lips rubbing against my neck, hot bologna breath steaming in my ear.

"I'm going to kiss it," she said, chasing me around an elm tree one summer day. Her braces flashed in the sunlight. I didn't know what the *it* was, but I didn't run as fast as I could have, and when she caught me, I only pretended to put up a fight while she fumbled around with my belt and zipper. A dry breath tickled against my groin, and then I felt her mouth, warm and slippery. Her chalky tongue, combined with the meaty smell of her head, was somewhere between horrifying and religious. It was the first time I ever had sex.

I was twelve.

I always remember that time with excitement, but also with disgust. Her freckled face, her acrid kiss that heated my mouth, my teddy bear's glass eyes watching us as we jerked clumsily around on my bed on top of my Sacramento Zoo animal comforter, cartoon giraffes stretching their long necks from their cages, trying to watch the show.

It was the year my older sister started to party. Whenever she'd babysit my little sister and me, her friends would come over right after my parents left, bringing the little bottles of alcohol they'd swiped from their parents' cabinets. They also brought joints to smoke in the backyard; they'd stumble around, screaming into the cool summer air. They sat in a circle and told secrets, and whenever I'd get close enough to hear, they'd tell me to fuck off and throw rocks at my head.

It was the same year Sunshine changed her name. Her teacher was a stern but perceptive man. I'd heard many kids call him an asshole, but he must have sensed an unease in Sunshine. One day, he asked her if she wanted to be called by her middle name, Rebecca.

"Sure," she said, and that was that.

Her name was Rebecca now. Nobody seemed to have a problem with her new name, as if everyone had been waiting for her to change it. Everyone went along with it. I wondered if everything could be that easy.

One night when they had gotten too drunk, her friends left, and Rebecca crawled into the house crying and vomiting. I thought she was dying, so I wrapped a cold towel around her, pulled her to her bedroom, and tucked her into bed. I spent the rest of the night cleaning up her barf and hoping she wasn't dead. When my parents came home, I told them she'd gotten sick from some brownies we made and that she needed to rest. I spent the rest of the night crying into my giant teddy bear, which had an opening I'd cut into his asshole to hide my fireworks and cigarettes inside.

When my parents finally hired a babysitter, they got a mean old German lady named Heidi. She liked to smoke cigarettes in the front yard until my parents came home. Once, my mom arrived home early, and Heidi was out front smoking cigarettes. Heidi panicked and shoved the entire lit cigarette into her mouth. She pretended nothing was wrong while my mom choked back laughter.

My parents worked a lot, so after they got rid of Heidi, I had time to explore the house, and I preoccupied myself by rummaging through the kitchen cabinets to find spices to smoke. I don't know why I thought of that, but there I was at three in the afternoon, tearing a page out of a cookbook, rolling up a joint full of oregano.

I squeezed into a bush between our house and our neighbor's and lit the joint. Lighting the match, then holding the cigarette to my lips and inhaling, ignited something inside me that elevated my existence. My heartbeat flickered double-time, and my shallow breath barely swallowed enough oxygen. The oregano didn't work, but doing something that I wasn't supposed to be doing was a better high—and infinitely more erotic—than being chased around the backyard by Alley and her slippery mouth.

I was twelve when I changed.

Everything was different.

The world swirled around me and sucked me up like a tornado.

I wasn't a boy anymore.

I held my anger toward my dad and his sudden departure, my new dad, and my shitty teachers like an explosive device, one that I could either tuck away somewhere safe or lob away, taking me out along with anyone who happened to be nearby. I wanted to see what kind of damage I could do if I pulled the pin, but instead of throwing the grenade I just stood there. To see what would happen.

Skipping School

I discovered John Holmes—a skinny white porno star with an enormous dick that he'd use to skewer women half his size—when I skipped school with my friend Jason, who we called Bubba. We sat on the couch with coagulated Doritos dust covering our fingers, our orange-tinted mouths agape at the freakishness of his dad's pornography collection.

Halfway through the day, high on porno, we'd wander outside and find the bottles of vodka his dad kept hidden in the garage and take cautious sips, gagging until we curled on the cement, laughing hysterically. It tasted so rancid that we couldn't get drunk. We had so much fun that we decided to skip school again the next day. And the next. The day after that, we recruited some classmates to cut with us. We forged notes and more notes.

A whole week had gone by. I knew we were going to get caught. But I didn't want to go back to school. I wanted to skip school for the rest of my life. As if fun was an electrified fence protecting me from the consequences I was about to face. Every time the phone rang at the house, my stomach tightened, my blood went cold, and I'd nearly shit my pants. Usually it was some ordinary call for my mom, but one afternoon the phone rang and I immediately knew it was the school. My mom's voice changed whenever there was trouble. It deepened, and she did her throat-clearing thing when she answered.

"Oh, okay," she said, her tone sharp. "*Ahem.*"

The footsteps up the stairs were hard and quick.

"I will ask him. *Ahem.*"

She opened my door.

"Hi, Josh," she said. "*Ahem.*"

That night she spanked me by the washing machine and struck me so hard that her wedding ring nearly snapped her finger in two. She screamed, jumped up and down, and rubbed her finger until I exploded into a fit of laughter and tears.

When I finally went back to school, I was full of rage. A fresh hatred for everyone who looked like they were going to tell me what to do. It was more than rage, though. It was bloodlust. Something changed in me. I wanted more than just for everyone in charge to leave me alone. In fact, I wanted them to not leave me alone. So I could hurt them. So I would be justified in hurting them.

I spent much of my time in the back of the classroom, tuned out, watching my classmate Drakul, a Romanian who had a bowl cut and wore thick glasses. For some reason, all his sweaters were holiday themed. He was always looking around, taking in his surroundings, happily in his world, even though he was picked on relentlessly.

He barely spoke English, and it seemed like half his week was spent stuffed in a locker or the bathroom, wiping some liquid substance from his pants. But he always came to class smiling, as if whatever horrible thing that had happened the day before was gone and the new day would bring some good fortune and cheer. It made me wonder about Romania; it must have been a horrible place if being stuffed into a locker for half of the year was some form of paradise.

Everybody called our teacher Dicknose, mostly because he had a short fuse and lost his temper at least once every class, but also because his nose was so long that it looked like a giant dick. One day, he was already three minutes late for class, and when that happened, which it rarely did, restlessness began to mount in our faces, like the first rumblings of an earthquake that would level the entire city.

Drakul was staring at the fluorescent lights, as he often did. Every few seconds, he'd break his gaze, look forward, and blink his eyes as if drugged by the sharp light. And then he'd look up at the lights again, sometimes letting out a little giggle.

Bubba wadded up a piece of paper and threw it at Drakul, which started a cruel chain reaction.

Persephone threw an eraser.

Jeremy hurled a handful of paper clips.

Markie chucked a science textbook.

The rest of the class followed suit, hurling whatever they could find at Drakul, who closed his eyes, waiting for the hail of objects to run its course. When the torrential downpour of paper, books, backpacks, and staplers failed to stop, Drakul calmly crawled under his desk and waited with his hands covering his head.

I hated watching Drakul fall victim to the cruelty of my classmates. I took out a sheet of paper, and instead of crumpling it up and throwing it at Drakul's face, I wrote out D-R-A-K-U-L in big letters vertically on the page. Next to the D, I wrote -angerous. By the R, I wrote -omanian, and so on, until the page looked like this:

Dangerous
Romanian
Always
Kissing
Ugly
Ladies

I walked over to Drakul, whose eyes were still shut. Our classmates had run out of things to throw, but Drakul wasn't taking any chances. He stayed under the desk.

"Here," I said, showing him the paper. Drakul blinked his eyes until they were focused and leaned toward the page to get a closer look.

"Look!" he screamed. "Lookit!"

"Stop it, Drakul." I put my hand on Drakul's shoulder to calm him down. "It's for you. It's *only* for you. Just stop." But it was too late. The rest of the class was out of their seats, fighting for the piece of paper.

"I want one," Michelle said, and in a matter of seconds, everyone was clawing at my shirt for their own piece of paper with their own names on it.

I didn't get it. All I did was write words on a page next to their names.

"You do it yourselves," I pleaded.

"We can't do that," Markie yelled, shoving a blank piece of paper into my hand.

Of course they could do it. Anyone could. It was just words. It felt like I was upside down and they were all right side up.

I did Markie's name, then Michelle's. When she saw it started with *Magnificent*, she let out a little squeal of joy.

"Keep going!" she screamed in pleasure.

When I got to Bubba, my hand was cramped, but the thought of keeping the classroom's collective attention shifted away from Drakul eased my physical pain. I must have scribbled names for all thirty-three of my classmates when Dicknose finally showed up, his huge nose glowing with the rage of a thousand suns. He stood in the doorway, his tightly curled hair framing a tiny face as red as an angry planet on the verge of an explosion. Everyone rushed back to their assigned seats. Drakul went back to staring at the fluorescent lights.

Dicknose approached Jeremy's desk, picking up his paper. He saw that the *J* was for *Jewish*, which I was particularly proud of because Jeremy was, in fact, Jewish, but Dicknose wasn't impressed. He walked to each desk, collecting the papers, hand outstretched until each student produced one.

He stood at my desk for an excruciating five seconds before he spoke. "Yours," he said with his hand out. He smelled spicy, like he'd bathed in cinnamon before he got to class. I didn't dare look into his little eyes.

"I made them," I said. "I don't have one."

A dead silence fell over the room.

I felt my heart beating in my chest.

Bubba screamed out, "He's a poet!"

The class erupted in laughter.

Dicknose slammed his hand onto my desk. "This is a science class," he said.

I laughed too, first out of my nose and then from my mouth, in a rolling, uncontrollable wave. I buried my head in my hands and hoped everything would disappear, but that made me laugh harder. I looked into my teacher's face hoping that maybe he was laughing too.

But he wasn't.

Dicknose was not pleased. He remained poker-faced, pointing his finger toward the door. Still laughing, I picked up my book, put it in my bag, and walked to the office. It wasn't just the poems. It was skipping class, being a dick, everything, and this was the tipping point. I was suspended quickly and painlessly.

After Principal Gary tried to call my mom and had no luck, he wrote up the suspension and sent me home with barely a lecture. I walked up Beaconsfield Road, trying to figure out a way to tell my mom I'd been suspended from school.

I kicked a rock toward the sewer drain. It scattered across the grates and plunked into the sewer's mouth.

When I got home, my mom and stepdad were waiting on the couch. They asked me what happened, so I told them I skipped school to go to the library, which seemed to soften the blow. They grounded me and we never talked about it again. But I saw something in my mom's eyes—a dullness, and a lowness in her voice that told me there were levels to her disappointment and we were only at the beginning.

It was the start of a pattern of misbehaving and getting caught, stewing in anger, and then suppressing it all at the bottom of my gut. What happens when you wire up an explosive and leave it under a carpet in the middle of the living room?

I thought about the poems I had written, mostly how Persephone touched my shoulder while I wrote them. I dreamed about her that night. I was writing my poems, and she was floating, rising into the sky.

"I can fly now," she said, her feet lifting above my head.

"Okay," I said. "What do I do?"

But as soon as she appeared, she was gone, and it was just me, alone, suspended in the clouds.

The Second Russian War

The electrical buzz running through my belly was constant now. I was suspended for skipping school but never told my mom or stepdad. Instead, I learned the art of forgery. I'd wait until my parents were sleeping, then go through their file cabinet where they kept all their handwritten notes, find their signatures, and copy them. Sometimes I'd write out a letter letting the office know that I had to be out of school for an extended period, then cut the individual letters out of their notes, glue them to a page, and trace over them so it was a perfect replica of my mom or stepdad's handwriting.

I don't know where this level of deception came from, but it came naturally. I had a keen sense of right and wrong from an early age and simply preferred to do the wrong thing. The world was more fun that way. I wanted to see what would happen. The threat of trouble was a precursor to the electric current, to sexual intercourse, the closest sensation I had to arousal, like the first time I crafted a joint out of oregano. My need for delinquency accelerated rapidly after that.

I skipped school one day. It was close to summer; it didn't really matter if I was there or not. I didn't have any plans, so I walked around Brookline, peeking my head into stores. I turned a corner and saw Sasha lurking in the distance. He was with Andrei, a little weasel-ass servant who did whatever Sasha said. If I had caught Andrei alone, I could've whooped his ass. Throughout fifth and sixth grade, I watched every Bruce Lee movie ever made, and I was pretty sure I could fuck shit up.

But Sasha was another story. He was still mad at me for crushing the bird. Or for my Russian slur. I couldn't tell which. I think between that time and now he had grown another inch. Nobody fucked with him. Not even the teachers. One time when Sasha got caught passing a note, Mr. Jacobs stopped the class and told Sasha to stand up.

"Fuck you," Sasha said, and remained seated.

Mr. Jacobs approached his desk.

"You sure you want me to stand up?" Sasha said in his broken Russian accent.

"Stand up," Mr. Jacobs repeated.

Sasha stood up, the classroom collectively gasped, and he laid a smack on Mr. Jacobs so hard that Mrs. Sanchez ran in from the other room to see what was happening.

Sasha got expelled that day, and from then on, he lurked around the greater Boston area looking for people to terrorize.

I watched him as he tried to hide behind a tree, a yellow water balloon in each hand. Andrei was next to him, laughing. I knew he was going to throw the water balloon at my face, but I kept walking in his direction anyway. I didn't want to punk out. I was a punk, but I didn't want to look like one. That was the Boston way.

My pride led me to walk closer.

And closer.

If I had turned around, I would've looked like a coward, so I kept going.

The inevitable smack of the water balloon against my face stung, but it didn't hurt. My stomach ignited and bile shot up my throat like a burning hand, squeezing when it arrived at my brain. Andrei was doubled over on the ground, laughing.

I inspected Sasha's stupid face, how his dirty little mustache curved into a smirk. Ever since I'd squashed that bird, I couldn't stop thinking about slamming his face into a brick wall. Everything tightened into a thick ball. My vision blurred. A wad of vomit threatened an escape from my throat.

Sasha stood next to a short stone wall and I hopped onto it to get as close to him as I could. My heart was beating out of my chest as I jumped and kicked him in the dead center of his face. His lips turned inward at the force of my shoe. I landed on the ground and turned to face Sasha. His sausage fingers covered his mouth. Andrei had stopped laughing and lay on his back in the grass, paralyzed by confusion. A cascade of blood poured down Sasha's chin. His eyes widened like two stars expanding. He held a bloody front tooth between his forefinger and thumb.

That's when I ran—through manicured yards, down the alley behind the deli, up the flight of stairs toward the park, up the dirt embankment toward the church, across the parking lot, and behind the dumpster where sometimes we found entire pizzas from the shop next door. I wedged myself behind the dumpster, dry heaving and crying, trying to make myself small. My toes began to throb like they were all broken, and I could feel blood soaking through my sock. I vomited onto my shoes and tried to catch my breath. A tiny nun in a starchy blue dress walked by slowly, shaking her head and muttering something—probably a prayer—under her breath.

When the pain dulled into a steadily beating drum, a new section of my brain opened, like a sped-up video of a stream of water carving out a groove in rock over eons. A new pathway. I wasn't afraid anymore. I wanted desperately to fight again.

COMMUNITY SELF-DEFENSE

I turn on the lights to the community center and let the turquoise walls lined with paintings lift my spirits, like I live in my own gallery and all the paintings were painted for me. The jagged patterns of the oversized papier-mâché skeleton and the cartoonish bust of a ghostly Mexican woman fill the room with bright colors that invoke ancestral spirits—Xiuhtecuhtli, Tonalli, Teyolía, Ihiyotl (fire, shadow, soul, breath)—keeping close watch as I arrange the room to prepare for our ritual.

I head toward the back, where we keep the gear and the wrestling mats, and start to configure the puzzle pieces. Little by little, people arrive for the free mixed martial arts class. A few friends started this class after Trump was elected as a way for Black, Brown, and queer people to find strength in exercise and learn how to defend ourselves as the world turns angrier in the last gasp of white supremacy. We get a surge of new people every now and then, usually after a news story, a Proud Boys rally, a white nationalist march, or a police shooting of an unarmed suspect. We started this thing to give our people something to keep, a gift of fitness and self-determination, a way to hold our heads up high when everyone is telling us to bow.

Every time we get new students, we go back to the basics. Stance. Footwork. Breathing. Jab. Cross. Slip. Roll. Unlike traditional classes, everyone spars, regardless of their experience. If the point of self-defense is to prepare for a situation on the street, whether it's a protest or a robbery, the best thing you can do is practice what you've learned in a high-pressure situation.

The more experienced people go hard while the new people go light and focus on their breath. Most new people forget to breathe because they're nervous about the confrontation. They crap out after a minute.

The more you're used to standing in front of someone who's going to punch you in the face, the more you focus on your breath and the less spastic your movements. You're able to relax your body and anticipate the next punch or kick. When two new people are fighting, their movements are too exaggerated, they waste too much energy overstepping, overextending, they stop breathing. When you tell them to calm down, to relax, they look at you like you're insane. *I can't fucking calm down in the middle of a war.* But I say the same thing to my students when they first get to my writing class and they can't get past the blinking cursor at the top of the blank page: *Calm the fuck down. It's just writing.* But they're frozen, blinking along with the cursor. Their high school teachers buried a fear of language deep inside them that it's my job to uncover and toss into the ocean, along with all the other improvised explosive devices bearing the initials of the institution. Throw out everything you know and start over in a better world, the one we create together.

Jose and TJ arrive, and we hug and finish setting up. Jose is an Indigenous man, about fifteen years younger than I. He's a metalhead and one of the only people from our collective who trains in mixed martial arts at a proper gym. He works as a janitor two days a week and trains the rest of the time. Hard. Sometimes for several hours a day. Then he comes back and teaches us everything he's learned. We're essentially cheating, sidestepping the pricey gym memberships, like when students buy papers online to get through college.

Jose is training for an amateur fight, so he's looking lean and muscular. TJ is a therapist, but I know her as a tiny fighter and a Vietnamese revolutionary, one of the fiercest people I have met. Jose and TJ have been dating for a couple of years, a couple born in the struggle, two fighters, a janitor and a therapist, an unlikely pair.

I hug TJ.

"You okay?" she asks.

"Fine," I say.

Her eyes narrow. She always knows when my spirits are low. A detective of the human psyche. Lying to her is useless.

I forgot to eat, which is my first mistake. My second mistake is that I forgot my water. My third mistake is that I ran twenty miles this morning and my legs are shot. But I never want to miss these classes. There's something about fighting that makes me nervous, but once I'm in it, the fear, the quick decisions, and the pain offer a new perspective on life. Some ancient secrets are only revealed when you're desperately trying to avoid a shinbone to the ribs.

The room is starting to fill up with students, mostly Brown and queer people, the whole reason we started this thing, a place for the underrepresented people in our community to train in a supportive environment. I'm not feeling good, but I don't want to tell anyone. They'll tell me to sit it out. They'll tell me to get some food. *Fuck it*, I think. We run through a warm-up and some quick drills.

It's time for me to spar with Jose, and I'm looking forward to it.

"What do you want to do?" he says.

I feel like it's a trick question, like he wants me to say grappling so he can fuck me up by twisting me into a human pretzel. The truth is, whatever we do, he's going to beat me. He used to be a wrestler in high school. And he's like a little rat when he fights, scurrying around to every position, never running out of energy. But I love fighting him. The more he trains, the happier he gets when he's facing off with an opponent. He loves violence more than he loves most people. So who am I to damper his joy?

"Kickboxing," I say, which I know is a tragic mistake.

We slide on our shin guards and set the timer for three minutes.

When the bell rings, we touch gloves, a little act of respect and love before we start kicking the shit out of each other.

I move in quickly with a jab, which he sees coming.

I jab again, and he slips it.

I watch Jose setting up a kick, so I jump away.

My head is light. A flash of light fills my eyes.

A barrage of fists comes at me, and I cover up, move out of the way, and return fire with a flurry of punches, then follow up with a front kick to keep him away.

I look at the timer, and twenty seconds have passed.

I am exhausted.

Jose comes at me again, and I gear up for his fists, keeping my chin tight to my chest and my elbows tucked in, in case he hits my body. *This is like a game of chess*, I think. *It's only a game.* I feel his palm on my forehead, and I don't know what he's trying to do. I can't see anything. It's like I'm blind. Everything is blurry. I feel a thud on the side of my head from his shin.

I'm asleep.

This asshole just kicked me in the head, I think. *That sucks, because I think he knocked me out. He couldn't have knocked me out, because I'm still standing. Look at me! I'm still standing!*

But I can't talk.

The problem is I don't know anything about chess. I've never played.

I should have learned to play chess, I think as my legs soften, then bend. I am going down.

A pair of hands rest under my head, and I can feel myself being gently set on the ground like a newborn kitten. I snap back to consciousness, and everyone is crowded around me.

"Fuck," I say.

"Are you okay?" Hamid asks.

"I got knocked out."

"Sorry," Jose says, grinning. "I was trying something new I learned in Muay Thai."

"It worked," I say. I walk over to the corner of the room and sit down. Someone brings me a wet towel, which I wrap around my head. The cool water stops the throbbing, and I watch the next round of sparring, TJ versus one of my former students.

TJ puts in her mouthguard, and she looks like a mountain lion. She's tiny, but she scares me a little. Fighting can change small people into vicious animals, and it can turn vicious animals into something worse: those who know how to use their rage in the calmest, most controlled way, those who utilize the economy of energy and exertion to cause as much damage as humanly possible to the people who deserve it, and sometimes to those who don't.

CROSS-COUNTRY

At the end of sixth grade, my stepdad announced that he'd gotten a job and that we were moving. Right when he said it, I ran upstairs to pack a bag so I could run away from home and live with Russian Mark and his weirdo sister down the street.

I could hear my stepdad stomping up the stairs, so I prepared to attack him with my fingernails.

"We need to move," he said, sitting on my bed next to my contraband teddy bear.

"I'm not going."

"I got a job there," he said. My stepdad had a calm demeanor—his psychiatric training rendered him monotone and Zen-like—that reminded me of a serial killer. "It's in California."

I thought for a second about California. Skateboards, beaches, palm trees, probably a lot of girls.

"Okay, fine," I said. "I'll go."

And that was it. I said goodbye to my friends, and we promised to call each other.

I stood in the middle of my street and breathed a huge breath through my nose. I registered an overwhelming smell—sweet, slightly citrusy, rich, and chestnutty. To this day, the wind will blow a certain way and I'll catch a whiff of that exact scent. It'll transport me right back to Brookline, my older sister holding my little hand while I sniffed every flower, with that impatient look in her eye.

Davis, California

We flew 3,010 miles across the dirt-brown sections of America, my mom, my stepdad, my Rebecca, and my little half sister, Lauren, suspended over the green mountains and cutting through the clouds that rattled the plane, and into Sacramento, where we rented a car and drove through the endless pastures and farmland—California. Not the California non-Californians think of. No beach. No surfboards. No golden-skinned white people. We drove to the tiny college town of Davis on a road that could've been the road to Montana—sprawling fields reaching across the horizon like outstretched palms, empty as they were dry. Cows chewed grass near electrified fences while green tractors plowed deep into the earth. There was no subway system, no back alleyways in which to hide from Russian oafs, no taxicabs, no strange men who sold fireworks on the corners of Chinatown, no liquor stores that sold *Playboy* to kids, no homeless men to chase you down the street after you stole their change.

"That's a cow," Lauren said.

"Yup," I said, wondering the best way to escape this agricultural hellhole.

In Davis, kids pedaled leisurely to class on their bicycles. There were no Puerto Ricans or Black people. Just packs of white children, like schools of goldfish, weaving across the wide streets and down tree-lined paths to brick institutions tucked neatly into residential neighborhoods. Sometimes a trash can was kicked over, and a neatly bearded homeowner, still wiping the sleep from his eyes, would dart from the front door and into the street shaking his fist at the kids who pedaled faster, laughing so hard they could barely catch their breath.

In my first few months at school, I ate lunch alone. From the middle of the soccer field, I watched boys hang from metal poles, kick balls around large grass fields, and climb trees. Girls huddled in packs, giggling. I wore the wrong shoes, ate peanut butter sandwiches, and watched the sky, hoping to find patterns in the clouds that would give me some direction. But there were no clouds at all. I had never seen a sky so ridiculously blue. Every now and then a bird sailed through the air and perched on a tree, something I don't remember ever happening in Brookline. I'm sure there were birds there, but I don't remember them, at least the flying ones. We had other things—buildings and trains and Hasidic Jews walking in packs, their long beards wrapping around their bodies like boa constrictors. At thirteen, a boy from Boston who landed in Davis, California, might as well have been a speck of space dust floating around the atmosphere of Mars.

My parents had bought me a skateboard in Boston, and I carried it on the plane. I'd desperately wanted a skateboard after watching my friend's older brother bombing down the hill in front of our house, lying on his back, his hands on his chest in the coffin formation. He was four years older than I but looked like a man. He wore denim jeans and a denim jacket; whenever I saw him, I felt different. It was like nothing I'd ever felt before. He had long, curly hair; I'd never seen anyone wear hair like that who wasn't a girl. I couldn't tell if I was in love with the speed at which he flew past our house, if I was in love with the fluorescent skateboard against the gray concrete, or if I was in love with him. Maybe it was all three. He bombed past our house on that bright green skateboard wrapped in fluorescent pink grip tape, and that's all I could think about. Every other toy became obsolete.

Finally, for my birthday, my stepdad brought me to Beacon Hill Skate, and I picked one out, a bright green deck with a graphic of a man's melting face. When I brought it home, I didn't know what to do with it. I didn't account for all the moving and my lack of coordination. I set it on my carpet and looked at it. It became a decoration.

I wasn't good at skateboarding, but I brought my skateboard to California on the airplane. I bought some skate clothes, an Ocean Pacific shirt with a picture of a skater doing a wallride. Under the picture it said *Natas Kaupas: Frontside Wallride*.

I wore that shirt to school, and one day at lunch a chubby Black kid and a couple of his friends surrounded me.

"Natas Kaupas frontside wallride," he said, pointing at my shirt.

I wasn't sure what to say.

"Natas Kaupas frontside wallride," he said, louder this time, in a mocking tone, his friends laughing in response.

I wanted to crawl inside of a hole and never come out. But as they laughed, I laughed along, like I was in on the joke the whole time.

They became my friends—the chubby Black kid, my best friend. It seemed like he had the only Black family in Davis. His mom was a veterinarian, and his dad was an alcoholic, like mine. Once when he was waiting on my porch for me to get home, my neighbor, a liberal Democrat, called the police because she saw a Black boy on her cul-de-sac. That's Davis in a nutshell: a blue wave of overeducated racists.

I don't remember any of my classes. Math, history, English, I suppose. All our teachers looked the same—old, enthusiastic white people. I sat in the back of the room with my head on the desk, waiting for something interesting to happen, daydreaming about skateboard tricks I wanted to learn.

I didn't know what to do or how to act under the fluorescent lights of the seventh-grade English classroom while our teacher, a nameless woman in a plaid dress, used me as a lightning rod to channel her rage.

"Hey, you," she called to me.

"Me?"

"You," she said. "Do you understand *Les Misérables*?"

I stayed quiet.

"Hey, you!" she shouted at the top of her lungs while the rest of the class chuckled at her anger. "I'm talking to you."

"I don't know anything," I said into the crook of my arm. I made sure not to look or lift my head from my palms. I traced a line with my middle finger along the desk's false wood, and like clockwork, the nameless teacher flew into a fit. Something in her eyes snapped, just as my father had snapped. One second everything was fine, and the next her hands flew into the air, teeth clenched, fists trembling. She wanted to punch me in the face but couldn't. Instead she sent me to the principal's office, where I sat until the bell rang.

It went on like that for days. Weeks passed. Months. Years. Fistfights by lockers. Smoking cigarettes in the bathroom. And slowly enough, I made some more friends. We skated from morning till night, sliding along the yellow-painted ledges at the university until the cops rolled up, lights flashing, and we ran serpentine across parking lots and through the maze of lecture halls until we lost them. Until the next time.

After a few years in Davis, I didn't call my old friends as often. The memories of Boston, the squeal of the T as it ground to a halt in Copley Square, pushed themselves deeper into my mind. A small voice nagged at me, tucked in the membrane of memory, telling me to go back and see my father, who'd by then lapsed into full-blown psychosis, sending cryptic letters about God crafted from pages cut from *National Geographic*. One Christmas, he sent a Walkman he'd picked up at a thrift store with a message that said *HE LISTENS* in mismatched ransom-note letters. His return address was in Boston. I wondered if he had followed us from California to Massachusetts. I wondered if he would follow us back. I wondered what he looked like, if he still talked like a surfer. If he still had a ponytail.

The older I got, the more confused I became.

Everyone around me was telling me what to do; some was conflicting information. My English teacher told me I was going to jail. My mom told me I was a smart boy full of potential. My inner dialogue told me to cut holes in my clothes, ride around on my skateboard, and flip off everyone who stood in my way.

That year, in Davis, the thermostat reached 114 degrees. Our neighbors, locked in the culture of suburbia, trudged around their yards with trowels, gardening in their little sun hats, panting like dogs. The grass in our backyard wilted while the neighborhood cats sprawled under trees, dying of thirst. On that day, the hottest day of the California summer, the phone rang. It was Russian Mark, from the old neighborhood. I hadn't talked with him in two years.

"Did you hear about Charlie?" he said, his voice humming with puberty.

"Nah," I said, placing my hand on the window. The heat burned my palm through the glass.

"He got shot," Mark said.

"For real?"

"For real."

I hung up the phone and sat in the kitchen among all my parents' modern furniture, the granite countertops, the turquoise tile floor, and the dark wood cabinets. The house smelled of cedar and citrus. I didn't cry. I tried to remember him, but I couldn't. Charlie made us laugh; I know that. We made fun of him sometimes. When his mother died, we skipped class and rubbed his back in the corner of the lunchroom.

A few days after I hung up with Mark, I was expelled. I got into a fistfight with the principal when he wouldn't let us play rugby at lunch. My mom slapped me, and I slapped her back. I ran away from home, but then I came back. I didn't know what I was doing. I wanted to kill myself, but I was too much of a coward. I hated the sight of my blood.

I was trying hard to be good, but I could feel the wires configuring themselves into a dangerous formation, something that would spark, catch fire. Something that I couldn't control on my own.

When my baby sister, Monica, was born, a perfect blend of my stepdad and my mom, who looked more like a baby cupid than an Irish Mexican, everything seemed to calm down, as if someone had stopped the timer, the countdown no longer relevant. Monica saved me from an imminent explosion. She was a tiny baby, a little potato who couldn't do much but fart and smile, but we were buddies, and that's all I needed at that moment.

Punk as Fuck

We tried so hard to be punks, but none of us really knew how, so we messed up our hair and wore cutoff shorts that showed off our pale chicken legs. We'd go to punk shows at the Veterans Memorial Center, and I'd try to hide my excitement at the energy, how everyone looked like peacocks preening for a mate. We hated everything, but I was secretly in love with the attitude, the dancing, the throwing ourselves around the pit while the bands played. We were little anarchists in training. Angry tadpoles swimming in the moldy pond of Davis, California. We wanted to be tough. I wore a shirt that said SLAPSHOT, a hardcore band from Boston, with a picture of a pair of hockey sticks and a growling bulldog. I didn't care about dogs and didn't like sports, but I thought nobody would fuck with me when I wore that shirt like a suit of armor.

There was an all-day punk festival in the park, and I wondered what I should wear.

I sat on my bed and slipped on my Converse, tying the laces into a triple knot.

"Hello," my two-year-old half sister Monica said, her little head poking into the doorway. My third sister, a little angel who looked at me with longing in her eyes, like I was some kind of superhero and she was my sidekick. Monica's hair was comically curly. She was so much older now, but she still looked like a cupid, piercing blue eyes that lit up whenever she smiled, which was always.

I don't know what I would have done without my sisters. I was such a dark little fucker that their brightness acted as a seat belt in a car that was about to swerve from the freeway.

"Hey, Monica," I said, standing up, checking my outfit in the full-length mirror.

"Going?" she said.

"To a concert," I said. "I'll be back later."

That seemed to be enough information. Her head popped out of the doorway, and she clomped down the hallway toward her room.

The park was only a ten-minute walk from my house. When I got there, dozens of kids in different stages of punkness—skaters, skinheads, girls with colorful spiked mohawks—formed loose circles in front of the metal slab that acted as a stage. I'd never seen so many hairy-faced, shitty-tattooed punks in one place. They smoked cigarettes and drank beer while I hung in the corner to scope the scene.

I found my friends, who were propping themselves up with their skateboards, like crutches.

We talked for a few minutes before the first band started.

Almost immediately, a group of five Nazi skinheads picked us out and formed a little circle around our crew. The skins grinned and got closer, their acne pustules ready to burst. They grabbed Atif and his fists balled up. He got that look in his eye like he was going to fuck some shit up. I wanted to cry as the skins closed in, but I didn't have time. The skins pummeled us like we were in the path of a hurricane, fists like boulders rushing past our heads, some of them connecting with hard thuds. It didn't hurt. The singer screamed over a grainy guitar, "Don't ask me where I'm at, cuz I'm a million miles away!" I wanted the song to end so bad, as if we were all controlled by the music and the end of the song would freeze the boneheads, giving me enough time to escape before the next song began. But the music didn't stop. It just got louder. They kept playing. They only had a handful of songs, and it seemed like they were playing them all, over and over, back to back. I caught a fist to my tooth, and it came loose. I felt around my mouth with my tongue, relishing the taste of blood. None of us said anything. Nobody begged for them to leave us alone. We didn't want to look like pussies in front of the other punks.

Even in the tornado of the punches and kicks to the flesh, the fists to the back of the head, and the boots to the ribs, ideas swelled like giant bruises. How my stepdad was so nice to me but I hated him anyway. How he'd brought me to an AC/DC concert for my thirteenth birthday, so I could watch Angus Young spaz out in his little schoolboy uniform. When my stepdad showed me the tickets, I couldn't believe he was going to bring me. I was still at the age where it wasn't embarrassing to be seen with my parents, so all I could think about was watching Angus Young strutting around the stage like a pale Chuck Berry. At the concert in the smoke-filled arena, my stepdad told me to go up front if I wanted, so I made my way through a crowd that smelled like body odor and cigarettes. A shirtless rocker put me on his shoulders so I could see better. He smelled like chemicals, and he danced with me on his shoulders until the very last song. At the end of the concert, I made my way back to the sound booth, where my stepdad had told me to meet him, and there he was with a content look on his face, exactly where he said he'd be.

I thought about how I'd gotten kicked out of school for fighting. In poetry class, I'd plagiarized lyrics to a hardcore song, and the teacher had pulled me aside and pointed to the line "I faced odds so strong that I used both fists." She'd looked hard into my eyes and asked me with a straight face if I was a homosexual. It was a good question, and I'd often wondered the same thing.

The skinheads left me on the ground. All my friends were gone. There were no clouds in the sky. No birds. I don't even remember the sky being blue. The band stopped playing, and another one started. I felt nothing, not even a twinge of pain. I pretended I was at my funeral and was no longer afraid to die. Like a punk. A real punk.

SOME HAPPY MOTHERFUCKERS

It's November 8, 2016, the day Donald Trump is elected as president. A grifter and a con man. A white nationalist who uses tax codes and investments as his weapons. In some ways, he's the perfect man to lead our nation.

My first mistake on this shitty day is signing up to attend a conference about diversity and education, the kind of conference that always ends in a pile of feel-good, neoliberal bullshit. But this one counts for the professional development credits that every professor is contractually required to maintain, so I cancel my classes and prepare for eight hours of the institutional version of smashing racism, which involves extreme politeness, following the rules, and, apparently, lots of crying white people.

I grab a chair at the back of the room with some other English faculty and try to look like a guy with nothing to add. I'm too angry for this. Hordes of white supremacists roam the streets in red hats, harassing anyone with an ethnic last name or a particular look in their eye. I want to flip a desk. Rip the shitty fluorescent lights from the off-white ceiling. Light some shit on fire. But I've half committed to this life of relative comfort as an English professor at a community college, so here I sit, internally raging in the off-white walls of a classroom turned guilt-laden echo chamber. I'm not going to rock the boat. I'm not going to set fires. I'm going to go along with the agenda. That's what I tell myself at least.

The facilitators for the day are an approachable white guy and an even more approachable Black guy from Oakland. They're both wearing pastel. Two nonthreatening people, wearing nonthreatening colors, who are going to both-sides every issue. I imagine they live above a yogurt shop and bump into each other every morning, yoga mats slung over their shoulders, ready to stretch their limbs in a ninety-seven-degree room surrounded by an endless Enya remix.

They have a good rapport, laughing and telling jokes back and forth like they're part of some ad campaign for Dove soap. They appear to be the happiest motherfuckers on earth, probably because their only job is to travel around and talk about race so workers can get professional development credit.

The first order of business is to share our origin stories. Another professor, an old hippie who's known to tell students nauseating stories about her college days, goes first. She rocks back and forth in her chair, crying about how difficult it was growing up as a white girl in the Midwest. My temples start to throb, so I try to remember my serenity prayer:

"......................."

I can't remember anything as the rage builds in my chest. Maybe I should move. I get up for more coffee but can't take my eyes off my colleague. I watch a long booger slide down her lip into her mouth. I look around the room, and everyone is crying. The lady who works at the front desk is slumped forward in her chair, sobbing uncontrollably about being white. She feels guilty about being born a Caucasian lady.

"I'm so ordinary," she says. "I don't know what to do."

I have many suggestions, but they'd get me kicked out of the room and possibly arrested, so I sit back down, patiently sipping my coffee and quietly watching everyone in horror. Imagine a room of middle-aged white people all in the throes of existential crisis, like being trapped in a Golden Corral buffet that's just run out of food. For a Mexican, academia is strange in that most of it is simply enduring humiliating rituals, mostly involving white people publicly atoning for their sins.

The white facilitator immediately notices that I'm not crying, and he approaches.

"Are you okay?" he asks. In this upside-down bizarro-ass world, not crying is a major offense.

"I'm fine," I say.

He puts his hand on my back, as if to say, *That's the wrong answer, my friend*, and I want to bend it back into an arm bar until I hear it snap. "Can you tell the group what you're thinking?"

"I'm angry," I say.

The facilitator nods, as if to say, "I'm angry too, brother." We're probably not angry about the same shit. For instance, I notice his pastel sweater tucked into his khakis and I want to choke him to death.

"Tell us," he says.

Fuck you and your shitty sweater, I think. *Go back to your condo in Oakland.*

I get up and walk outside, leaving my colleagues to weep under the fluorescent lighting.

Earlier in the morning, when I dropped my son off for school, the school's director pulled me aside to tell me that my son's best friend had gone to the hospital with complications from leukemia. I walk around campus and think about the little boy in the hospital hooked up to the buzzing machines, his mom by his side telling him everything will be okay. I think about his cute little face, the way his fingers interlocked with my son's fingers as they stood on the playground, holding hands under the jungle gym while their classmates jumped and swung around them.

I look out at the quad; the modern angles of the college seem straight out of a glossy architecture magazine. A student from the Queer Straight Alliance club is outside with a handful of little homemade flowers, handing them out in protest of our new president, Donald J. Trump, the billionaire con man who is rapidly returning our country to the pre–civil rights era. Most take a flower graciously. Some people offer a hug. This student was born a girl but doesn't feel like one. They're nonbinary, something I understand deeply because I, too, am upside down in a world of people who are right side up. We are pockets of warm air floating between the earth and the heavens. I refer to the student as *they*, which some people won't. Some insist on using *she*, if only to make a statement about American moralism. It's a war being waged on language. A war being waged on values. On tradition. And I'm here for it. I've grown to love war.

Another one of my colleagues, a sociology professor, walks over to me with her daughter, a lanky girl who loves to climb trees, and I tell them about my son's friend, a three-year-old boy tangled up in clear plastic tubes and dying in the hospital, and her daughter hugs me. We both stand there crying. I wonder what the diversity facilitators are doing back at the workshop I left. I want them to see me like this, with tears streaming down my face. They'd probably be proud of me for experiencing so much pain and expressing it openly. Maybe they'd relay my bountiful capacity for emotion to my superiors so they'd never even think of firing me. *Damn*, I think. *Here I am, crying like an asshole with no administrators in sight, wasting all my professional development diversity credit.*

I can't get myself to go back to the workshop, so I stand outside in the heat. In the distance, a group of boys huddle around each other. One produces a giant blue flag that says *TRUMP* in big white letters. I can tell they're laughing self-consciously, like high school kids who haven't yet grown into their bodies and minds. The group moves toward the student handing out flowers and surrounds them, the flag billowing in the wind. The student tries to hand one of the boys a flower, but he snatches it and throws it on the ground. The boys are laughing, waving the flag high in the air. An employee sees what's happening, and she yells at the boys, and they scatter like cockroaches in daylight. The student with the flowers is hunched over, crying, their homemade decoration falling onto the patch of perfectly manicured lawn. I walk over and pick up one of the flowers from the grass. Tiny words are printed on the petals. *We are all allies.*

I Held Her Fingers in the White Room

I was fifteen when my mom and stepdad went out and left me to babysit my little sister Monica, the blond-haired angel with a smile that always managed to break my teenage angst clean in half.

That night, we ran circles around the house until neither of us could breathe. We lay side by side on the carpet, panting and holding our burning chests.

"Blue," she said, breathing heavily.

"Blue?" I asked.

"Blue," she said. "The sky."

"But we're inside." I could barely catch my breath.

"Blue."

"But it's nighttime."

"Sky always blue," she said, laughing.

When I put Monica to bed, I kissed her on the forehead.

"Goodnight, little sister," I said, but she was already sleeping.

I went to the kitchen, found a bottle of vodka in the liquor cabinet, and twisted the dusty cap. It smelled like poison. I gagged but mixed it with orange juice and drank it down. And another. By the fourth glass, my head swirled, and I gave myself a field sobriety test by walking a straight line across the cracks in the tile floor and fell over in a fit of laughter. I made another drink and tried to watch *The Wizard of Oz* on the television, but my head filled with helium and spiraled into a windstorm. I crawled to the bathroom and vomited a heavy stream of orange juice and vodka into the toilet until the bowl glowed orange. The acid burned my throat. I crawled into bed. The room spun me to sleep.

I awoke to the sun stabbing through the blinds. My head burned like all the moisture had been sucked away by nightmares. I shot out of bed, afraid that I had left the bottle of vodka out for my parents to see or that I had vomited all over the bathroom floor. A pain blasted through my skull and escaped from my sandy eyeballs.

"Mom?" I called out. Nobody was in the kitchen.

The house was empty. I found a note on the kitchen counter:

Josh, something happened to Monica. We are at the hospital.

> *Love,*
> *Mom*

It was 10:30.

Something happened to Monica.

I read that part over and over again.

Something happened to Monica.

I repeated it over in my head until it became something like a mantra.

Something happened to Monica.

Until the words carried no more meaning.

A friend of the family drove me to the hospital. He was a plain man with cartoonishly large glasses. He looked nervous when I glanced at him through the rearview mirror. I hated him for that. He was supposed to be strong. But there he was, an adult, breaking eye contact every time I looked.

What a fucking coward, I thought.

We pulled into the parking lot and entered the mouth of the building, which swallowed us like a tan giant.

We made our way to the wing of the hospital where everything was blinding white.

My family was in the white room, crowded around Monica's hospital bed.

I couldn't tell if she was breathing.

Everyone was crying.

I hugged my stepdad and I wasn't crying. I felt bad that I couldn't get any tears to form.

What a fucking coward, I thought. *Now I'm the fucking coward.*

My sister lived in the hospital until the end. A rare intestinal disease. The doctors were confused, standing around scratching their heads in their white coats. I could hardly look at Monica. A machine breathed in and out in place of her lungs, her fingers purple as raindrops.

The doctor asked if I was ready, and I said, "Hell no. No way. Don't pull that goddamn plug."

"Do you want to hold her hand? You should hold her hand."

I tried to feel the life in her fingers, but I couldn't feel anything. I wondered for a second why I wasn't crying. I couldn't believe I wasn't crying. I was supposed to be crying. A real human would cry.

The doctor cut the machine off, and it stopped beeping. The room flickered white. When my mother cried, it sucked all the air out of the room until there was nothing left but white light on the white walls and the white doctor in his white coat, his eyes darting around the room, searching for an exit.

Our family held each other so hard that it left a bruise on my shoulder.

Monica died and our already-broken family would never recover.

The Teacher's Daughter

Mr. B was the only teacher in high school I didn't hate. He taught creative writing and was horrible at his job, a slow talker who seemed like he was always half-asleep. He had no passion for anything, like he was running his class from a feedback loop from the '70s, a monotone sepia reel that lasted exactly fifty minutes. But he wasn't vindictive. Or on a high horse. Or mean. He didn't wield his authority like a weapon. He didn't blame me for my anger, for sulking around the school with the pain of a dead sister written into my frown. His only crime was being boring as fuck, which is something I could deal with.

His daughter Josephine went to the same school. She reminded me of Tatiana, a pale, beautiful girl with a face full of freckles. She came over when my parents were at work, and we fucked in my room until I heard the front door open. We scrambled into our clothes, and I threw her out my window into a rose bush. The next day she showed up at school with scratches all over her arms and face. She never talked to me again, and I felt bad, mostly because I liked her dad, who kept teaching, his script never breaking, droning on and on until the bell rang. He left me alone to stew in my rage against the world, images of my dead little sister swirling around the toilet bowl of my mind. Then I'd go to math class with the teacher who kicked me out every time I didn't do homework, which was every day; then on to Spanish class with the teacher whose eyes furrowed like a cartoon villain. I stopped attending classes for good; the idea of education was poisoning my mind until I had to remove myself as a form of self-preservation. *There's nothing here for me*, I thought. *I'm not meant for this.*

I was traumatized by my education. I hated almost every teacher I had, enough that I treated each one like they were one of those cops and FBI agents charging at me and my sister in Samoa. Authoritarians. Angry as my dad and just as fucked up too. I hated them so much that maybe I wanted to be one. That whole running-face-first-into-the-wrong-situation thing. Maybe I was dumb enough to think I could be a good teacher. A great teacher, even. I could change the education system. Or the whole world.

Anti-Racist Action

We marched along K Street in an unruly line, a bunch of angry sixteen-year-olds chanting out-of-sync rhymes in cracking voices—rejects with fucked-up haircuts trailed by a crowd of cops whose hands clutched their batons like beefy GI Joes.

The Nazi skinheads seemed to be spawning, infesting all the punk shows, flaunting their swastika tattoos, flying *Sieg heils!* into the crowd of kids who were there to watch bands and get rowdy in the pit. The Nazis were bigger than us. And older. Nobody knew what to do. Any sign of opposition was met with a savage beating, a flurry of fists, and steel-toed boots delivered to the gut.

There was a meeting hosted by Aragorn, an older college kid who had a way with words. He had heard about a group in Minnesota called Anti-Racist Action—a bunch of kids, punks like us, who were dealing with the same Nazi problem. They went to shows together. They brought weapons. It was working.

"We can do it if we're organized," Aragorn said.

Aragorn was a loudmouth. A straight-edge kid who loved to cause trouble. He made long-winded flyers about the ills of drug use and posted them all over Sacramento. There were ten of us at the meeting, held at Aragorn's tiny apartment in Midtown Sacramento. He had a pile of records as high as my head. He told us some Nazis were having a rally and we were going to do a counterdemonstration. None of us knew what that was, but we all nodded, because it seemed right.

On the day of the counterprotest, we marched. Some kids carried cans of spray paint and, under the cloak of the crowd, sprayed messages like *FUCK RACISM* or drew a big *A* with a circle around it on the sidewalk and windows of businesses.

"An! Anti! Antifascista! An! Anti! Antifascista!" we screamed as we marched. Out of nowhere, three bald heads appeared, and we stopped, mouths agape, as if none of us had realized who we were protesting: actual people in uniform, with boots and braces and swastikas tatted in blue ink.

They screamed, "White power!" and held their middle fingers up to the crowd.

We watched them watching us, and the space separating us grew into its own city of volatile ideas. We had no weapons—no bats or knives or sticks—only our voices, held like black flags under the California sun. I found a Coca-Cola in my backpack—twelve ounces of high fructose in a red can, its elegantly sloped cursive as iconic as the American flag—and I hurled it at the closest bonehead I saw. I remembered my dad telling me that Coca-Cola was once considered a wonder tonic of cocaine and caffeine; it had helped calm the souls of the terminally nervous. I laughed at the image of nervous old people jittering around the world, coked out of their goddamned minds. They had probably thought they knew everything, even while slowly killing themselves one bottle at a time.

I lobbed the can at the skinheads, and it sailed through the air like a little red fighter plane, crash-landing onto a Nazi's cheekbone and opening a gash the size of a fist, spilling blood and soaking his white T-shirt. The police froze in confusion while the bonehead wiped at the blood. His red hands glowed under the sun as he smiled and took a solid step toward us, but then his knees gave out and he fell hard to the concrete. One of his friends rushed to help while the other launched a *Sieg heil!* high above his head. I half wondered if the guy *Sieg heil*ed whenever his reflexes were tested, like at his general practitioner's office after the rubber mallet banged under his knee.

The other bonehead ran off and disappeared behind the Bank of America. We cheered and laughed as the hurt Nazi tried to get up. I almost felt a little sorry for the guy as he laid there greasy and crumpled on the light-rail tracks, like a discarded bag of McDonald's.

A woman from the street dropped her Macy's bag and wagged a finger in my direction. "Who are the *real* Nazis?" she said, and pointed at one of our Anti-Racist Action banners. She turned to the police and demanded an arrest, but they were still frozen by idiocy and profusely sweating under their thick blue uniforms, all probably younger than I am today.

When the sirens blared, we dropped our banners and took a hard left through the alley. The cops gave chase for a while but quickly fizzled out, either unable to keep up or struck by boredom. Nobody went to jail. Our group met up later at a hardcore show in the basement of a rented house, where we circled the room like blood cells racing toward a fresh cut. The first band's singer wore a dog collar and screamed about chaos and destruction as the room steamed and filled with the stench of angry adolescents stomping around endlessly, never tiring of kicking and punching each other for fun. The show stopped short when a cruiser pulled up; its familiar lights and orders barking from a megaphone gave us a thrill. We lived for the opposition. Once again, we scrambled out the back door, over the fence, and into the night, running and laughing and cursing like soldiers after a great, bloody war.

Aragorn got bigger and became a brawler, scuffling whenever he could. He shaved his head and wore combat boots. He became a SHARP—Skinheads Against Racial Prejudice—a group that opposed Nazis theoretically and physically. In the early '90s, Nazi skinheads were crashing every punk show, getting more brazen—and stronger. If you wore a SHARP patch, you were going to fight.

As Aragorn muscled up, I felt myself becoming smaller and weaker. Maybe it was the vegetarian diet. Maybe it was all the positive hardcore music I was listening to, as if Youth of Today and Bold was entering my bloodstream and sucking out all its nutrients. Whatever it was, I was on the sidelines for many fights. Maybe that was better. I wasn't disciplined. I didn't know what it would take to learn to fight or build my muscles. All I knew was that I hated those Nazi skins with all my soul and I wanted them dead. I just wasn't ready to do it myself.

One night in Sacramento, there was a show at the Cattle Club. Lots of SHARPs showed up, their bald heads sweating under the sweltering heat. New, different energy buzzed through the nightclub. Something sinister. Enough bad energy to short out the sound system.

It wasn't long before a group of Nazis showed up to find some SHARPs. Quickly after arriving, a Nazi pulled a knife and charged. Aragorn fumbled with a canister of Mace and sprayed it into one of the Nazis' eyes. A fight broke out. The blinded Nazi wildly swung his knife around. He stuck

Aragorn in the kidney and spleen. Aragorn's roommate Paul, another SHARP, tried to intervene, but the Nazi stabbed him, once in the chest and again in the abdomen.

Aragorn recovered in the hospital.

Paul died the next day of stab wounds.

It wasn't so foreign anymore, the violence, some abstract idea from a movie or television show, and it wasn't just relegated to my family. Death was everywhere now.

Bad Advice

I brought my girlfriend to Monica's funeral, which I remember being at a church, but why a church? None of us were religious in the slightest bit. It made no sense, other than my parents' dedication to traditionalism and normalcy.

She was a wild mess, my girlfriend, a hurricane of hairspray, eye makeup, and spandex shorts. She was horrible for me in every way, which is why I loved her, my own little form of punishment, wrapped up in a beautiful package.

I sensed angry eyes burning my back when we walked into the church. I didn't look at my mom, but I could feel her seething with rage.

How dare you bring that slut to my daughter's funeral?

But I loved my girlfriend. I wanted her there with me as I listened to echoes of crying in the dark wooden room. My little sister was dead, but I wasn't. I still had all the time in the world to make the worst decisions, and my girlfriend was my latest. We held hands in the pew, and I listened to the priest. He was talking about God, how a dead child was fortunate to be with the Lord now, and some other bullshit. I could only focus on my girlfriend—wearing white spandex underneath her dress—and her leg, pale as lamb's wool.

She eventually broke up with me. She was courted by every badass kid in a fifty-mile radius, and I knew my time would eventually come, and when it did, it hit me like a bag of bricks. My stepdad noticed I wasn't feeling well and invited me for a walk.

"It's rough," he said, and as we walked on the burning pavement, sweat pouring from our faces, he told me a story about when he was dumped. He was in high school. The girl broke up with him, and he was the saddest he'd ever been. He couldn't take it. He was nearly suicidal.

"You know," he said. "I'm not sure why I told you that story."

We walked back into our cul-de-sac, the modest suburban homes finally cooling under the shade of the valley oak trees. My stepdad was trying to make me feel better, trying to relate to me. He had been young once too. He'd had a girlfriend. And a dick that he wanted to stick into his girlfriend so badly that he thought he was in love. When she dumped him, he thought it would be his last chance at that sort of thing, so he thought of plunging himself off a building in a dramatic show of sorrow, but he was too cowardly for that, so he kept going, only to realize that it wasn't the end. Not even close. There were so many more horrible things to come. I love the story, not because it was supposed to be a didactic tale, but because it was so fucked up. I got to see my stepdad in a new light—he was like me, like my biological father, like every man. We have bad plans. We make mistakes because of our refusal to calculate. We make impulsive choices that end up making us look like complete fools. We're all time bombs, but not everyone has to explode. He's no different than I am, but somehow it's like we come from two separate planets on opposite ends of the galaxy. He was able to disassemble his most dangerous elements, while I was crafting my own mechanism without a safety switch, just a timer and the detonator, set for the inevitable explosion.

Half Sister

It was the middle of summer in Davis, California, which meant one hundred degrees. I was sixteen, completely upside down, and mad at the world, always on the verge of dropping out of school and jumping onto the nearest freight train, or in front of it, but too soft and too long fed by the comforts of suburbia to do anything but dress like a hobo and keep a middle finger up to the world.

I sat on the edge of the soccer field, using my skateboard as a chair, and watched my little sister Lauren's soccer team, a horde of eight-year-old girls scrambling up and down the field. There was no strategy or grace, just a gang of kids frantically rushing toward the ball. It was beautiful to me, their rejection of the rules. They went to practice. They studied the fundamentals and techniques of proper soccer. But come game time, all that shit went out the window and those girls did whatever the fuck they wanted. The game turned from soccer into "get the fucking ball by any means necessary." I loved watching them, especially Lauren, a curly-headed angel, half of my stepdad and half of my mom.

An Irish Mexican with a gap-toothed smile who temporarily eased my teenage angst.

When she was five, we still lived in Brookline. Her head was so full of curls that her hair bounced around like a tiny bobblehead as she walked. She never stopped laughing. When she looked up at me, I felt taller and stronger, like somebody wanted me in the room even though I was a fuckup who couldn't do math and skipped school for weeks at a time.

My parents had gone to take care of errands, so we had the place to ourselves. I pulled her on a blanket across the hallway, through the kitchen, and around all the rooms, taking corners like a rally car, our laughter echoing through the house. We played for an hour until I took a corner too hard and her face banged into the coffee table. Her lip split like a little pomegranate, blood pooling onto her chin and shirt.

She screamed in horror at the pain and the blood until my parents came home. Their disappointment seared into me, my stepdad's serious face, their fingers wagging while Lauren bled, screaming in the corner.

After the soccer game, Lauren ran to where I was sitting at the edge of the field. She was a little sweating ball of energy. The smile on her face sent a wave of joy through me, like radiation to cancer cells.

Sometimes now, as an adult, she'll bring up the time I showed up at her soccer game even though I was in the midst of a juvenile delinquency crisis.

"Do you remember you came to watch my soccer game by yourself?" she'll say.

"I do."

"That meant a lot."

I know what she means. I was a fucked-up teenager. I didn't care about anything. I wanted to split from our family. I wanted to burn down my school with all the teachers inside. I wanted to watch cops get run over by trains. I wanted to put on my headphones and turn up Black Flag's "Rise Above" while the world exploded into a billion pieces. But I also wanted other things. I wanted to feel love—real love, not the transactional kind where my GPA needs to be at a certain level or I don't come home with a fucked-up haircut. I wanted to feel the love of a sister and brother who would do anything for each other.

Nobody in our family talked about Monica, my parents' dead daughter, our dead sister. We grieved silently and in our own ways, my parents quietly visiting her grave on her birthday, my sisters burying their heads in books, and me finding new and interesting ways to self-destruct.

Skatepark Wetback

They shouldn't have hired me at the skatepark in Davis. I was a sixteen-year-old kid and all I wanted to do was skate. I didn't need money. I didn't want to work. But I took the CPR classes with a couple of friends, and by the next week I was working as a skate park attendant, a city job that consisted of me sitting there, watching people skate. Suddenly, I had authority. If anyone I didn't like showed up, I'd tell them to get the fuck out, and they'd leave. It was the most power I'd ever had, and I intended to wield it like an American flag at every inappropriate opportunity.

The shifts were only a few hours long, but they seemed like an eternity, especially for a hyperactive kid who didn't like being left out. It felt like the world partied while I sat in the concrete park baking under the sun. Now and then I'd take a run around the park, carving the bowls, ollying the transitions, sliding the rails, and then I'd sit back down and see how many minutes I'd used up.

When Jerry, the ginger-haired scumbag from Sacramento, showed up, I was tempted to bar his entry, but I let him in out of boredom and watched him skate for a bit. His idiotic skateboarding provoked my nerves. He wasn't good. With every push, he struggled to steady himself. By the time he hit a transition, he was already off-balance, and he'd fly off his board. He never changed his approach, just kept doing the same dumbfuck shit he was doing before and falling dramatically on the concrete.

Jerry pulled a picnic table from the corner of the park and set it on top of the funbox at the bottom of a hill we'd use to gather speed. The hill was perfectly placed so you could do a huge trick over the funbox while you were hauling ass. People skated the table this way all the time. But for Jerry, it would've been certain death.

"Ay," I said. "Put that shit back."

"What?" Jerry said. He took off his baseball hat, his orange hair flying in the sun like a bonfire.

"Pull the fucking table back."

"Fuck you," he said. He stuffed his hair back into his hat and angled the table on the funbox like he was going to try to fly over the thing lengthwise.

I skated over to him. He was bigger than I remembered. Like an out-of-shape football player. "Put the table back."

"Or what."

"I'll fuck you up," I said. I debated saying it, but I thought I could take him. I was strong for my size, and I was good at wrestling. If anything, I could choke him out on the ground. Or run away.

Jerry ripped the hat off the top of his head so his orange hair stuck straight into the sky and opened his arms wide, skateboard hanging in the crook of his arm.

"Faggot!" he yelled.

"Get the fuck out," I said, trying to sound calm. I smiled, but Jerry was losing his mind, his freckled face turning a deep shade of purple. I jolted at him, and he took a step back.

He wasn't going to do anything.

I ran toward him, and he ducked behind the big bowl and then out of the park. Once he was safely on the other side of the fence, he hit his skateboard against a metal pole, sending a loud smack through the air.

"Fucking wetback!" he yelled.

"What?" I moved toward the fence so our faces were inches apart.

"Fucking dirty wetback," he yelled again. He spit a loogie toward me and it dissipated against the fence, the spray spritzing my face. I wiped his saliva from my eye as he stomped across the field toward the parking lot.

Nobody had ever called me a wetback before. Not many people even identified me as a Mexican person. Nobody bothered to classify me beyond *babyface with big feet* or *skateboarding punk*. People saw me and thought, "Now there's a racially ambiguous child. Wonder what happened there?" *Wetback*. There was something interesting about being called a wetback.

I walked back to my post. The park was empty again. I followed the smooth concrete dipping gently into the earth with my eyes, appreciating how it jutted up again at a sharp angle, the metal coping on its edges ground down from months of metal against metal.

"Wetback," I said to myself.

I liked it.

A minute later, I heard an unmistakable smashing of glass. And then another. And another. I ran across the field into the parking lot, where Jerry was heaving a metal trash can over his head and breaking another car's windshield. He threw the can, hopped in a truck, and took off screeching down the road.

Like in an old karate flick, an entire karate class in white gis ran into the parking lot with their hands on their heads, pointing to their trucks and then at me, standing at the top of a hill.

"What happened here?" asked a large man with a black belt cinched around his waist.

"Guy freaked out," I said. "In the skate park."

"Freaked out?"

"Yup."

"How?"

"Called me a wetback."

"A wetback? Why?"

"Cuz I'm Mexican."

The man looked at me and back at the parking lot full of cars with bashed-in windshields, surrounded by chunks of glass.

"Do you have a name?"

"Josh," I said. "It doesn't sound Mexican, but my mom named me that because—well, I don't know why, but my last name is Fernandez."

"No, I'm saying, do you have the name of the guy who smashed my fucking truck?"

"Oh," I said. "No."

The karate man shook his head and went to look at the damage.

"Which one is yours?" he called up to me.

"Mine?"

"Which car?"

"Oh," I said. "I don't drive."

More Violence

I stopped listening to hardcore music and started smoking weed. I stopped caring about the ideals learned from listening to punk day and night. I found the principles of antifascist and anticapitalist rage too tedious for my hormonal mind, which preferred only to retain information pertaining to finding a girl who would get naked with me. I was seventeen. My friends were a bunch of jumpy kids with peach fuzz mustaches and raging boners who didn't have time for politics.

We hung out at Woodstock's, the wood-paneled shithole where high school and college kids skipped class to flirt and score beer. AC/DC's "Dirty Deeds Done Dirt Cheap" blasted from the speakers that lined the restaurant, Bon Scott's nasal voice sleazing up every corner. My friends scattered around the pizza place like fire ants, frantic and ready to bite. I took my own table. I didn't want any part of their energy; too many clustered on each bench, shoveling hot slices in their greasy mouths, yelling in between bites, like, "Yoooo! Your mouth looks like a pussy, yo!" and other dumb shit. I got a whole pie to myself, a Wild Bread: dough cooked till golden, no sauce, cheese with some herbs on top, and when you dip it into a tub of ranch, you're transported to a blissful otherworld, which I wanted all to myself. It felt right to be with a group of friends and totally alone.

I remembered that AC/DC concert I went to with my stepdad, when he had bought me tickets because I used to dress like Angus Young: school-boy shorts, long socks, a little baseball cap, and a sports coat. I could name every lyric to every song, Bon Scott or Brian Johnson. I hugged my stepdad when he showed me those tickets. A real hug. He always tried hard to find me through all my anger, and I always managed to shut him off and sprint in the other direction.

I went back to finishing my pizza. When I looked up, all my friends had finished their slices and were playing arcade games in the back. A new group arrived with three pitchers of beer. They were older and beefier, two sporting UC Davis football sweatshirts. I stood up to fill my drink and walked toward the fountain, and when I passed the football players, one of them stuck out his elbow and hit my thigh. I pretended not to notice, filled my drink, and sat back down without looking up until the last greasy rectangles were gone.

"Fuckin' *faggot*," one of them called. He clutched a pitcher of beer with his meaty fist, wiggling his middle finger at me with his free hand.

I smiled pleasantly at the football player and slurped down the rest of my Coke. It's funny that he called me a faggot. I'd often wondered if I was a faggot. Now and then, another boy would catch my eye. The last one was a dark Mexican I'd met at the skatepark, skin the color of wet earth. I couldn't stop watching him, the most beautiful person I had seen in quite some time. We had skated in the heat until we became dizzy from the sun. We sat facing each other. His shorts crept up his leg, and I could see his testicles clinging to the side of his thigh. I couldn't get the image out of my mind.

I was a good-looking teenager by American standards. My Mexican features gave my face the angles of a young, possibly non-American boy who had never seen the sun. I blamed my pale complexion on the Spaniards who had conquered my motherland and created a nation of soap opera Mexicans—delicate, light-skinned people with hooked noses flattened to a point and broad faces chiseled into thin angles. My *abuela* was the color of a slice of whole wheat bread, and she often admired my light skin, pinching my cheeks as if I'd achieved greatness. She spent a good portion of her life driving to Tijuana to procure the cheap makeup that she'd slather all over her face to appear a couple of shades lighter. I secretly hated my heavily European features, so I spent summers shirtless under direct sunlight, baking my flesh until it was the color of wet earth.

White boys hated me—especially the all-American types, the baseball players and football players. The sight of me, an ethnically ambiguous hoodlum who wore bandannas and Timberland boots, was enough to drive them to violence on more than one occasion.

The boys got up, and the biggest one, who wore a white T-shirt one size too small, pushed me when he passed. They laughed in unison and left a trail of beer stench in their wake, then loitered out front in a half circle, smoking cigarettes. I turned my head to watch them on the sidewalk. They glared at me, trying to look scary. The big one motioned me to come outside, so I walked toward them. I had no fighting skills at this point, just a head full of anger and a body buzzing with teenage angst. A song I didn't recognize blasted from the speakers. I think it was country music, twanging guitars and a man's voice shooting from a high squeal to a corny baritone in a couple of bars. I hated country music. It reminded me of everything I disliked about people, the cheesy, *yes ma'am*, shit-eating bravado that was supposed to represent the proper image of a real American.

The crisp air was shocking, like someone taking me by the shoulders and shaking me to wake me up. The temperature outside had dropped ten degrees, so cold that the big football player's nipples were hard, poking through his tight shirt like tiny googly eyes. The boys all wore the same deceptive smiles, trying to mask hate with friendliness to appear more badass.

A cloudy mixture of hot breath and cigarettes rose from them. The big one got in my face first.

"Wussup, faggot," he said, his orange goatee curling hatefully toward his cracked lips. Before I could say anything, he cocked back and punched me between my nose and my eye. The force pushed me back a few steps. He stood there in a half daze, his beer breath egging me on. There was a little pain, but not much. Unbridled revenge acting as an aspirin.

I shot a jab at his chin and put my hands up, bracing for a flurry of punches that never came. They would've killed me had it not been for my friends, who swarmed out of the restaurant. Sonny, a short, stocky

Mexican who only wore red, ran at my attacker and swung a huge over-hand that landed directly on his temple with a dull thud. The large boy's knees buckled under his own weight, and he dropped like a sack of bricks. Leon made quick work of the smaller one with a hook and a jab to the nose. The guy's hand flew to his face as he shrank and crouched next to a parked car, his free hand waving like a white flag of surrender.

The last one didn't want any part of the violence, and he tried to run away, but a group of three caught him in the middle of the street. Someone stuck out a leg and tripped him while the other two jumped on his back and pummeled him until he curled into a fetal position.

In a perfect, violent grand finale, my friend Clifford ran into the middle of the street and landed a kick that connected with the side of the football player's face. A trail of blood leaked from his ear into a tidy pool on the concrete as he lay there motionless like a gigantic question mark.

A crowd started to form. Onlookers pointed at the bloody football players, then at us. We quickly split up and ran in opposite directions, knowing the cops would arrive soon, the crowd only too willing to offer descriptions of the different shades of Brown assailants.

As I ran toward my parents' house, my nose started throbbing. I tried to think of a lie I could tell my stepdad about the black eye that was surely forming. A fall on my skateboard? A play fight with friends? A robbery? Any lie would do. I was a liar. I'd lied thousands of times to my parents. They knew when I wasn't telling the truth but rarely said anything, like a little game we played, not for fun but out of necessity. Nobody wanted to spend eternity yelling at each other, so we picked our battles and tried to leave each other alone when we could. I loved my mom and stepdad, but we existed on different planes, maybe in different universes. I didn't understand their obsession with success, their insistence on following a traditional path from academic achievement to office work. I wanted to drop out of school. I wanted to fight, and fuck, and roll around on the floor with my friends, laughing until we choked on the smoky air. I wanted to break the world into pieces and leave a mess for everyone else to clean up. When I got home, my stepdad was working in the garage, my mom in the backyard spraying her plants with a hose. In my room, I sprawled on the bed and let my throbbing face lull me to sleep.

When I woke up, it was dinnertime. The house smelled like baked chicken.

I pulled up a chair at the table where my mom and stepdad sat.

My face pounded, but I tried not to let it show.

It worked. Nobody noticed. Or maybe they did, but they just didn't know what to say.

I poked my fork into the chicken and watched the juice squirt out of the holes I had made.

HOW TO TALK TO COLLEAGUES

I'm trying to cook dinner when my colleague calls. He's out of breath, like he'd been running a 5K and remembered that he needed to tell me something important.

"I have something to tell you," he says. "You can't tell anyone we talked."

Even when he's not handling covert operations such as this, he's perpetually nervous, a Rockstar energy drink forever clutched in one hand, amplifying his anxiety issues. I keep telling him to quit drinking the fucking things, but he laughs sheepishly and blows it off. One time, another colleague told me he gave her the creeps. I guess I can see why. He's an oversharer on social media, and he's always looking to be lauded as the good guy—typical liberal progressive stuff, but I've never really had a problem with him. Sometimes men who aren't afraid to show their emotions get a bad rap. They're misunderstood. He has a good heart, but many people have those and don't know what to do with them.

"What's up," I say, pushing an uninspired tofu stir-fry around the pan.

"This is confidential," he says.

"I know," I say, wondering how many polite phrases he'll invoke for telling me to keep my mouth shut.

"I was by the instruction office, and a few students were waiting for the investigator to see them," he says.

"Oh shit, okay," I say. I know this already, because another colleague called to tell me that the investigator was poking around the campus and wanted to interview her, but she told the investigator she wouldn't participate.

"Don't worry," he says. "The students won't say anything."

"What do you mean?"

"They were talking about how you're a good person, and they're not going to say anything to the investigator."

I know this too. The students all called me right after their interviews. They couldn't wait to tell me what had happened. One of them told the investigator that I'm one of the only LGBTQ community allies on campus and that I've saved lives, which is a little dramatic, to be honest. But if there's one thing about my creative writing students, it's that their sense of melodrama is finely tuned.

Other colleagues and students begin contacting me with stories about the investigator, how they're poking around the campus, conducting interviews about my affiliation with Antifa and my ties to violent leftist activism. I've been involved with antifascist organizing since I was a teenager. I could tell a million stories about how the punk scene was infested with neo-Nazi skinheads, boneheads who'd try to ruin every show until we got organized and started showing up with bats and crowbars. I wish the investigator would have come to me first.

My union rep and their lawyer have different ideas on handling the investigator. They've already started coaching me on what to say when it's my turn to be grilled.

"Don't say too much," the lawyer said. "They're trying to catch you with an inconsistency. The more you say, the easier it is for them."

My lawyer's plan is to make me play it safe. One-word answers if possible. I already know I'm going to say too much. I always say too much at the wrong time. It's part of my charm. Plus, I feel like I have nothing to hide. I can tell this investigator everything, starting from day one. I mean, what the fuck is she going to do? They can't fire me for being against racism, can they? I'll tell her so many stories that she'll die of boredom right there in the interrogation room.

I stop listening to my colleague. Everything he's saying I already know, but I don't want to be rude, so I don't hang up. I know that my students are being pulled into the administration office one by one. I know that the investigator is grilling them about my affiliation with Antifa. I can't control what they say. I don't even know them that well.

I look at my lifeless dinner. I never learned to cook, and I don't want to start now. My son, Ezra, is three, and he eats hot dogs for his meals. I hear a homeless man rustling around our bushes, probably pissing, but I'm too tired to tell him to go away. *Let him piss*, I think. *Who gives a flying fuck?*

I catch my reflection in the kitchen window. Sometimes I forget that I'm covered in satanic tattoos. It makes me laugh when I see them reflected at me. What do I care about some homeless dude pissing in a bush that's still owned by a bank? I'm still a punk. Right? Could it be that I'm more punk than ever? No, I'm a college professor. I live in a house now—a big house in a nice neighborhood. That's no way to be punk. But my neighbors, the ones with SUVs plastered with military stickers, still look at me like *I'm* the crazy one. On the first day of class, my students always gasp. They're horrified by my tattoos. They see something in my eyes, and it fascinates them the same way caged lions fascinate small children. They try to impress me with their punk rock knowledge, which extends only as far as the Warped Tour. *Professor, did you go to the Aftershock Festival?* they ask. I wonder if it's professionally ethical to kick them out of the class for being lame. *What does that tattoo mean?* one always asks.

It means nothing, I think. *None of this does.*

When the investigator finally calls me into the interrogation room and asks the inevitable question about violence, I'll give her the exact look I give my students. I'll tell her how to stick a skinhead with a ballpoint pen, how to carve an anarchy symbol on your forearm, how to make a weapon from a flagpole. Or maybe I'll just shrug my shoulders and say, "I don't know," like my union rep and the lawyer instructed.

"Just don't tell anyone I talked to you, okay?" my colleague continues, as if being associated with me is some heinous act of domestic terrorism.

"Don't worry," I say. "My lips are sealed."

I get off the phone and immediately call my union rep to tell him everything my colleague just said.

"It's okay, buddy," he says. "You have nothing to worry about."

That makes me feel better for a second, but then I start thinking about all the money the school district is spending to conduct an investigation. It can't be cheap. They're gunning for me. I open my laptop to check my job prospects. A job alert pops up.

You would be a good fit for a job at Google writing UX!

I don't even know what that is. I don't know what UX stands for and I'm too lazy too Google it. I know nothing about computers, but I submit my resume anyway and hit send.

THE GREYHOUND

I finally failed out of high school when I was seventeen, with only a few credits left to complete in summer school, but I didn't want to waste any more time, so I decided to split. I couldn't stand California any longer—its angry summers and empty spring breezes, its overabundance of slack-jawed football players who roamed in packs, ready to start some shit, its university economy, snake eating its tail—professors spawning children of professors who were all expected to one day become professors. With $365 in my pocket, I packed a duffel bag and waited at the Greyhound terminal in Sacramento for the next bus across the country, back to Boston.

The ride took seven days. On the third, somewhere in the Midwest, I met a metalhead so illiterate he could barely form whole sentences. When he spoke, he brushed the long, greasy hair from his eyes and concentrated as hard as he could, as if it took all his brain function to create a string of words. We sat next to each other in the back of the Greyhound. His name was Christian, and like any man of faith he shared a bag of cocaine, and the rest of the ride was a blur of rambling conversation about the nuances of death metal. Halfway through the trip, my eyes bugged from my skull. My teeth jittered. In the middle of the night, I touched his dick a little bit under his blanket.

When the bus finally peaked over the rugged Connecticut terrain and screeched into the Boston terminal, my body ached, my jaws tight like I'd been chewing on lug nuts for a week straight. Chemical electricity buzzed all around me, mainly from the drugs, then the subsequent lack of drugs, and something else. Maybe it was the absence of my parents, the realization that I couldn't rely on anyone except myself, an utterly unreliable person.

Boston's thick, wet air was a detail I'd forgotten about and hadn't prepared for. The city, murky with smog, carried a serious atmosphere. People, even well-dressed adults, contended with an aura of deranged energy hovering about them. Everything seemed dangerous.

My disheveled father greeted me at the station wearing a loose ponytail and black bruises on each of his cheeks. He looked the same as I remembered, although deep lines now cut into his face and the schizophrenic sickness had hollowed out his brown eyes.

For years he'd been wandering from place to place, renting any room that his monthly social security check would cover. Sometimes he'd stay in residential hotels or on the street. Every now and then Rebecca and I would get a hastily scribbled letter letting us know where he was and rambling about the importance of God.

"Oh, my son," he hugged me with frail arms. His sweater smelled of dirt, grease, and weed. "*Mijo.*"

On the way back to his apartment in Boston's Roxbury area, we walked fast, talking about my father's legal trouble. He'd punched a cop for harassing a homeless man just down the block. But mostly, he spoke about God. We walked quickly through downtown along crooked brick sidewalks, past the old brick churches and the marble library. He spoke about Jesus Christ, spit flying from his lips as he ranted.

"I'm a lawyer, you know," he said suddenly with a furrowed brow. "I'm a lawyer for God and the four points of the compass, the kingdom of heaven on earth."

I couldn't understand what he was saying.

We entered a park, and my dad introduced me to Damon, an old man so drunk his daughter had to keep him propped up with her shoulder. Her name was Rasha, a licorice stick of a girl my age. Her muscled arms had more definition than I'd ever seen on a girl, probably from holding up her father for the entirety of her life.

Rasha nodded to me, embarrassed, tugging her father's shirt toward her as he leaned like a cable on an old swaying bridge. Damon reached out to shake my hand. His rough palm slid into mine, and he pulled me real close and laughed.

"You ain't surviving a minute out here," he said, his breath reeking of pure vodka. It's like he could see in the chubbiness of my face that I had been infantilized by the comforts of suburbia. He slapped my back so hard that the sting lingered like an aura as I walked up the stairs to my dad's apartment. My face burned with anger.

My dad lived at the top of an old brick building. It wasn't even an actual apartment, just an attic nearly unfit for human life, with a shared bathroom at the end of the hallway. We sat on milk crates, smoked a bag of dirt weed, and talked about God. My narcotic bones jonesed for something stronger and trembled beneath my skin. He opened a dirty Bible and read passages from pages that smelled like cigarette smoke and mildew.

"You see?" he said, and pointed to a passage that said:

> Overthrow their altars, and break their pillars, and burn their groves with fire.

I said it aloud, again and again, and we laughed at its beautiful violence.

That night, we drank and smoked and repeated that line over and over until our teeth chattered and the neighbors banged up against the wall.

I Can't Fight

The last time I saw my father was in San Diego. I took the bus across the country with no plan. I was twenty-one and got a job working at a smoothie shop and living in a rented house with my friends, who were all attending UC San Diego. We lived at the edge of Pacific Beach. Every day, after they got back from class, we'd go skateboarding at different ledges or banks or sometimes we'd do the Hillcrest Bomb, a steep downhill path that started at the top of a gigantic hill and snaked downtown, with stairs and ledges along the way.

My dad insisted that he didn't want to bother us and he wanted to act like a normal father, so he pitched a tent in our backyard, where he slept and ate meals that he cooked on his little Bunsen burner. Pretty normal dad stuff. We were ten people packed in a three-bedroom house. We never cleaned. We drank all day and rode our skateboards. My roommates didn't want him there. My father scared them, those dull eyes, craggy cheeks, the bald spot with a long ponytail, and his insistence on sneaking God into every conversation. He was homeless and worn from schizophrenia.

One day I was on the phone with my sister, and he came in through the back door and opened a beer from the refrigerator. He often wandered in to steal our beer and smoke our weed.

"Who is that?" he said. "Who you talking to?"

"It's your daughter," I said. "Rebecca."

"Sunshine?"

"She goes by Rebecca now," I said.

He wound his arm up and punched me in the stomach. The phone flew out of my hands. The air left my body. A voice in my brain told me to kill him, so I reached for his neck, and he stood there while I choked him. I hadn't realized how small he was. A good two inches shorter than I. And frail. Like a little Mexican ragdoll. He didn't try to stop me. His hands hung by his sides and his face turned red, then gray, his watery eyes bulging from their sockets. Under his long, wispy hair, I saw a vein popping from his forehead. I think I was yelling. I must have been yelling, because the neighbor shouted over the fence, "I called the police."

"Fuck you," I said. "I'll kill you next."

The neighbor ducked his head under the fence and slid his door shut.

My father wouldn't die. I let go of his neck and tried to punch him, but I didn't connect. I ran to the refrigerator, found a gallon of milk, and hurled it at his face, its contents spilling over the living room, the couch bathed in a translucent film.

"You pussy," he growled. "You can't fight for shit."

Everything was over by the time the cop showed up. The cop was tall and fat and tired and out of breath. His bright red nose peeled under his sunglasses. I thought of taking his gun and shooting him in the face, then turning the gun on my father, then myself. He told my father to pack up his tent and go, leaving me alone in a messy house bathed in milk.

I remember when my sister changed her name in fifth grade, how effortless it was. She came home with a new name and everyone went along with it.

I wish everything were that easy. I wish I could change everything I've ever done, start over knowing what I know now, but that's impossible. Everyone would notice and nobody would go along with the plan. All I can do is study the machinery, learn its mechanisms, and carefully remove its most volatile parts so it's less dangerous in the event of a malfunction.

Meth on the Coast

Leo was so drunk that he could barely hold up his head. It was 2 a.m. The lights in the diner were too bright, and my head started hurting after fifteen minutes of not drinking, as if my brain were already drying up with sobriety. I ordered some toast, and Leo managed to order a stack of blueberry pancakes. Somehow the waitress understood his order of *boo-borry manka* as "blueberry pancakes." Likely she was adept at the language of the lonely and depressed drunkard. Leo was a jolly Mexican man who craved more affection than anyone could give. He constantly sought out a girlfriend and often settled for internet porn. His eyes were half-shut, and his head waved around until he put it in his arms. He looked like he was going to barf.

"Goddammit," Leo muttered. "I wanna fuckin—"

"You okay?" I asked.

"No," he said. The waitress set his pancakes next to him with a set of utensils wrapped in a paper napkin and gave us an eye roll.

"Don't need fork!" he yelled.

"Okay," she said without a smile.

Leo eyed his plate of pancakes and lunged open-mouthed into the stack. His entire face was covered in pancake, smashed blueberries, and butter when he emerged. It was the best thing I'd ever seen.

"More, more, more!" I yelled.

Leo dove back into the stack and emerged once again. He finished the entire plate of pancakes using only his face. By the time he was done, his face glistened blue. He left too much cash on the table, and we got into his compact car, both of us too drunk to drive.

Our house was only about a mile from the diner. Leo started the engine, pulled out of the parking lot, and skidded onto Balboa Avenue. It was a straight shot home to Clairemont Drive. We lurched forward after the stop light and headed into the early morning.

Leo pointed to a yield sign glowing in the distance.

"Leo," I said.

He ignored me and shifted into a higher gear.

"Leo, no," I said. I braced myself.

The car merged onto the round edge of the sidewalk with a *thump*, the sign now in our direct path. I clung to the sides of the seat and gritted my teeth. The car slammed into the sign, which folded easily underneath the bumper. We jumped a little, and then Leo swerved back onto the road, leaving the folded sign in our wake.

"What the fuck!" I yelled.

Leo grunted.

He was not happy.

When I looked over, tears were streaming down his face. He banged his head on the steering wheel before glancing back at the road. We were young and lonely and crazy and addicted. That's probably why we got along so well.

A few months later, I was staying on a friend's couch in Pacific Beach, and a bunch of Korean dudes came over to visit one of my roommates. That night, we were all playing video games on our little TV, and one of them pulled out some weed and started rolling a joint. I wasn't good at smoking weed. It made me too paranoid. I lost my ability to talk whenever I smoked, so I tried to stay away.

"Try this," the Korean guy said, pulling out a little baggie of clear crystals that he sprinkled over the weed and then rolled up into a perfect joint.

"What is it?" I asked.

"It's speed."

They passed the joint around, and I took a hit. As soon as the smoke filled my lungs, I was struck with a bold new sensation, a tingling in the body, a clear head, the clearest head, a divine head with the ability to parse the bullshit of the world and feel empathy for every living being. And I was the horniest I'd ever been. I could have fucked anything in front of me. A man. A woman. A pillow. It didn't matter. I couldn't wait until the joint came my way again and again. Until there was no more left in the baggie. I turned the baggie inside out and licked its insides. I took a walk into the night. A cool breeze touched every part of my body, even through my clothes. I pictured a hundred angels breathing on my neck, licking my balls. I could see each star in its entirety. The moon bulged and throbbed against the black sky. I walked toward the beach, breathing in and out, each breath filling me with the most intense happiness I had ever known, and I knew right then I was in serious trouble.

NOT THE POET, THE PUNK ROCKER

When our son, Ezra, is born, I stand in the hospital, the morning light splitting the room into abrupt angles, a clear delineation of light and dark, weeping at the sight of our baby boy resting like a tiny bear on Crystal's breasts while she kisses his tiny head.

He makes an easy exit.

He's an easy boy.

He probably won't make trouble for anyone.

I don't know if I'm crying because he's so cute, like a fuzzy bear cub, or because he was born to an unworthy father—an addict, a thief, a liar, a thug, a loser. It's probably a little of both. I'm still crying when the nurse offers me the scissors.

I look at the jagged scar on my palm from when I sliced my hand open trying to cut a bagel, the knife sliding easily into my palm, blood pouring out of the gash. I had no insurance or any money, so I chugged the rest of a bottle of Jack Daniels, heated a needle until it glowed orange, and sewed the bloody flaps of skin with black thread, tears of pain rolling down my cheeks. When I finished sewing, I held my hand up to the light, and a wave of drunken pride ripped through my body. I gave myself stitches. I fixed myself without the help of a hospital.

"No, no, no," I say to the nurse. "I don't want to use those scissors."

But she insists. "They're for you," she says, handing them to me. "It's a father's duty."

Peer pressure, I think. *This is bullshit.*

I hold the scissors in my shaking hands.

The umbilical cord makes a ripping sound as I cut him from his mother.

BITER

I get a call from Ezra's day care downtown, right across from the Sacramento County Jail, where I'd spent many weeks locked up and where I would spend many more.

"He bit a friend," the school director says.

Everyone in the same class is referred to as a friend, even if they're your enemy.

"Oh no."

"He'll be in the office," she adds.

"Be right there," I say, searching for my keys under a giant stack of student work.

When I get to the day care, Ezra is sitting in the office, away from all the other kids, waiting for me. He smiles when he sees me and outstretches his tiny arms.

"Bite," he says.

"Bite," I return.

Ezra laughs.

God, how many times I've wanted to bite the shit out of my acquaintances.

The next day, we get another call. Another bite. And the next day. I'm so confused. Crystal is confused too. Ezra is a good boy. He's jolly and doesn't give us any trouble at home. He laughs day and night at everything, even things that aren't that funny. His biting gets so bad that the day care calls a social worker to observe him. She sits next to Ezra with a pad of paper all day, taking notes on his every move, investigating him.

At the end of the week, her report is finished. I pick it up and read it in my office. It says that she's impressed. Ezra is smart. He speaks in complete sentences, which is rare at his age. The report says that when he's done with lunch, he tells the teacher, "More quesadillas, please." He's polite, she says. At the end of the report, the social worker notes that Ezra needs more stimulation at school. She gives the teachers a list of things to do that might help, like be clearer about expectations and continue to provide him with more words to satisfy his need for a large vocabulary.

Ezra bit some kids, sure, which is clearly illustrated by the photocopied picture of a red bite mark on a little white arm in the perfect shape of Ezra's mouth. But the social worker's report also determines that he's blameless, not of the bites, but of the situation that led to his penchant for biting his classmates. His environment is not right for him, and he's a baby. He wasn't sure what to do, so he chose the most violent path.

Plus, he's not ugly, and I hate to say it, but that plays a part. Ugly babies don't get much leniency. Maybe it's a Fernandez trait, one destined to get us in and out of trouble over and over again. When backed into a corner, we'll bite our way out, but we'll look cute as fuck while doing it.

When I return from work, Crystal and Ezra are on the couch. Ezra is lying with his head resting on his mother's leg. He's mumbling or singing, his eyes getting heavy with each word. I'm at the kitchen table, but I don't want to move, as if the slightest movement will break the perfect moment, like jumping feet-first onto a thin sheet of ice over a frozen lake, hoping the layer is strong enough to hold.

San Diego to Davis

I woke up in the back seat of my car, which was always out of gas. All I could think about was food and drugs, and my hands trembled constantly. I had parked two blocks from my parents' house in Davis, in a maze of neatly trimmed cul-de-sacs dripping with exotic flowers. Even though I'd been exiled from my family, I wanted to be near them, safety in proximity. Maybe I was still a little boy unprepared for a life on my own.

The little bird spotted me and jumped onto the hood of my car. He hopped around, flapping his wings in a tiny ritual of dance. He'd done the same thing the day before. At first it was funny how he strutted back and forth. But he wouldn't leave me alone. For days he stood on the car hood, jumping around like a deranged version of *Dance Fever* in the natural world.

I took a lot of drugs back then, mainly cocaine and methamphetamine, so I don't remember a lot, but I do remember always being hungry, and yet when I tried to eat, my body beaded with sweat and my face trembled, turning gray with nausea.

I tried to distract myself from hunger by propping my scrawny yellow arms on the steering wheel and scribbling poems onto the backs of old receipts. Almost too weak to move, I once wrote a poem that looked like this:

favorite son
of a bloodless father
gimme
ten bucks for two salami sandwiches

It's embarrassing to look back on my old writing. Whenever I see photographs of myself from those days, drugged and disheveled, I can laugh and shake my head in embarrassment. I looked like an elementary kid's drawing of a hobo in ill-fitted clothes and with crooked Xs through his eyes. When I force myself to look at my old writing, it gives me a deep, cold shiver down my entire body.

I learned later in therapy that we're supposed to talk about our feelings, all of them, even the scary ones, even the ones that make you want to cringe yourself into oblivion, and if you don't, you're bound to explode.

That poem was supposed to be about my father.

Back then, everything was about my father.

And food. Always hungry in one way or another.

I couldn't stop thinking about him. The old-school patriarch. The alpha male. The longhair who strutted like a brown rooster around Boston's Roxbury neighborhood. My father was always too poor to live in an apartment with a kitchen, so he cooked all his meals in a toaster oven—disgusting, soppy messes. He made chocolate chip cookies once, and we ate them out of a bowl with a spoon. He loved nature but always lived in the city, so he plastered his walls with forest-themed wallpaper to make his tiny apartment look like the wilderness.

He carried around brass knuckles, but only to be used for cops.

People loved him on the streets.

Bobby Fernandez.

He was smart enough to have finished law school at USC, and he hooked the whole ghetto up with shoddy legal advice. He didn't know shit about the law. He'd failed the bar and didn't put too much time into learning legal matters, so he simply told people what they wanted to hear.

"Hey, Bobby," our neighbor Joe said, knocking on the door. "Open up!"

I lived with my dad on and off back then, splitting time between friends' houses and his little apartment. All our neighbors were Black and Puerto

Rican men who carried guns under their waistbands. Whenever my dad became too much to handle, I'd head back to one of my friends' couches.

"What, Joe?" my dad said.

"I need help, man. My ex-wife is trying to take all my money."

"How much?"

"All of it, man. But I ain't got money like that," Joe pleaded from the other side of the door.

"Tell her fuck off," my dad said.

"Really?" Joe said. "Like that?"

"Sure," my dad answered. Joe's footsteps pounded away as if he'd just gotten news of his entry into the gates of heaven. My dad was a prophet to everyone in that neighborhood because he was so full of shit. It's wise to never get legal help from a guy who digs around in trash cans for new clothes. It's wiser never to trust a grown man named Bobby.

Dad constantly gave me two pieces of advice: stay away from girls and get closer to God. I did the opposite of both. I loved girls. I loved them so hard that they tore me to tiny pieces. It tore them to pieces too. I didn't know what to do with them, especially with all the drugs. So we just tore each other apart, our pieces fluttering to the ground until the wind picked us up and blew us in different directions.

Dad told me about Christ and his connection to the human soul and gave me a Bible. And I read. I smoked his brown weed and turned its thin pages. I only remember the Song of Solomon:

> *Let him kiss me with the kisses of his mouth: for thy love is better than wine . . .*

And:

> *I am the rose of Sharon, and the lily of the valleys.*
> *As the lily among thorns, so is my love among the daughters.*
> *As the apple tree among the trees of the wood, so is my beloved among the suns.*
> *I sat down under his shadow with great delight, and his fruit was sweet to my taste.*
> *Stay me with flagons, comfort me with apples: for I am sick of love.*
> *His left hand is under my head, and his right hand doth embrace me.*

It was the saddest shit I'd ever read, but I rejected God's love entirely. And there I was, having listened to none of my father's advice, starved from drugs and living in my stationary car. Which meant I had a lot to think about in my Honda Civic with almost 200K miles on the odometer. Every night I'd buy two forty-ounce bottles of Steel Reserve malt liquor and sit in the back seat, listening to Nina Simone's version of "Rags and Old Iron."

My Song of Solomon. It was the only thing that made me happy, the only song I owned, found while going through a trash bin, in a CD case mysteriously labeled *SAD* in thick Sharpie letters. When I put that song on, I didn't even know who was singing. I just heard her voice, so heavy that no man could ever lift it. That voice penetrated everything earthly.

That morning when I woke up in my car, I only had $32.25, presumably all the money I would ever have for the rest of my life. And, of course, I planned to spend it all on drugs. A funny thing happens when I tell people about addiction. They say, "Well, you say you were hungry. Wouldn't you use that money to buy food?" Some out-of-touch people will say, "Why wouldn't you put gas in your car and drive to job interviews?" It's hard to explain to somebody what it's like to be a drug addict. It's like when you open a bag of deli meat in front of your cat. No matter what it's doing, the cat runs to the meat and won't stop eating, even if it's full, until it's vomiting the salami back onto your carpet. And maybe after a few minutes, it will eat its vomit just to taste the salty meat once again.

The only guy I knew in town who sold good drugs was Peter, a Polish Nazi skinhead, which always seemed an odd combination. He had the insignia of the Polish trade union Solidarność tattooed in big red letters on his back, but he never had a job in the time that I'd known him.

The taste of hard drugs boiled my soul, burning all the goodness and distilling my body into a vessel for meth and cocaine. Peter's political views took a back seat. My fifteen-year-old self would have kicked the shit out of this new version of me. I walked through town toward the trailer park where Peter lived. The sun felt good on my face. There was no breeze, and it must've been 105 degrees outside. I loved the Northern California heat, the sun killing me slowly like a serial murderer tearing away strips of my flesh. As people walked by, the pained expression on their faces made me feel better about my horrific life.

Most of the college kids, the happy ones whose lives seemed so distant from my own, had gone home for the summer, back to their happy families in their happy hometowns. The streets were empty, aside from the occasional businessman who carried his jacket slung over his shoulder, collar loosened at the neck. Women fanned their faces with file folders. The world melted, and I didn't care. It felt good to be in pain and know they were suffering along with me.

Peter lived in the trailer park at the end of town by the freeway on a street shaded by so many olive trees that the temperature dropped fifteen degrees. A group of dirty white kids played swords with fallen branches. Where the sidewalk ended, the dirt road began, spilling into a lot full of rusted RVs that seemed like they'd been there for the past hundred years— white trailer shells sporting large dents accented by deep orange patches of rust. Old Black men with spotty hair and cutoff jeans sat in lawn chairs drinking beer under the shady trees.

Nobody seemed to notice I was there.

Peter's trailer sat toward the back of the lot. I knocked, and the flimsy door opened.

"The fuck?!" Peter said. "I thought you were dead." He wasn't wearing a shirt but had a pair of thin red suspenders holding up his pants.

"I'm basically dead," I said. Peter didn't laugh.

We stared at each other for what felt like five hours.

"What the fuck do you want?" Peter finally asked.

"Can I come in?"

"Fuck you," Peter said. "Do you have beer?"

"No," I said. "I don't have anything."

"You know who died?" he said.

"Huh?"

"Alison," Peter said. "Pregnant Alison."

"Pregnant Alison?" I asked, confused.

"The punk girl," Peter said. "You fucked her!"

"You mean Betty?" I asked. "The Colombian one?"

"Oh," Peter said. "Yeah, maybe."

"Did the baby die too?"

"No, she had the baby, and then she died."

"The baby killed her?"

"I guess," Peter said with the pained expression of a man who was overthinking. "But that's a negative way to put it."

"Is the father around?" I asked.

"Goddamn," Peter said. "You ask the stupidest questions."

"Can I come in?" I asked again.

Peter motioned me inside.

The trailer looked exactly how I'd expect the trailer of a Nazi skinhead to look, like the backdrop of one of those molesty Calvin Klein ads. The walls were made of wood grain laminate, and various sketchy political posters clung to the walls with the help of Scotch tape. The TV in the corner flickered in and out of commission, playing an episode of some talk show where a pasty man with a mustache talked about being raped by his mother. The volume was turned down, but I'd seen the whole episode before at my dad's apartment in black and white. The show's host tilted her head in fake sympathy for the entire segment. On Peter's color TV, the old bag had an electric yellow dye job that made her appear twice as insane.

I stepped over a pile of clothes and beer cans, and we sat on mismatched foldout chairs in the corner of the room. A baby slept in the middle of a mattress shoved into the trailer's back corner.

"Don't wake that thing," Peter said, pointing to the baby. "The first time it stops crying, you come to my fucking door."

"Is he yours?"

"She," Peter corrected. He flicked out a Marlboro Red and didn't offer me one.

"Some n***** bitch stole my bike," he said, changing the subject.

"How'd you know it was her?" I asked.

"I just know," Peter said.

"Then get it back."

"She got a brother," he said. "And he got friends."

"You know where she lives?"

"They live right next door," Peter said, moving toward the window and lifting the blinds. "I am looking at my bike right now."

I peeked through the window, and Peter's silver BMX was leaning against the trailer next door.

"Can't you just take it back?"

"What?"

"I mean, there's no lock on it," I said. "It's yours. You can just take it back."

Peter took a drag of his cigarette and seemed to be calculating his words.

"Fuck you," he said. "Why did you come here?"

"Seriously?"

Peter looked defeated. I hadn't realized how skinny he was, but I could see his collarbones jutting through his skin. His ribs made him look like a racehorse too old to compete. The dark circles under his gray eyes were a sure sign of malnutrition.

I felt bad for him, even though he probably hated me. He'd probably spit on my grandma, who spoke English with a thick Spanish accent and lived in a bullet-ridden apartment in East LA.

"I need some speed," I said.

"Yeah, I need some fucking money then," Peter said, shaking his head.

"I only have twenty bucks," I lied.

"Okay," Peter said. He picked up a little music box on the cluttered shelf. A plastic ballerina popped out when he opened the box, and Beethoven's "Für Elise" played softly. The baby let out a little groan and stretched her arms.

"Fuck," Peter said. "If she wakes up, I'm going to kick the shit out of you."

"Do you have her forever?" I asked.

"What do you mean? She's my kid."

"But where's the mother?"

"Fuck her mother," Peter said, producing a plastic baggie filled with chunks of meth. He unrolled the plastic, chipped off a few chunks, and placed them on a digital scale.

"There," he said.

"Come on, man."

Peter let out a dramatic sigh, chipped off an extra shard, and put it on the scale. He ripped a piece of newspaper, made a little pouch, poured the meth in, and handed it to me.

"Thanks." I gave him a twenty and stood up. My palms started to sweat. I could feel the pouch of drugs touching my thigh. It gave me a little high just thinking about it.

"I gotta get out of here, man."

"Yeah," Peter said.

I closed the door gently behind me. I decided to walk over toward Peter's bike to see if it was his.

When I got closer, the trailer door swung open and a Black lady leaned out, probably in her thirties. She wore a tight ponytail and short denim shorts.

"Can I help you?"

"Is this Peter's bike?"

"Who?" she asked, squinting her eyes.

"The guy who lives right there," I said, pointing to Peter's trailer.

"Yeah," she said.

"He said you stole it."

The woman's face registered surprise. "Stole it?"

"Yeah."

"I ain't stole shit," she said. She probably thought I was a Nazi too. I couldn't blame her for the look of hatred in her eyes.

"But it's here."

"That muthafucka," she said. "So high he fell down. And when he got up, he left his bike right where he fell."

"He didn't tell me that part," I said.

"I leaned it up against here so he could get it back."

"Why won't he get it back?" I asked.

"What do you think?" she said.

"I dunno."

"He sure has a different perspective."

"Yeah," I said. "Does that bother you?"

"Don't bother me none," she said. "But I'm pretty sure it bothers him."

"Oh yeah?"

"How would you feel if you was a skinhead surrounded by a gang of Black folks?"

I didn't understand how to respond to that question. But maybe it was a good one. The woman went back inside.

I took the bike, rolled it back to Peter's trailer, and leaned it against his door—gently, so I wouldn't wake the baby.

The sun was almost set when I started my walk back to the car. The delta breeze chilled the air, and people began to emerge from their air-conditioned houses. I practiced smiling at people as they passed but couldn't quite get myself to make a full smile. The closest I got was pressing my lips together so my cheeks bulged out a little. Nobody smiled back.

I crossed the city on foot, thinking about the time I'd spent as a teenager forming Anti-Racist Action with my friends, sitting in messy apartments fussing over the language of our anti-Nazi propaganda flyers. We'd post around town and at the packed hardcore shows, where we'd be stopping by anyway to hide our bats and lead pipes in the bushes for when the Nazi skinheads inevitably showed up.

When I returned to my car, I fumbled through the glove box to find a blown-out credit card. I poured the last shards on the back of a parking ticket and crushed them against the dashboard. I chopped up a line of speed the size of a toothpick and snorted it, the chemicals burning my throat on the way down.

The next morning, I was still awake in the back seat, buzzing from the night before. The bird didn't land on my car. I saw him, though. He waited on a tree branch low enough for me to watch him spread his wings and hop around from side to side. He had red feathers in the shape of a heart on his belly. He jumped to and fro on the tree branch, dancing for me. Then he flew up to a different tree branch, just above my car. He looked smaller; his gestures didn't look so jovial anymore. If I squinted hard enough, it looked like he was challenging me to a fight.

HOW TO FORGET

I'm watching my son sitting on the carpet with Crystal.

She's reading him his favorite book.

It's about a puffer fish who has a resting bitch face.

The problem is the fish can't fix his sourpuss until someone comes along and kisses him. I think the book is supposed to be about the overwhelming importance of happiness in one's life.

But I'm not sure.

It seems a little rapey to me.

Ezra enjoys it nevertheless, his fingers poised in anticipation over the pages, ready to turn them as his mom reads, even though he can recite the story word for word.

The house smells rich and spicy, like brown sugar and cinnamon. The house is clean. Everything is in its place. The early afternoon light cuts through the living room, dividing our house into sections of light and dark. I stand in the middle, like an actor at center stage, hoping to create some dramatic symbol for the world to enjoy, a fucked-up man made good, now the star of the show, pulling off a life despite all odds. Something to that effect. But they're focused on the Pout-Pout Fish. Nobody sees what I'm doing. My family is ignoring me, lost in their cartoon world captured within the pages of a book. I'm standing half in the shadows, half not, in our clean, good-smelling house.

Nobody is calling me, bugging me about work.

My phone isn't buzzing with emails.

This is one of those moments I'll probably forget. The globe of happiness that surrounds me, if only momentarily, which I live perfectly inside without thinking of the pinprick past or future that gets too close and . . .
pop.

I would never remember this moment. I only remember the bad ones, the body of the bird, squelching underneath my feet, its innards shooting out of its ass. The fist of a neo-Nazi skinhead landing on my temple. Teacher upon teacher, fumbling for their pink slips, sending me away to the office. The administrators at my work, finger on the panic button, ready to start a war.

This is none of that. It's the opposite. And I don't want to forget.

Maybe *this* is life, the moments we create on our own. The traumas of our past are wires that don't connect to anything dangerous; we simply move them out of the way and create our own pathways to something that never explodes. It's not even a bomb. It's a machine. A beautiful machine that exists with all the other machines, but when something gets in its way, its blades rotate, spinning as it moves forward, mowing down anything in front of it.

HOW TO MOVE ON

Sometimes when I'm listening to Ezra, I have no idea what he's saying, as if I'm underwater and he's on a pier. His mouth is moving, his little hands are waving, and I know he's telling me important things as he leans over the cold water trying to communicate. And through the watery blur of his face, I can see he looks worried, and I think about how sweet it is that he cares, even just a little.

But he's only a baby, so who knows. Maybe he's wondering why I'm not talking or why I don't drown, or why not even my eyes say a word. Perhaps he wonders why I don't reveal every secret buried in the graveyard of our family, like my other sister, Monica. The dead one. The one I never mention.

I gave her language, you know. Did you know that I taught her how to run?

We ran through grass fields, away from our little house and family, laughing until we cried. She slept in her crib and woke up in the hospital, choking on her vomit. Two years old. *The same age as you, Ezra.* She held my hand when the doctor pulled the plug, and my mom sucked all the air out of the room.

"What is that, Daddy?" Ezra asks, pointing to the burning church tattooed on my arm. I could teach him everything I know, everything I've ever learned, but why the fuck would I want to do that?

It's strange how little you know when you're a child, but ignorance can be helpful. What if you knew everything you know now, but as a child? I don't think many kids would make it past ten. If I had known that my parents were fighting, that they hated each other, that my father was descending into madness, I probably would've run away and never returned. Or maybe something worse. The nature of the world, the weight of everything we've learned, rattling around our tender little heads, would be too much to handle.

I told Crystal that I didn't want a boy. I don't know what to do with boys. I never played sports. I don't fish or fix shit around the house.

But here he is, so I teach him what I know. I teach him how to punch.

We both have our gloves on and stand barefoot in the front yard with all our gear. Our conservative neighbor across the street tries to ignore us, but I say hello anyway, and he waves back begrudgingly.

"Remember, slip, slip, roll, jab, cross, roundhouse," I say. "Got it?"

"Got it," Ezra says. He's grinning. He loves kicking me. Sometimes he'll use his hips and turn his leg at the perfect time and, *Pow!* A crack to my thigh so hard that I let out a little yelp, and he'll howl with laughter.

I jab, and he slips. I cross, and he slips in the other direction. I telegraph a hook, and he bows like he just encountered royalty.

"No!" I yell. "What happens if you bow like that?"

"Kick me in the face."

"You want me to kick you in the face?"

"Let's do it again."

"A roll is a slight movement," I say. "Just barely move and keep your eyes on me the whole time."

"I knowwwww," Ezra says. He's itching to start again. This time he rolls perfectly and launches an impeccable roundhouse into my thigh.

Goddamn my teachers, sending me to the principal's office.

Goddamn all the drugs I ingested.

Goddamn the jocks who called me a faggot.

Goddamn the cops who slammed me against walls.

Goddamn the school administrators snitching on me to the law.

"Goddamn!" I yell.

"Goddamn," Ezra repeats, grinning bigger than the universe.

HOW TO FIGHT

It's been a long day, meetings upon meetings with administrators trying to micromanage every aspect of my job, but I care less and less. Have my job. Take it. I can get a job driving a truck. I can work on an Alaskan fishing boat. I can collect unemployment. Anything other than listening to liberals shouting about diversity and equity while making $250K per year.

I'm drifting off, watching my six-year-old son in his mixed martial arts class, marveling at the ease with which he switches modes from an untethered wild boy who has grown up in a household light on restrictions to a focused, disciplined fighter who listens intently and takes directions without batting an eye. He's the only boy I've seen his age with a bright green mohawk. One day he confided in me that he thinks of his hair as an island that exists within him. What he meant, in his poetic way, was that each one of the characteristics that compose his soul claims a piece of his body. The parts exist by themselves but are still connected in some way, like islands connected by water. His hair meant something special to him before he knew it was a unique style. People ask him about it; they turn their heads when he enters a room, try to figure out what kind of kid he is, why a kid would have such a fucked-up haircut. He thrives on it. He's quick to thank people for taking an interest, then starts a conversation with them. He's hungry for humanity, and his odd hair is just one entry point into his exploration. He understands the power of his appearance, and he uses it to connect himself to the world.

I watch him in class, standing in front of a heavy bag as his sensei, an overgrown and severe man with a black belt dangling at his waist, gives instructions for the drill. He reminds me of every slobbering jock who ever called me a faggot and punched me in the face.

"You're going to jab, cross, front-kick," he says. "You're not going to drop your hands, yes, sir?"

"Yes, sir!" the class screams.

Ezra takes a breath and focuses on the bag in front of him. He jabs, crosses, and front-kicks, taking care to keep his hands up, not letting his guard down. Unsatisfied with his performance, he tries the combo again, this time with an increased focus and a *Kee-yah!* at the end. Sensei walks around the room correcting the students and stops at Ezra.

"This is a future black belt," he says, proud of his green-haired student. "Watch Ezra."

Ezra shows the class the combo again, all eyes on him, his green mohawk flopping with each movement. I can see him trying to hide a smile, and I wonder for a second why he's hiding it, why he doesn't just smile like his spirit is telling him to. It's probably one of those things we pass down, the fear of emotion, the fear of rejection of emotion, the fear that someone will see you for what you are, call you a faggot, and then walk away for good. Or maybe that's all a silly projection. Maybe it's just that he's proud of himself. And humble. Like a regular person.

Family of Dirtbags

My uncle told me this story about my mom as a kid. He said she used to kneel on the sidewalk in front of their apartment in LA to find cigarette butts to smoke. He never mentioned her age, but for some reason, I imagine her as a five-year-old, an age that makes no sense. My daughter is five and too lazy to get a handful of cereal from the kitchen cabinet. But still, I imagine my little mom in a black floral dress, searching the dirty sidewalk for something to smoke and finding a half butt, setting it between her lips and pulling a lighter from her dress pocket, tilting her head back as the smoke billows toward the sun.

My mom denies this ever happened, but I wish she didn't. It fills my heart with love to think of my little mom dragging on a filthy cigarette, the edges of her dress dusty from the LA sidewalk.

Now and then, this version of my mom will surface, like when she visited me in San Diego and we took a trip to the mall. In the parking lot, my mom pulled a hard right into a parking space just as a white lady in a minivan tried to pull a hard left. My mom won. She's from East LA— she knows how to drive her car better. She knows how to cut a corner. The white lady stood no chance. They both got out of their vehicles, and my mom held her purse over her head like a *macuahuitl*, her turquoise earrings dangling above her shoulders. The white woman made a quick calculation and slunk back to her car. She drove away, screeching through the lot.

There's that saying, *You can take the chola out of the hood, but you can't take the hood out of the chola*. I don't like that saying. It's wrong. If you spend most of your life attempting to disown your past, maybe move away from LA and marry a white dude, go to college and graduate from medical school, little by little your past becomes a distant memory. It loses its pull.

This is why when I'm fifteen (then sixteen, and then seventeen) and I come back with a report card riddled with Ds and Fs, my mother looks at me as if I'm an alien. My stepdad sits in his chair and glares at me with crystal blue eyes. The success and stability they've created in their own lives is not evident in their son. They believe the way I live my life is a complete rejection of their values and hard work. My mother forgets the little girl scrounging for cigarettes in the middle of Heliotrope Avenue. Maybe if even a tiny part of her could remember what it was like, she would be gentler with me.

"Well, Josh," my stepdad says. "We need to figure something out."

"What have you been doing all year, Josh?" my mom spits. She has hatred in her eyes.

My stomach turns. The feeling I get when I don't want to answer and have nothing to say anyway. It feels like a gallon of acid rising from my belly and into my throat, into my brain. Like fire. My fists clench, and my only choice is to fight or to run. And I do both.

HOW TO LIE

My union's executive director, Robert, is a soft-spoken old man with the gruff presence of a mob boss. People listen to him when he talks, so maybe that's why the investigator doesn't put up a fight when he tells her we wouldn't meet at her downtown office. We meet instead at our union hall, a familiar spot, where I'd spent every other week with the executive board arguing about how to get paid more, eating catered lunch, and watching my colleagues grow sleepy with beers in their hands, listening to the clock ticking toward dinnertime.

The building has a soul, something I can tap into if the interview gets too tough. Plus, the union hall is in Midtown, where much of my adult life was wasted away, barely surviving in cheap apartments with shared bathrooms, working at the bottom rung of various office buildings, cooking breakfast for state workers, doing dishes, drinking Bud Light in walk-in refrigerators. Back then I knew every street, every alley, every bar, and every apartment that sold crystal meth. Like old trauma, the place, for better or for worse, is ingrained into my DNA.

Midtown saw me mostly at my worst. No money and rent always due. I didn't pay bills; I just let them stack in the corner in an ecosystem of neglect. I learned to harness the feeling of desperation, waiting in the night, just around the corner from here, for a drunken whiteboy to stroll by. When one did, I told him I had a gun and to give me all his shit. I'd never seen anyone sober up so quickly. He ran as fast as he could before I could catch up. I was probably drunker than he was, crumpling his wadded fives and tens into my pockets.

One time I stood in defeat, penniless and desperate, next to an old man's apartment. I'd been watching him for weeks, every day at 3 p.m. parking his Toyota Celica, shuffling to the back seat to pull out his walker, then moving at a snail's pace from his car to number 14. I calculated how long it would take me to shove him inside and rifle through his wallet until I found enough to pay rent (twelve minutes and some change). My body froze as if God himself wasn't allowing me to commit a felony. If only I believed in God. My prayers were to the chemicals that sustained me. I stood shaking under the long trunk of a palm tree next to his Celica and crying, not in the shame of my willingness to rob an old man but in the shame of my cowardice, pure as the California sunlight.

The secretary ushers me into the conference area, a room not quite big enough for the long, dark wood table, and the investigator is already sitting—a blonde, maybe five years younger than I. She offers a cold smile, and I give her a tight-lipped nod.

"We'll just wait a few minutes until it's time," she says into the morbidly quiet room. Robert takes a seat next to me. I adjust in my seat to hide my stomach gurgling and take my phone out of my pocket, staring at the black screen in fear that if I hit the power button, "Antifa Hooligans" will start playing at top volume. I pretend to scroll, thinking, *What if she sees my phone is off? She'll think I'm a sociopath.* I put my phone back into my pocket and look everywhere except in the investigator's direction, so I don't have to make eye contact.

My lawyer instructed me how to behave: give short answers and don't go into detail. Don't start babbling. I've practiced over and over for the past week, providing answers to questions I made up myself. *Are you an Antifa? Have you ever punched a Nazi in the face? Do you arm your students with knives? Do you stab old ladies wearing Trump hats?*

I try hard not to think about the gravity of the interrogation, how my entire fate is wrapped up in this one interview, but that itself is a form of thinking about the interrogation. If they did fire me, a part of me in the back of my mind would say, *Yeah, sure, I get it.* It's a terrible feeling knowing my history, knowing I'm a sinister piece of shit, but also knowing that I'm innocent of this one thing.

My mind spins in a vicious cycle that always ends in the same dark place: I'm fighting an entire school district, and if they want to fire me a few weeks before I'm supposed to be tenured, then they'll fire me. But I'm ready. I can't possibly be more prepared. All I need to do is to inhale and exhale.

Their accusation that I'm leading students to commit violence at protests is entirely made up. Yet I still feel like I need to lie. Maybe it's the nature of being a scumbag—a juvenile delinquent turned adult delinquent. Or maybe the investigation process creates a cycle of self-doubt paired with intense overconfidence. I haven't lied to them specifically, but I am a liar, because I'm human. All they need is one lie to prove their point, but if all of us in that room told the truth about everything, we'd probably all be locked away for eternity.

I've spent the entire week letting the darkness of my thoughts eat my brain until the only possible outcome of this interview was me ending up without a job and possibly in jail. Every time I think to myself, *Wait a minute—I didn't do anything wrong*, my negativity kicks into overdrive, and within minutes I'm sweating profusely, looking up one-way tickets to Mexico, Googling "How much money do you need to open a bar in Puerto Vallarta?"

Robert shuffles his paper and checks his notes. I wonder if he's also pretending. What if we're all pretending to be busy to save ourselves from being devoured by our thoughts? The mind is a ticking time bomb crafted by our own hands. It once could be dismantled, but its wires are too confusing after all these years. Or maybe we never learned their configuration. It seems possible to deactivate a bomb, but it's probably best to leave it the fuck alone. A sudden movement can shake the wrong part loose, so we stay perfectly still and wait for fate to explode naturally.

"Are you familiar with Antifa?" the investigator asks.

"Yes."

"Can you tell me about it?"

"It's an ideology that seeks to rid the world of fascism." I see Robert scribbling furiously in his notebook out of the corner of my eye.

"Are you familiar with the group called the Campus Antifascist Network?"

"Yes," I say. "It's a broad group of clubs at different college campuses that align with antifascist ideology."

"Have you ever solicited students for potentially dangerous activities?"

"No. I try as hard as I can to protect students, to lead them away from danger," I say, and I think for a second about saying too much. *Which, by the way, is precisely the opposite of what the army recruiters on our campus are doing.*

She asks me more about my relationship to violence at protests, and I tell her that I've seen more fights in the parking lots of baseball games than at demonstrations. It goes on like this for two hours, the questions, the brief answers, my union rep scribbling notes, Robert stopping me midsentence when he thinks I'm starting to babble.

Amazingly, she never digs into my past. Even just a cursory glance at my previous debauchery—all the fighting, the stealing, the drinking, the driving while drugged—any number of acts that could have easily landed me back in jail.

But, of course, none of that would come up in this investigation. How could it? It only exists in the vault of my guilty past. Maybe worse than a trip down memory lane is the silence after I answer each question. The quiet room is an interrogation unto itself.

I am here.

The interrogator is here.

My union's executive director is here.

We're all in this room with the table too big for the space, the silence a thick pressure on our chests, squeezing our lungs with all its weight to see who will be the first to run out of air.

The Biggest Dirtbag of All

I had a little baggie of cocaine in my coat pocket to help the writing process. The plan was to get a cheap motel in San Francisco so I could get some poems out of my brain. I was waiting until I got to the city to snort the coke, but it was all I could think about, so I gave in and pulled over to the side of the freeway. It wasn't good coke. It had a wet consistency, like old toothpaste, and I wasn't even sure if it would work. I sat for a minute on the side of I-80, whizzing cars shaking the Toyota Camry my stepdad gave to my little sister, Lauren, who then gave it to me. The car was on its last bit of life, making noises that surely meant it was on its way to the junkyard. Any problem bigger than a flat tire I couldn't afford, so I would run that thing into the ground. Wherever it eventually broke would be its final resting place.

I lined up the coke on an *Enter the 36 Chambers* CD cover and shook the bag. Maybe two more lines left. I rolled up a dollar bill, snorted one of the lines, and then the other into the other nostril. I didn't feel a lot. There may have been a little rush, but my body was so full of chemicals that any drug I ingested was like throwing a safety pin into the ocean and expecting a wave.

The scenery from Sacramento to San Francisco is a path of farmland and gas stations and the Budweiser factory, where they used to let people drink as much beer as they wanted at the end of the tour. When I got to Vallejo, I had to pee, so I pulled over and ran toward the Safeway. When I got to the automatic door, I realized I had left my keys in the car. The car that locks its doors automatically. I ran back and tried the doors while a few feet away a homeless man screamed the butchered lyrics for the national anthem.

The car was locked. My keys sat in the passenger seat inches away, completely out of reach.

"O-oh say can you see? Like a dog's early eyes!" he yelled.

If I wanted to get in the car, I'd have to break a window.

"When so frowny we fail!"

I didn't want to cause a scene. Surely if I stood there in broad daylight breaking a window in the Safeway parking lot, I'd be beaten by good Samaritans and hauled off to jail.

"At Carmine's last beating!"

"Ay," I called to the singing man.

"Whose broad pipes and light scars!"

"Excuse me," I said.

The man stopped singing and sized me up. I waved him over.

He looked like he'd been on the streets for most of his life. Two long dreadlocks hung over his eyes, and a patchwork of dreads and bald spots covered the rest of his head. His crusty eyes were as yellow as Dijon mustard.

"Look, man," I said, trying to figure out what I would say. "If you find a rock and break into my car, you can have all the change on the floor."

I pointed into my car, and he looked inside. There were probably ten dollars in quarters down there. "All of it?"

"All of it," I assured him. "Just make sure my car is open by the time I get back."

I ran back toward the Safeway. Before I reached the doors, the crash of rock against window filled the parking lot. I peed, power-walked through the alcohol aisle, grabbed two forties of Steel Reserve and slid them into my pants, then returned to my car, where the man was kneeling in the front seat collecting change. A rock-sized hole decorated my passenger window.

"You got everything?" I asked.

He kept scraping change and putting it in his pocket. When he was done, I reached in my pants, grabbed the forties, and handed him one. He took it with no comment and wandered away.

I pulled out of the lot, a cold breeze shooting into my neck.

Back on the road, I drove past the residential motels in Richmond and the sprawling strip malls of Albany toward Berkeley, where the Pacific Ocean opened to a view of San Francisco, a pile of broken window glass my only passenger.

I thought about the man who broke into my car, how he didn't hesitate to smash a hole in the window for a handful of change. How I had been too cowardly to do it myself, and he could've ended up in jail. How I'd looked into his eyes and he into mine, and all I saw was a tool to my own freedom.

The cocaine wasn't working, because otherwise I wouldn't have been thinking like this. My breathing shallowed, lungs shrinking to the size of peanuts. No matter how hard I tried to breathe, I couldn't get enough air. I reached over, grabbed the Steel Reserve and set it in my lap, twisted the cap to let the acrid mist fill my nose with familiarity, and took a long swig. I drove through the intestines of the Yerba Buena Tunnel, the yellow light cooling my shorted brain, and came out on the other side, where the San Francisco skyline was so close that I could almost touch it.

To San Francisco

I worked at Macy's in San Francisco's Union Square, the best place in the world to be entertained by the freakshow of humanity, like an improv circus streaming twenty-four hours a day. I sat on the sidewalk to eat lunch and people-watch. I always ate the same thing, a cheese sandwich and a tomato soup from the deli across the street. A cute girl worked at the counter, so every day I'd order my meal and smile at her, hoping she'd smile back. Sometimes she did, and I would read the world into her smile and walk back to my work with my greasy bag, fantasizing about her while I chewed my disgusting sandwich. Inside San Francisco existed a giant subculture of the retail class, who served each other during the day, flirted at work, then ingested every drug imaginable at night and fucked each other senseless in the nightclub bathrooms until the next morning.

"Excuse me, do you have a minute?"

A slender man in a tight azure suit bent down so he was at eye level with me.

"Sure," I said, hoping he wasn't trying to sell me anything. I was broke.

The man pulled up a chair. "Are you a model?" he asked.

"No."

"Would you like to be a model?"

"I don't know," I said.

"Well, I'm going to give you my number, and if you want to get into some modeling work, then give me a call."

He handed me a simple business card with his name and number and continued up the sidewalk, leaving me to my meal.

I called him that night.

"I'm in," I said.

"Good," he said. "I have a job for you."

"What kind of job?"

"It's a billboard," he said enthusiastically, "for a salon."

The following week, I met him and his team of people at a salon right in Union Square. I was surprised that it wasn't some scam where I'd be beaten in an alley, stripped bare, and left for dead. Or I'd open the salon door and find the man naked, his azure suit crumpled in a pile next to him.

I got a haircut, and the wardrobe lady picked out one of the gayest blouses I'd ever seen. I loved every second of it. "Ohhh, so many broken capillaries," the man doing my makeup said as he brushed my face into an even, pinkish tone. Then the photographer led me to a studio, where I did my best impression of a model.

"Can you stop doing that?" he said, visibly annoyed with me.

"Doing what?"

"The thing with your eye."

"That's just how my face looks," I said.

"Fine," he said, and snapped away.

I don't know what happened to the billboard. I never saw it. But they paid me $700 in cash, so I didn't care.

A week later, I got another call from the man in the azure suit. "I got another one I think you'll like," he said. "It's for a television commercial!"

I was excited by his excitement. A television commercial!

"How much?" I asked.

"I don't know the details yet, but I'll let you know."

The commercial ended up being for Coca-Cola, I think. That's what he said, but I'm still not sure. It was at the height of reality shows like *The Real World*, and I lived in a room in Oakland. The producer wanted to come to my place and follow me around for the day.

"Do what you'd regularly do," she said.

I couldn't drink myself into a coma, so I took her to some skateboarding spots and messed around, then we sat by Lake Merritt and she interviewed me about the future.

"The commercial is about young people and their possibilities in the future," she said. She was a sweet blonde, maybe in her early thirties. I didn't have the heart to tell her I had no future.

We talked by the lake for an hour, and she handed me a check for $500 and let me keep the wardrobe she'd brought for me to wear during the shoot. I don't know if the commercial ever aired. I didn't have a TV and wasn't interested in anything but getting fucked up and having sex with random strangers.

A few weeks later, I met a girl at a party. Her name was Nancy, and she was a photographer and a poet. We got drunker than we'd ever been, on a rooftop in East Oakland. I carried her on my shoulders and jumped up and down until the roof almost caved underneath my feet. We fell in love, and I packed up my belongings the next week and moved to Los Angeles to be with her. She would take my pictures for a portfolio, and I'd be a successful model and actor. Her apartment sat on top of a hill in Silver Lake. It was small but neatly decorated with fluffy colorful pillows and plants that hung from the ceiling.

It wasn't long until I had an interview at a talent agency. I took the bus to a business park and waited with nine other handsome boys in the lobby. We didn't speak to each other, but we all sat in the same rigid and unmoving way—the posture of people who've relied on their looks for their whole life and are unable to express their personality in other ways. One thing I admire about movie stars, they're good-looking, yeah, but they also have charisma and talent. It's not as easy as you think. Most good-looking people are as dumb as a bag of turnips.

We shuffled into a large office covered in pictures of famous people. I couldn't tell who any of them were. I only knew they were famous because they stood on red carpets wearing clothes I couldn't afford, surrounded by paparazzi. The man in front of us looked like a Hollywood agent in his fifties with wispy, dyed black hair and a shiny dress shirt unbuttoned low, so his hairy chest showed through.

"Before we do any one-on-one auditions, I want each of you to tell me a little about yourselves."

We all nodded.

"Excuse me," he said, looking straight at me.

"Yes," I said.

"Are you slouching?"

"Slouching?"

"Yeah," he said, sitting straight in his chair like he was about to get up and attack me. "Slouching."

"I don't know."

He gestured to the pictures of all the famous people surrounding us. "Talent. Doesn't. Slouch."

"Okay," I said, making a point to slouch a little farther down in my chair.

"Get the fuck out of here," he said, pointing to the door.

I got up and left the room. The Los Angeles sky was brighter and crisper than everywhere else. Even the bland business park lot gleamed with a layer of wealth. The door behind me opened, and the Black kid who'd sat next to me appeared.

"Got kicked out right after you," he said with a grin.

"Why?"

"Fuck if I know," he said, and offered me a cigarette from his pack of Newport.

I hated menthol but took one anyway. My fellow Hollywood outcast lit my cigarette, and we smoked, our minty cloud momentarily dulling the crisp sky. Maybe I could find a job in some nearby shitty restaurant to keep me alive for the time being. Or maybe I'd just wither away and die in the middle of this freakishly clean parking lot.

Back to Sacramento

The explosion.

It's a familiar feeling.

I'm bad at jobs.

I hate work.

I dislike people getting in my shit or telling me what to do. I've been broken up with by every girl I've ever dated. Even Nancy, the sweet artist, saw what lurked behind my looks and gave me the boot at the very first sign of trouble. I don't blame her. I've gotten fired from every job I've ever had. Big explosion. Up in smoke. Even my favorite job at Starbucks, where I drank free coffee, ate all the food I could steal, and kept a cooler of beer and some hard alcohol in the back under the pile of lost and found coats.

I constantly drank—whiskey and beer before, during, and after work. One of my supervisors, Leigh, drank more than I did, and his breath always smelled like Guinness. He had a big, smelly beard; everyone hated working with him because he never smiled and had a short fuse. One time, we were helping customers, and there was a line stretching out the door.

"Get me a fucking latte," he yelled.

"Fuck you," I replied.

All the businessmen in line looked nervous and pissed off. Leigh and I kept arguing until we dropped everything and tried to strangle each other. One of our coworkers had to pry us apart. Leigh apologized a few hours later, and I could tell by the way he looked at me that he meant it. I apologized back, but I slashed his bike tires on the way out just in case.

When I returned from lunch, I walked into the back room, and Arthur, the flamboyant senior citizen with a mustache, was snorting meth from an empty lip balm jar. He freaked out when he saw me and ran back to the floor like nothing had happened. Nobody cared that he was a tweaker, because he was less depressing when he was high. Sometimes he'd come to work sober, eyes drooping, voice an octave lower than it should've been, and he'd spend his entire shift telling us the most demented stories from his horrific childhood.

Once he told me a story about how his cousin had molested him, and he started crying at the espresso machine. I was twenty-two years old and unequipped to handle his emotional outburst.

"Damn, Arthur," I said. "Are you . . . crying?"

"No," he said, wiping the river of tears from his cheek with his green apron.

"Why don't you go take a break in the back," I said, hoping that he'd find some meth in his backpack and snort himself into a good mood. Luckily, there was nobody in line, only a few people studying at tables nearby. Arthur went in the back, grabbed all his belongings, ran out the front door, and never returned to work. He became a legend among the workers there.

"Remember fucking Arthur?" we'd say.

"Fuck yeah," returned the chorus of admiration.

This was before Starbucks became the company we know today. It was still a chain but smaller. It wasn't as corporate. Everybody stole. We never came to work on time. Nobody followed the dress code. It was like a thriving slum inside a store, complete with whores, junkies, drunks, and thieves. I thought it was clever to take the STARBUCKS COFFEE shirt and scratch out the letters so it read FUCK OFF. None of the supervisors noticed. We drank all the coffee for free and took all the food.

One day after a busy shift, my boss sat me in her office.

"You're a really good employee," she said. That's it. She wanted to compliment me.

I felt bad because I wasn't a good employee. At all. I must have cost that company thousands of dollars in free food and beverage. But I took the compliment. I could tell she thought of me as a relative, like maybe a little brother who always got in trouble. She was rooting for me.

After several months working there, I went out one night, got into a fistfight, and ended up in jail. After two days of missing work, I called my boss from the phone in the jail.

"You're going to have to come in and talk to me," she said.

I could tell she was crying.

"Can you tell me now what you're going to say? Because I can't just walk out of here."

"Just come in when you get out," she said.

I never went back in. I was a coward and didn't want to face an awkward situation. I wanted to remember her as the boss who gave me a compliment. I never returned to that Starbucks, even though I lived down the street. My plan was to move on to something else, another shitty job, another shitty apartment. There was plenty of that to go around.

Sacramento Sweeper

At the height of my addiction, I lived in Midtown, Sacramento, where I had a landlord named George. Everybody hated him. He was mean and rude, a real prick of a landlord, one of those old white people who talked too much about the Civil War. I'm not even sure which side he rooted for. He wore overalls and an engineer hat and yelled at me whenever we saw each other.

"You're a loser," he said maybe a hundred times. He was correct, so I didn't take it personally. I lived on the third floor of his old teal Victorian that looked nice on the outside but inside was infested with human cockroaches. The building smelled dead and sour. The window that faced our neighbor's house was the one I liked to sit in to smoke cigarettes. The neighbor was an old lady. Her hair was orange because she dyed it that way, and she was always outside watering her plants. Under certain light, the sun would shine through her thin orange hair and onto her scalp, so her head appeared on fire. This one time, I was in my window smoking a cigarette, watching her tend to the garden. She gave each stalk, leaf, and petal individual attention. It was impressive. She was out there for most of the day with her fingers touching each part of every flower. She glanced up at the windowsill and saw me sitting there, smoking.

"Aren't you afraid you're going to fall out of that window?" she yelled with her flaming head.

"No," I answered. "Are you afraid?"

"I don't care what you do," she said, and went back to her plants.

I flicked my cigarette down into the little walkway between our apartment building and her yard.

"Hey," she said. She carried a hose spewing water. "Where are you flicking those?"

"Down there," I said, pointing to the walkway.

"Don't you have an ashtray?"

"No," I said.

"If you need to smoke, get an ashtray."

"My bad," I said.

Her mouth looked like a wilted orchid.

The next day, I set a Budweiser can near the windowsill and ashed my cigarettes into that. When I smoked my cigarettes, my neighbor didn't look at me anymore because I had my little makeshift ashtray, which made her happy. I still watched her tend to her garden. She treated each flower like an infant. I wondered if she had any kids. If so, she should have known that kids are capable of much worse than littering.

The guy in the room directly across from me was named Josiah, an MC who liked to take the microphone at rap clubs and battle other rappers. Every day, he'd see a girl he liked, and even if she were with her boyfriend, he'd sit down and talk to her. He fucked quite a bit using that strategy. Sometimes I'd walk into his apartment and he'd be fucking like a large tugboat putting through the sea. He had no rhythm or style when he fucked. He introduced me to his friend Mike, this goofy-looking white guy dressed like he worked at a country club. Mike loved to do drugs. Hard drugs. I met him right when he was getting into speed. My girlfriend and I went to his apartment once and did a big bag of speed together. We were so high that night, we could barely stand. Mike kept pacing around the apartment, asking if he could fuck my girlfriend.

"I'm fucking horny," he said. "It's killing me."

He was wearing this hideous salmon-colored polo shirt tucked into his chinos, and he looked like a young investment banker whacked out of his goddamn mind. He marched around the house for about an hour, then put on some porn and tried to jack off, but his dick wouldn't get hard. His penis flopped around in his hand for a few hours while my girlfriend and I talked. When we left, it was about 6 a.m., and Mike was still sweating on the couch, tugging at his little red cock.

I knew it wasn't good when I heard George coming up the stairs. For such a withered old man, he generated a lot of power in those footsteps. Especially when he was ascending stairs: *clonk, clonk, clonk.* He banged on the door.

"Open up," he yelled. "Get the fuck out here."

I put on a pair of boxers and opened the door a crack. George slammed the door with his elbow into my big toe. I jumped up and down, and he stepped into my room. George looked around with his hands on his hips, surveying the room while I stood on one foot and massaged my hurt toe. His engineer hat was so fucking ridiculous that it took all my sensibility not to laugh out loud.

"Don't you have any self-respect," George said in a way that told me it wasn't a question.

"I guess I do," I said, picking up a few Bud cans off my chair and placing them on the floor so I could sit down. My toe throbbed.

"Mrs. Boleto said you gave her a hard time," George said. His hands were still on his hips.

"Mrs. Boleto?"

"Your neighbor, over there, in the house next door." He pointed toward the old lady with the orchid mouth. "Don't you give me hell too, you little shit."

"I didn't know that was her name," I said. "She doesn't look like a Mrs. Boleto."

"Why are you giving her a hard time?"

"I wasn't."

"Don't lie to me," George said. His face was red, and he had large purple veins in his nose. "You flicked your cigarettes on the ground and told her, 'I'm bad, I'm bad.'"

"No," I corrected him. I explained to George how I had said "My bad," not "I'm bad." It was supposed to be an apology.

"Oh," George said. His face softened, and his hands came off his hips.

"I even made an ashtray," I said, pointing to the can on the windowsill.

George didn't look at the ashtray.

We stood there in my dirty little room for a few minutes, watching Mrs. Boleto hunching over her infant flowers down below.

George made me the building manager that night, which meant that I was in charge of sweeping up once a week, collecting rent, and making sure the other tenants weren't fighting or smoking drugs in their rooms.

"You're the most responsible one I got," George said. The other tenants were drug addicts like I was, but they were happy being fuckups. My saving grace was that I was wholly uncomfortable with who I was. Or at least that's what George told me.

"Look at you," he said. "You're crawling in your own skin. You can't even look me in the eye. All Kwan down there does is look me in the eye, the creepy little bastard."

Kwan was an Asian man who lived in the tiniest apartment on the first floor. He was the kind of guy you'd see on the street and wonder, "Where does *that* guy go at night?" He came back to this little teal Victorian. He was a speed freak. He'd wake up every morning, snort some speed he kept in a Carmex jar, then set off with his huge boombox to stand in the middle of downtown blasting A-ha. He'd return to his tiny apartment every night at about 9:30. On my twenty-second birthday, we broke into his apartment, snorted all his speed, and replaced it with crushed-up aspirin. On the second floor was Bernt, a Swedish guy who gave me the creeps, but I couldn't figure out why. He had a job that he'd get dressed up for every day, but he seemed off, like maybe he'd once studied to be a priest or kept a laptop full of child porn. When there's a normal, productive member of society living in a building full of degenerates, there must be something he's hiding. Something big. His name was pronounced *Bay-r-nt*, but everyone called him *Burned*, and he'd flip out and tell them to fuck off and eat shit.

That's the kind of stuff I was supposed to manage.

When George started coming by the building now and then, it wasn't to scold me but to give me fatherly advice.

"You know how you stay out of jail," he told me once.

"No."

"Quit acting like an asshole." And then he smacked the back of my head.

One day, he came over while I was sweeping the hallway downstairs. He watched me for a second before he grabbed the broom out of my hands. "Didn't anyone teach you how to sweep properly?"

"No," I said. "It seems pretty easy."

"It's not easy," he said. "Watch."

I watched him sweep. He swept like he was angry at the ground. Like he was trying to sweep a hole into the goddamn earth.

When I finally moved out of that place, I cleaned my apartment so thoroughly that it looked better than when I'd moved in. I even painted. When I was finished, my hands were bright red, and blisters covered my palms. When George came in for inspection, he stood there with his hands on his hips and said, "This is beautiful. I didn't know you had it in you." He gave me my deposit back in cash. Then he patted my back and almost said something but didn't. He just grabbed my shoulder so hard that it left a bruise.

A few years later, I talked to an old friend, and we got to the subject of that old apartment building.

"Did you hear about George?" she asked.

"Apartment guy?"

"Yeah." She told me that one of the foreign exchange students who lived in one of the spare rooms in his mansion came home after school one day and found George sitting in his favorite chair wearing only a pair of tighty-whities and clutching a bottle of Jack Daniels. She wasn't surprised, because that's how she often found him when she came home after 4 p.m., but usually when she came back, he'd tell her to stand in front of him while he barked orders like *Clean the sink better next time* or *Come here and let me massage your neck.* But this time he didn't bark anything, so she went up to him and saw that his eyes were open but weren't looking anywhere. He was just sitting there, dead, clutching his whiskey bottle.

"And then what happened?" I asked.

"What do you mean, what happened?" she said, confused. "He was dead."

"But what about the student?"

"She went back to Japan, I guess."

"Did she say how his face looked when he was dead?"

"What do you mean?"

"Was he smiling?"

"What are you talking about?"

I didn't know what I was talking about. George died in an old leather chair with his hands wrapped around a bottle of whiskey. And that was it. It seemed so simple, but I didn't think it should've been. He deserved something more dramatic.

Bar Fight

I ran out of options. All my job prospects dried up, I couldn't afford a place to live, and the only light in my life was emanating from behind me, from all the bridges I had burned along the way.

Rebecca took me into her tiny one-bedroom apartment in Sacramento. I was as aimless and wild as a kid who'd never finished high school could be, a boy who took the bus everywhere with a skateboard slung in the crook of his arm, mooching off friends, stealing from grocery stores. I set out at night starting with alcohol and not stopping until I found hard drugs. And then came the women. And sometimes violence. That was my life then, and I loved it a little bit. Maybe it was the romance of living every day with no future in mind, or maybe it was the constant buzz, but I was content in the exciting cocktail of unknowing and not caring.

I slept on the couch. I owned a pile of clothes and a skateboard, which was more than enough. I got a job at Macy's downtown and hung out with Rebecca's friends whenever I could. They were the fun kind of white people who drank too much and had barbecues at any given moment. Cocaine flowed freely, and nobody seemed to care if you were high out of your mind.

The first week I was in Sacramento, Rebecca and her boyfriend, a shifty-eyed country boy, brought me to a bar on the outskirts of the city, a good ol' boy hangout called the Purple Place. The parking lot was full of gigantic trucks with mud all over their fenders. Something was wrong with the energy in the bar. Meaty country folk played pool. I didn't fit in, so I ordered glass after glass of beer. I don't know how I paid. I sat near the pool table to watch the show. An argument started, and two whiteboys began shoving each other. I turned to a man beside me and punched him in the face. It was a bad idea. The look on his face was one of pure surprise. Like I hurt his feelings. He cocked back and punched me. It seemed like he hit me a hundred times. His friends rushed over to help him even though he didn't need any help. The entire bar erupted into a brawl. It was like the movie *Roadhouse*, but I wasn't Patrick Swayze. I was one of the extras where the camera panned to him lying in a bloody pool, then panned away for the rest of the movie, only to be forgotten.

Rebecca's boyfriend pulled me out of the bar and dragged me back to his car. She was there trying to comfort me. I could feel the hot wind blowing through my hair and see the stars when I hung my head out the window.

"Fuck you, motherfucker," I yelled.

"I'm trying to help you," he said.

"It's okay, Josh," my sister said.

I was crying. My face was full of knots and bruises. Blood poured onto my lips from my nose. "I'm going back in there," I said.

Her boyfriend kept his hands on my shoulders and pinned me to the car seat so I wouldn't do something so dumb.

The next day, I woke up to an unrecognizable face. Deep purple bruises underneath my eyes painted my face into a piece from Picasso's blue period. Rebecca woke up and asked me how I was doing but didn't push too hard for answers. It was life. She didn't scold me or judge me. We went out drinking the next night like nothing had ever happened. It's what I needed at the time. I couldn't survive life with any more judgment. I needed to exist with whatever trouble was coming my way.

We Also Held Hands under a Tree

When I met Crystal, we were both community college students, and I was still struggling with addiction, barely on the edge of sanity. I had to drink a glass of whiskey every morning to steady my hands enough to hold a pencil. I started running in the mornings, because I could feel myself getting fat. I'd set the alarm for 5 a.m. and get out of bed, still drunk, to run laps around the park, past the homeless people sleeping underneath the trees, past the other runners, who were probably sickened by the cloud of whiskey surrounding my wheezing body.

By the time I got to school, I was hungover and exhausted, and I'd sit at the front of the class so I wouldn't fall asleep. I knew I needed that routine, the heavy drinking, the workout, the dead-tired fight for academic survival. Even though I had squandered most of my life, my parents had instilled in me a ferocious work ethic. When I found myself being lazy, an overwhelming sense of guilt set in, and it wouldn't subside until I had overworked myself.

There I was, slumped over my desk, still buzzing from the previous night of rum and Cokes and a few mushrooms, still confused by the idea of being back in a classroom. I was twenty-two years old, sitting with a bunch of eighteen-year-old kids in a college composition class.

After I'd taken the assessment test to place into a writing class, the lady administering the test accused me of cheating.

"Fine," I said. "I'll retake the test."

"It's just that I've never seen someone with this kind of score," she said.

"Look at my math score and you'll feel better," I said.

She must've looked at my dismal math score, because she left me alone after that.

I'd spent a lifetime reading books and writing dumb poems. I could read and write.

The English professor walked in a minute before class was supposed to begin, looking flustered, like she might have stayed up too late. She was a tall white lady who loved her students: stern, like the teachers I remember, but more playful, and something sparkled in her eyes when she talked about writing.

A cart with a television stood in the center of the classroom.

"I want to show you a part of this video," she said. "Not the whole thing, but I think you'll like it."

She slid a VHS tape into the player and hit Play. A raucous crowd cheered, and the camera panned to a woman bent over her chair while a tiny man painted her ass cheeks a bright blue.

I looked around at the class, and everyone was horrified.

She was right, I did like it.

I couldn't stop laughing.

"Um, Professor," a kid yelled from the back.

The professor was at her desk sorting through papers when she noticed the screen and ran in front of the TV. "Don't look!" she said, trying to cover the pornography with her body. She locked eyes with me. "Why aren't you helping me?!"

I got out of my chair and pressed the Stop button.

"This is the wrong video," she said, laughing, embarrassed, blaming her son for the mix-up.

The class erupted in laughter.

College was what middle school or high school could have been without all the angry white men wagging their fingers and touting their book of rules.

I kept drinking. Hard. I did cocaine when I could get it. I also kept going to school and working as a tutor, which made it easier to rationalize living like GG Allin, the degenerate punk who rolled around in glass and shit as a spectacle and died of a heroin overdose as his grand finale of treating life as one big rock 'n' roll show.

One afternoon, in between classes, I saw Crystal walking to class with a big smile on her face. She was dressed like Lara Croft in *Tomb Raider*.

Her eyes sparkled in the sun. I watched her make her way across the quad until she disappeared around a corner. The next day, I waited for her at the same spot, but she didn't appear.

I ran into her again at her desk in journalism class; I was next door in a poetry workshop. Her desk was a mess: papers, Tupperware, and trash cluttered her space, some of it falling onto the carpet underneath. I smiled, because everything was a metaphor then.

When my professor started reading his poem about growing tomatoes, I got up and walked into the journalism room.

"Do you know where the bathroom is?" I asked.

"It's over there," she pointed.

It was my pickup line. I used it all the time. Sometimes I'd ask if there was a store around or if they knew the time. Anything to get them to look in my direction. It had never worked until I used it on Crystal.

I asked her out to lunch, and we talked but didn't really get along. We got into an argument about the band Operation Ivy. I don't remember what it was about, but we both thought we were right, even though I was right. We saw each other the next day. And the day after.

Crystal invited me to meet her family. Before I left, I took a couple of mushrooms from a party the night before. I got in my car and started to drive, and then the shrooms started to kick in. I didn't know if I was driving too fast or too slowly or if I was even on the right side of the road. I pulled over, breathed in and out, and gave myself a little pep talk. "Look at the speedometer and go thirty," I said. "If you see a cop, act normal. Don't panic." I drove the rest of the way internally screaming, the road stretching and thinning like a wad of bubble gum between my fingers.

She answered the door, and a colorful swath of warm static bubbled between us. We sat on the couch and watched a hilarious basketball game with her little brother. The players were so long and fast. I loved every minute of it, sitting in their messy house, howling at the game, brain sizzling in my skull.

I crept into the other room, where her mom was watching a Chinese movie. I asked her what it was about, and she seemed annoyed at the question.

"It's a drama," she said. "Just like in English."

I didn't know what she meant, but I watched for a little while, then went back to the basketball game. We ordered steaks from Outback, and I couldn't look at the food while I ate. I could see each tendon and muscle, and I started to gag. I got up to throw my plate away, and her mom yelled at me.

"Don't waste it!" she said. "Look at that, Crystal!" She pointed at my steak, which still had some meat around the fat ring.

"It's okay, Mom!" Crystal said, slightly aghast.

It *was* a waste, I thought. I don't pay attention to the things I waste. I should be better at that. I called Crystal the next day and the next after that. I told myself I would stop drinking, but it was a lie.

UC Davis

I know I shouldn't have gotten through community college with all the alcohol benders, fights, hard drugs, skateboarding, girls, and at some point, a terrorist attack in New York City. I showed up at school still buzzed on 9/11 and nobody knew what to do, students walking around quickly with their heads down, nearly banging into one another, listening to the news on their headphones.

It was already warm by the time I walked into the quad at 9 a.m. My temples throbbed with dehydration. A crowd formed around a kid with a giant boombox that blasted the news. A plane had smashed into one of the Twin Towers. Then another. Fire and smoke filled the skyscrapers. Workers jumped from windows, falling to their deaths. The newscasters cried on air. We stood around the radio clear across the country with our jaws dropped.

I broke from the crowd and sat by a patch of flowers in between classrooms and breathed in and out, the sweet roses tickling the insides of my nose, the campus exploding around me, frantic with community college students with their heads buried in the news, clutching my chest because I was about to die of hyperventilation. A panic attack. Again. On this strange day mere months before I was to transfer from community college to a real college. A university. Without a high school diploma.

After two years at community college, I was a twenty-four-year-old man clutching a letter from UC Berkeley that I couldn't get myself to open, like a seventeen-year-old boy. If it's thick, that means you got in. I heard that so many times that I actually believed it. Mine wasn't thick. It couldn't have been more than a couple of sheets of paper. I opened it up and it said, "Congratulations!" I almost passed out at the idea of going to UC Berkeley. I accepted their offer, but when it came time to provide high school transcripts, I couldn't. I didn't have them.

"Isn't there anything we can do?" I pleaded with the admissions officer at other the end of the line.

"I'm sorry," she said, and hung up the phone.

I called the admissions office of my second choice, UC Irvine.

"There's nothing I can do," the man said at the other end of the line. "You need a high school diploma or a GED."

I made an appointment with a counselor at my community college.

"I don't have a high school diploma," I told her.

"A GED works too," she said.

"I don't have that either."

Her office was dark, with dark wood cabinets. Her diplomas hung in frames behind her.

"I can help," she said, her soft face filled with kindness.

The counselor worked part-time as an admissions officer at UC Davis. She'd pull some strings. "Don't worry," she said. I almost cried at her kindness. Everyone's kindness at that community college—the English professor who took me under her wing, the guys in the RISE program who offered me a job as a tutor, the professors who looked past my blood-shot eyes and into the content of my work . . . there was so much goodwill around me that something shifted in my soul, as if the hatred that had once filled the entirety of my body had been replaced with a new mechanism that I didn't quite understand yet, like driving a stick shift for the first time. I'd probably stall out a few times and look like an idiot, holding up traffic in the middle of a busy intersection, but I'd lurch forward nonetheless.

Home Invasion

I kept drinking and doing drugs at a ferocious pace in between community college and UC Davis. One night, I went out with my roommate to the bar down the street and ordered shots of whiskey until my eyes went black. I took a few more shots, got a Jack and Coke, and ordered several draft Budweisers. At some point, my friend wandered off toward a group of girls while I stayed at the bar. I didn't talk with anyone; I just sat and drank while the night progressed, until everything blurred and I felt trapped in the center of a tornado, looking up at the night's events swirling just out of reach. I don't remember leaving the bar, only walking home with my roommate trailing behind, talking to people with unfamiliar voices. I walked at a quick pace, enjoying the warm Sacramento night.

I stumbled home three blocks and sprawled on the couch. My room-mate, Roderick, a lanky Black kid who played basketball and wrote poetry, was there.

"Who these muthafuckaz?" he said.

"I dunno."

The stars were crisp, the moon huge. In the light, I got a drunken look at the two men who had followed me from the bar. One guy was dark brown with forgettable features, and the other was light-skinned with wild hair. The darker one went immediately for a beer run while I smoked a cigarette with the other guy on the front stoop.

"What set you rep?" the light-skinned guy asked, wondering if I belonged to an opposing gang.

"Nothing," I said.

Mexicans who ride skateboards don't join gangs, but I told him I knew some Tongans—Sivili, Joe, and Sufesi. They were Crips, but we only drank together sometimes. I wasn't a Crip. I once got drunk with them and shot guns at the moon until the cops came, and we all ran in different directions. I shouldn't have said anything. The words rushed from my mouth in a river of drunken language. But the light-skinned guy turned serious and said he was a Blood and flashed a quick hand sign that showed me what set he was from just as his dark friend came back down the street with a twenty-four-pack of Bud Light. I shouldn't have let them back inside, but we went in. A few minutes or an hour passed, and Roderick clomped downstairs, wiping the sleep from his eyes.

"Y'all play chess?" he said.

The darker guy nodded, and Roderick produced a chessboard from the cabinet.

While they played chess, I drank can after can of warm beer, the spin-ning room feeling more normal now.

"Let's play chess," someone said.

"I don't play chess," I said.

"What the fuck," another said.

"I never learned."

"Okay," another one said. "It's okay."

"Okay," I agreed. They were rude, and scary, but nice. They reminded me of everyone else in the world. I kept drinking until all the beer was gone. I couldn't tell who was in my house or why. I wanted everyone to leave. I wanted to be alone, to spin myself to sleep.

I got off the couch and the next thing I knew, I heard my bike clicking past me out the door. Someone walked down the stairs with my record player slung over his shoulder. Someone was trying to unplug my computer from the wall. I ran into the kitchen and grabbed a knife to stop the man lugging my computer toward the front door. I took a wild swing, trying to stab him in the brain, but missed, cutting drunkenly through the air.

Something whacked the back of my head. It felt like a car had driven into my skull.

I woke up in the hospital to a big, fat nurse sponging my naked body. She was beautiful. I told her she looked like Anna Nicole Smith, and she giggled. My parents stood over my hospital bed, and I said I felt like Kurt Cobain.

My Tongan friends came to visit right when they were allowed. They piled in the room and held my hand.

"You'll be okay," Sufesi said.

I believed him.

The next thing I remember is a detective. He showed up at our messy apartment. He didn't look like a detective. His slim body, pleated slacks, and awkward disposition betrayed the law enforcement stereotype. He sat on the couch and slid a large photo album across the coffee table, knocking over a near-empty can of Pabst. A vein of beer cascaded around a few other empty cans, pooling finally into a little pond near the ashtray.

"Sorry," he said, adjusting his wire-framed glasses. His nondescript vibe was comforting.

"It's fine," I said. "I'll clean it up."

"Now, before you look through these pictures, it's important to remember what the men looked like," he said. "Can you remember?"

"I think so," I said. I knew there was a lighter one.

"Are you picturing them right now?"

"The one I remember best wasn't the guy who tried to kill me," I said. "He was light-skinned, about twenty. Thin. Peach fuzz mustache. Thick eyebrows and relaxed, really messed-up hair."

"It's okay," the detective said. "You don't have to verbalize it. Just make sure you have the picture in your mind."

It was a professional way of telling me to shut the fuck up.

"Yeah," I said. "I got him."

"Mr. Fernandez, before you look through the photos, there's something you said at the hospital." The detective wore an impressive look of concern, as if he'd practiced it a thousand times in the mirror.

"Yeah," I nodded.

"You described one of the assailants as 'nice.'"

"He was nice," I said.

"Nice?" the detective shot back, confused.

"Kinda."

"How so?"

"Well, we hung out a little before—"

"Before he robbed you?" he asked, cutting me off.

"Uh-huh."

"And sent you to the hospital?"

"Yeah."

They were nice, like I was nice.

The detective straightened his posture, as if he'd caught himself lapsing out of professionalism. He took a deep breath, shook off his line of questioning, and changed directions entirely. "Do you feel all right? Do you need anything? Water?"

"No," I said, remembering that my entire head was wrapped in a bandage. It must have taken all his strength not to laugh while I answered his questions.

"So, you were saying you felt some empathy with your attackers."

"I mean, yeah. They bought beer."

"Mr. Fernandez, would you consider yourself an alcoholic—" He stopped at the tail end of the sentence before he could even get to the question mark. Had he continued, I would have answered. "You know what? Why don't you just look at the pictures now and see if you recognize anyone." He pointed to the photo album.

As I'd told the detectives in the hospital, I couldn't recall the exact details of the night in a linear sense. It was more like the facts came in unrecognizable segments, an unfinished puzzle with half of the pieces jammed in where they didn't belong.

I began to compile a list of all the things I remembered:

The dead yellow of the room.

Alcohol-soaked mop water.

Faces blurring into other faces.

Women with each drink becoming less and less exotic.

The warm breeze.

The shirt sticking to my back.

The cracked sidewalk.

Unkempt bushes forcing shadows to creep like demons in the grass.

These things were all useless to a detective.

Concentrating on a single face in the photo album was next to impossible, especially with the detective sitting there watching me, his steel eyes burning holes into the side of my neck. Each portrait shared a similarity with the next—the slow curve of the nose, the point of the chin, the tightly cropped curls, the yellowish eyes. Picture after picture of incarcerated Black men, like a bastard American history captured in a flimsy fifteen-inch photo album.

I had a few lines of coke left in a baggie under my bed. It felt wrong to identify anyone for sending me to the hospital.

"I smell some alcohol on your breath," the detective said sheepishly. He was a good man. He didn't want to upset me or pry.

I stopped at his photo and focused on it. He looked right at me, exactly as he had appeared in my apartment. Peach fuzz mustache. Thick eyebrows. Wild hair, like a lion's mane. He didn't look like a criminal. Even in his mug shot, he looked nice.

I tried to remember what he was like—his personality, and that night—how he had concentrated on his friend's chess game with Roderick, watching every move as if studying for an exam. Then it all came back to me at once. How I'd drank most of the beers, maybe all of them, and as the night stretched on, I could barely stand. The world had turned thick with drunkenness. Roderick went to bed. I tried to tell our guests it was time to go, but I could only look at the skinny one and smile. I tried to get up but fell back onto the couch.

I watched the darker guy steal my bike. It clicked as he wheeled it across the living room and out the front door. He unplugged my computer and carried it away. The skinny guy demanded money. I didn't have any. I was too drunk to argue. The room spun. I ran toward the kitchen, crashed into the wall, fumbled around the drawer, and found a small, serrated steak knife. I made my way back to the living room, where I showed them my weapon. I might have been crawling. *Was I crawling?* I waved the knife, and the light-skinned guy backed up toward the door. He pulled out a knife of his own. It was gold—even the handle. I couldn't understand why he had a gold knife. It wasn't like the movies. My movements were wild and clumsy. Everybody looked scared to death. I swung my steak knife at his face, and he backed out toward the door, trying to keep my eyes focused on his gold knife. There was a crack, and my head exploded into a wet mass of pressure, as if I was under the ocean and balancing a boulder on top of my head. I turned around to see what had hit me. Everything went black.

I woke up in the hospital with two tubes in my throat and could barely make out the two detectives, Crystal, my stepfather, and my mother. My older sister held one hand and Crystal held the other. Anna Nicole Smith rubbed my belly with a warm sponge. I heard machines humming and fell asleep to a cool river of drugs rushing through my system.

"That's him," I said, pointing to his picture in the photo album.

The detective straightened his posture. "Are you sure? Look harder. Make sure."

"It's him," I said. "I'm positive."

The detective sat expressionless, as if he didn't want to put his bias onto the situation. I admired his composure. Nothing seemed to faze him. Nothing was right or wrong in his world. Everything was a series of facts that all led to a specific point. He'd make a good father, I thought.

"So, what happens next?"

"Well, if your roommate Roderick picks the same suspect, there will be a trial."

"No," I said. "I mean, what happens to me?"

"To you?"

"Yeah."

"Well," the detective said, "I suppose that's up to you."

A wave of sadness washed over my body. *I don't want to make decisions*, I thought. *I'm not good at them.* When the detective got up to leave, I stayed on the couch, thinking about the last night I'd spent with my baby sister, Monica, who died before her third birthday. It wasn't fair.

The sky is always blue.

"Do you have kids?" I asked before the detective reached the door.

"Yeah," the detective said without turning around. "But we don't get to speak much."

He closed the door gently behind him.

It was 104 degrees, and everything was burning. I was working as an intern for a writing class at the community college. A stack of eighty student essays stared at me longingly. Instead of grading, I was tooling around the internet, wasting time, reading stories about celebrity coke binges gone awry. Charlie Sheen's face had grayed from narcotics. Lil Wayne had started skateboarding. I scrolled through Myspace and then checked my work email. Among the dozens of cryptic messages from the administration about potlucks and retirement parties, I found a message marked Urgent from one of the students:

> *Dear Mr. Fernandez, my fiancé left ... I feel pathetic and weak ... I'm not sure what's happened, and I stayed up all damn night crying ... he broke into my house and stole everything. I had to have my daughter picked up because I'm just falling apart, and after everything we've been through, this happens??? I don't get it! I hate this life, and I guess you can say I'm being a little bitch about it. I feel so stupid. —Whitney*

Part of me wanted to tell her, "Oh yeah? Join the fucking club." Another part wanted to say, "Yeah, fuck it, you're right. Life is fucked, and it probably gets worse." But still another part wanted to tell her something else. Something closer to the truth: that these things happen, these events that we think are the end of us. We think, *How can I possibly survive?* But we do. We're stronger than we think.

The detective called out of the blue. He said he'd been thinking about me, that he had wanted to give me some advice but was sure I wouldn't want to hear it. It plagued him to think that he'd left me there all bandaged up with an unanswered question.

"Do you remember what you asked me?" he asked.

"Not really."

"You asked me what happens to you."

"Yeah."

The detective's voice shook as he spoke on the other end of the phone. "Look, I gave you the wrong answer," he said. "I should have told you that when somebody invades your home, you get over it quickly. When they take stuff, it's only stuff. Your physical wounds heal. Time passes. You get your things back. Or you don't. But it's not about what they took. The real damage is done by what they left."

"What they left?"

"It's something like a little bomb they leave inside your brain, and one day—it could be a week, a month, or twenty years from now—that bomb will explode into a billion microscopic fragments, jagged and impossible to clean up. That kind of mess in your brain will cripple you to your death.

The only way to stop that explosion is to defuse it before it happens . . . are you there?"

"I'm here," I said. "I'm listening."

"Good," he said. "Then be with the people you trust. Hang on to the people you love. Don't let them go. And if they do let go, keep them in your thoughts, so there's no room for anything else. No anger. No bomb. No explosion."

I returned to Whitney's message and stared at the blank white field where I was supposed to type. Finally, I wrote:

> This is hard, but I got your back. This is a new life, maybe for the both of us, so let's do it right.

I pressed Send and worried the message might be too creepy.

A week later, I got a call from my doctor, who said he had some news I might not want to hear.

"What is it?" I said.

"Because of your brain injury," he said. "I think it's best that you hold off your first year at UC Davis."

I didn't have any words, but I'm sure my face said it all.

"I'm sorry," the doctor said. "I really recommend that you postpone your acceptance for another year. I know it's possible to do that."

"Okay," I said. "Thank you."

When we hung up the phone, I knew I wasn't going to listen to him. He also knew I wasn't going to listen to him.

Against Doctor's Orders

My first day on the UC Davis campus was like stepping into another world: hundreds of students rushing from place to place in the most disorganized ways, nearly running into one another, everyone late, like everyone was competing in a game show with no host and no clear end goal. I stood on a patch of grass under a gigantic pine tree with a crumpled printout of my class schedule, whiskey fumes protecting me like a force field. A tall Asian kid stood casually in the middle of the sidewalk, talking on the phone. Students walked around him, into the grass. He didn't move. He took up the middle of the space, looking down at his feet as a flow of students broke around him, reforming once they had passed, like a boulder in a shallow stream. I'm supposed to be at a Shakespeare class, but I can't find the room or the building. I've never seen so many bicycles. Students cross the streets without even looking up, bicycles swerving to miss them. At the roundabout, a bike speeds through the circle and slams into a girl wearing a Hello Kitty backpack and they both go flying. A group of students points and laughs. Everybody else walks around the pile of bloody humans. Nobody seems to care. It's like I've replaced one brutal world for another. I could probably get used to this.

YOU DRINK LIKE US

"You smell like my dad!" little Bob said, running away and pointing at me. All the kids laughed.

The sound of their laughter reverberated in my hungover ears.

Bob's Korean name was Bon-Hwa (Glorious), but Bob was his English name. All the kids had English names, even though their Korean names were much cooler. Eun-Kyung (Graceful Gem). Hee-Young (Joy and Prosperity). Joo-Chan (Praise the Lord). They were all flattened to American names. Rachel. Heather. James.

"C'mere, Bob," I said. "I got something to tell you."

I let out a huge fart and all the kids ran away, screaming, laughing, and dying.

Americans are weird and gross, and we drink too much and smell like cigarettes, so I like to amp it up, give them a real show.

After college, in a moment of panic, I had filled out an application to teach English abroad, and two weeks later I was on a plane to Korea. I left Crystal stateside, scratching her head, still finishing her last quarter of college at UC Davis.

"I'll call you whenever I can," I said. "They have phone cards. I'll have my own apartment. You can come visit."

"Okay," she said, trying to hide her disappointment.

When my plane landed in Seoul, a man with a shaggy haircut was waiting to greet me. He held a flimsy cardboard sign that said *Fernandez*.

"Welcome," he said. He wasn't friendly, maybe because it was 1 a.m., but he had the demeanor of a man who would rather be doing anything other than picking up new teachers at the airport in the middle of the night.

We got in his van and headed to Osan, a thirty-five-minute drive south. We drove through the country, mountains on the side of the road lit by crosses.

"Why are there so many crosses here?" I asked my driver.

"We love Jesus," he returned.

It was after 2 a.m. by the time we got to Osan, a small, architecturally confusing city of old stone and brick with utilitarian buildings colored with obnoxious billboards advertising restaurants, insurance agencies, bars, karaoke, and massages. He parked his van down a side street, and when we got out, a whiff of oily fried-chicken smoke filled my nostrils. A little corner store had tables and chairs set out. They were closed, but a man in a business suit sat hunched over the table, passed out.

"A lot here," the driver said, pointing at the man.

He gave me a piece of paper with a code on it.

"Door," he said. "You go."

I punched the code into a door, and it opened into a tiny studio apartment. He pointed out the stove, the air conditioner, and the bathroom, then closed the door behind me.

A whole gallon of Jack Daniels sat on the kitchen counter with a note from the last tenant:

Hello Josh,
I am Richard, the previous teacher.
I hope you enjoy teaching the kids as much as I did.
Everyone is wonderful.
This was a gift when I first arrived, but I don't drink, so maybe you can use it.

Best,
Richard

I unwrapped the plastic, took a long chug out of the bottle, and looked out the window at the streets of Osan. In the near distance was an alleyway with another man in a suit, sleeping on the ground.

I could get used to this place, I thought, and took another chug of whiskey.

I woke up with a pounding headache. A loudspeaker blaring from the market said something in Korean. I lifted the blinds, and the street was alive with activity. A woman and her small daughter struggled to get the man in the suit to his feet, but he still appeared too drunk to move. A woman with a straw hat and a broom resting on her shoulder ran past.

I felt like I'd arrived on a different planet.

I felt too afraid to leave the tiny studio but thought I'd try to get out for at least a few minutes. It was the end of summer, so the smoggy air was thick with heat. When I stepped onto the sidewalk, I could tell people were looking at me. It was the first time I'd been in a place where I was the only one of a kind. An old woman sweeping her stairs stopped sweeping and said something in Korean. It looked like she was lecturing me. I walked toward the market. The drunk man was gone from the table, and a white man with wispy brown hair was in his place. He was drinking a gigantic bottle of beer.

"Are you a teacher?" he said in a heavy Australian accent.

"I am," I said. "Josh Fernandez."

"Jake Marrs," he said, extending his hand.

We shook hands, and he gave me directions to a bar where some of the other teachers hung out. I was excited. I'd never talked to an Australian before.

That night, I followed Jake's directions and ended up at a sports bar on the second floor of a little mall. In Korea, everything is in a mall. When I entered the bar, I noticed Jake surrounded by a large group of people in different stages of drunkenness. Next to him stood an unsightly blond man, an odd, puffy fellow with searing blue eyes. I later learned his name was Cal, an expat whoremonger who spent every paycheck on his favorite prostitutes. He had a list of about ten that he chose from, and he talked about them as if they were his wives.

There was Stu, a hefty man from New Zealand, and his girlfriend, Eun Song, a beautiful woman with an unusually deep voice, and William, a Korean cop. William took to me right away, fascinated. "Do you need a ride?" he asked. "I have a car!"

"I just got here," I said.

"Later then!" he said. "I drive you."

We ordered pitchers of beer and talked about Korea.

"We'll go to Seoul tomorrow," Jake declared.

Everyone agreed. We ordered more pitchers. And more.

"You drink like us!" Eun Song said.

If she only knew.

I woke up the next morning unsure of how I had gotten home.

I spent the next few weeks getting acquainted with my school, or *hagwon*, an after-school program where students brushed up on their skills. The Korean students spent all day and night in school. They had private classes before school, then went to school, then more private classes after school. They were dead tired when they got to my class at 3:30. I was also tired, because the culture in Korea for *hagwon* teachers was to go out all night, stumble home when the sun started to rise, and then sleep until class.

I met a drug dealer from Thailand, a skinny kid who dressed in dirty sweatsuits.

He sat on my bed while I held the glass pipe up to my lips.

"In Korea, they kill you for this," he said.

"Good," I said, and watched the flame bubble the shards into liquid, then a pure white smoke.

The school I taught at was called TLC. It was on the second floor of a little mall. It was a nondescript building with linoleum floors and fluorescent lights. The walls were covered in scenes of America, flags and mountains. The Koreans had an interesting relationship with Americans. They loved the glamorous parts of the culture: the celebrity, the scenery, the music. But they hated us as people. One older Korean man, when he caught wind of an American in his path, he'd grab the nearest broom and smack them with it. Sometimes he'd hock up a loogie and spit. I got it. I'd have the same reaction, but I wished I wasn't on the receiving end.

"What is this, Bill?" I said, holding up a book.

"Book!"

"Nice! And what is this, Mary?" I said, holding up a shoe.

"Um, shoe!" Mary said.

They paid me a good salary for this, more than I'd be making in America, plus they paid for my studio and lunch.

I held up a pencil.

"What is it, Louis?"

"It's a pen!"

"No, it's a pencil!" I yelled, earning my keep for the day.

I woke up in an alley, cuddled up against Jake, using his flannel shirt as a blanket. An old man walked past us and laughed. Flashes of the previous night skipped through my head. *Bar. Laughter. Businessmen from Kentucky buying drinks. Subway. Fighting Jake in the alley.*

I had become the very American stereotype that I hated, the bullshit asshole who wastes every opportunity and expects another one to arrive right away, a pile of trash waking up next to a dumpster in a filthy alleyway. What had become of me?

"Where the fuck are we?" I asked Jake, who was trying to pull himself up. A giant knot sat in the center of his forehead.

"Itaewon."

"What time is it?" My face felt raw.

"It's almost one."

Itaewon, the "international" section of Korea that I insisted we visit so I could get Mexican food, was an hour from my school.

"Fuck," I said.

"Fuck," Jake returned.

We split a cab back to Osan. I didn't have time to shower, so I brushed my teeth and put on a fresh pair of clothes. I could make it to work in fifteen minutes if I ran, so I slammed my front door and bolted past the markets, through the park, past the old ladies stretching in the park, past the restaurant that sold dog meat in the evenings, past the strip of bars and the supermarket, and past the water where the factories cough black smoke into the gray sky day and night. It felt good to run. I could feel my lungs working, pumping in and out, my breath heavy and deep. I hadn't been so aware of my breath lately, like I'd forgotten to breathe for the past twenty years.

I was soaking wet when I got to work; my light blue shirt had turned royal blue. I slid into the bathroom to try to wipe myself down before my boss could see me, but she was already waiting at the top of the stairs.

"You're so late," she said, pointing to her watch.

"I thought I was early."

"Very late."

"What time is it?"

"What time is it," she mimicked, then let out a disgusted sigh.

It was 3:01. A minute late.

I started my daily cleaning duties, sweeping and mopping the floor and emptying the trash cans. I put in my earbuds to drown out my hangover.

The boss's mopey daughter, Soojin, walked into the front classroom crying.

"What's wrong?" I asked.

She was thirteen, a horrible age for anyone. I remembered when I was thirteen, so angry that I'd scowl around the school looking for someone to fight. I didn't dare cry though.

I set my broom down and tried to calm her down.

"My mom."

"Yeah," I said. "She can be tough." My boss was an asshole. When I messed something up around the office, like misplaced a textbook, she'd suck her tongue and call me stupid. "You're so *stupid*," she'd say with such conviction that I believed it.

"Tough?"

"Oh yeah," I said. "Like mean."

"Mean," she said. "Yeah, she's mean." Soojin wiped her tears and went to the office, where her mom was sitting. I could hear them arguing. Then it stopped. Footsteps clicked toward me.

"My husband talk to you."

"What do you mean?"

"Stupid," she said. "Tonight. In car."

"You have a husband?"

"So stupid," she says.

She slammed the door and stomped away.

She meant that her husband would drive me home that night, so I wouldn't have to walk or take the shuttle, which I appreciated. The shuttle was full of kids. I'd rather walk in the darkness of Osan, through the busy streets, dodging bicycles and unruly traffic all the way home, than spend another minute with my students, whose idea of a good time was touching my arm hair and yelling in unison, "Ooooooh!"

Her husband pulled up outside the school in a black luxury sedan with tinted windows. I reached for the passenger door, and he rolled down the window.

"Back," he said.

I sat in the back seat like he was a taxi driver. We took a route I'd never seen before, under a freeway and through a quiet residential neighborhood.

"You drink," he said.

"I do."

"Too much," he said.

"Yeah," I said. "I probably do."

"I drink too much too," he said. "But I stop."

"Oh," I said. "That's good."

"You stop too."

"Okay," I said. "I'll stop."

"Good," he said.

We didn't talk the rest of the way home, driving through the neighborhoods and back into familiar Osan with its four-story malls and little karaoke bars. When I got into my apartment, I opened a bottle of *soju* and poured it into a glass. It tasted like lighter fluid, but I drank it as quickly as possible. I went to the market to buy more *soju* to drink while I packed. I called the airline to check if my boss had purchased a two-way ticket. They told me it was, so I booked a flight back to Sacramento for the next day. I still had another four months left on my contract. I was supposed to teach the next day. Instead of finishing, I would abandon my students, abandon the director, abandon the friends I had made, abandon Korea, and never return. I would reenter America as a failure.

When I arrived back in Sacramento, I was out of money. All the money I had made I had spent on alcohol and drugs. My parents picked me up at the airport and took me back to their place, a big house on the outskirts of Davis. Everything was clean. The windows were spotless. The empty sink glistened. I couldn't stop shaking. My hands trembled. I spent my last money on forty-ounce bottles of Steel Reserve malt liquor. When my parents went to bed, I drank the forties in my room. I tried to write, but nothing made sense. I was trying too hard. I plagiarized Charles Bukowski. One line made sense:

Help me.

I wrote it over and over until I had to pee. I kept running to the bathroom to pee. I finally found an empty bottle and filled it with piss. I screwed on the cap and placed it underneath the bed. *I'll clean it tomorrow*, I thought, but I forgot about it. A week later, my mom was cleaning the house and found it.

"What is this, Josh?" she said, holding up the bottle.

She'd saved it to show me.

"It's a bottle of pee," I said, trying not to sound weird about it. "I didn't want to wake you." I was profoundly embarrassed. I didn't know what I was doing. I had failed in Korea. I had failed to find a job. I had no skills. I had lost sight of everything I loved—punk music, Anti-Racist Action, friendship. I had nothing of my own. I didn't even want to work. I had lost everything that I'd ever cared about, even my beliefs. Over the past year of this I didn't want to live. I turned that embarrassment into rage.

"Fuck you," I yelled.

My mom's face contorted into an angry question mark.

I ran out of her clean house and into the car they'd sold me but I'd never paid for. I had nowhere to go.

I stood under a palm tree in the middle of a park in the middle of the suburb of Davis, California, and the breeze was just as hot as the air. It was the middle of the summer and more than one hundred degrees. I was too tired to stand, but I kept standing. There was nowhere to sit. I was paralyzed.

The blue sky was perfect. The tall tree was good for perspective. The small person standing still in a large swath of unbroken lawn offered a symbol of insignificance. It would have been a good painting. But I couldn't paint. I had no camera. If I moved, the image would be broken. I wasn't sure what to do or where to go, so I kept standing until the sun started to dip under the horizon. My life loomed over me, the things I believed in hovering above my head, out of reach, but still visible—punk rock, antiracism, smacking Nazis with bats, education, writing. My breath started to get faster, like I was having a heart attack. I thought maybe I *was* having a heart attack, so I collapsed to the ground. The breathing came quicker, and there wasn't anywhere to go, like being inside a glass box at the bottom of a pool slowly filling with water.

I noticed a door. Right at the top of the glass box. On the door was a little latch. All I had to do was flip the latch, and the door would open. I could swim free to the top and take a gulp of air. It couldn't be that easy. I wondered if the door had been there the whole time.

Shooting Guns

On a Friday afternoon, I got a call from one of our freelancers. I had been out of college for a couple of years and writing for local newspapers when I'd scored a cushy editor position at an alternative weekly newspaper.

"Let's go shooting," he said. "Just buy the ammo."

"Okay," I said.

HOW TO PUT A BABY TO SLEEP

Our new baby, Luna, doesn't like to sleep, and when she finally stops fighting and drifts off in my arms, I try to set her down in her crib, and she wakes up and starts crying again.

It's midnight.

12:55 a.m.

2 a.m.

I cradle her in my arms, and we walk around the house in the darkness. I'm careful not to trip over the toys scattered on the floor or nick a table corner with my hip, and she's still crying. I bounce her up and down.

"Shhh," I say, but she's still screaming.

Nobody wants to be told to be quiet.

We go to the backyard, where the moon is full and glowing in the middle of the sky.

"Look at the moooooon," I say. "Look!"

She stops crying to study the moon. I wonder what she sees in it. Maybe it's the perfect shape or so bright against the black sky.

I sing her my favorite verse of Dio's "Heaven and Hell," the lines about black really being white and the moon being the sun and walking in golden halls and the gold that falls and heaven and hell, the ones that turned my dad against me, the ones that made him run out the door and never come back, "Oh noooo . . ."

Joey from the Time-Out Box

I spent months trying to quit drinking, but I couldn't, so I started running every morning, hungover, my body shrouded in a fog of whiskey fumes, running through the early morning darkness around the park near my apartment. No matter how shitty I felt, I ran every morning. I ran so much that I decided to run a marathon. I trained hard every day for eighteen weeks for the San Francisco Marathon. The rigorous training chiseled my normally chubby face into a strangely angular shape, giving it an athletic zombie look. I lost about ten pounds. Sometimes I felt sick and couldn't eat, followed by periods of severe gluttony in which I consumed pizza and pasta at an extraordinary volume. My mood often went from ecstatic to flat-out tired. By the time the race came, most of my toenails had turned black and fallen off from the constant pounding against my shoes. But it was the healthiest I'd felt in my life, and I'd successfully trained my body to run for almost four hours without stopping.

What the fuck are you running from, people would ask, sort of as a joke, but sort of serious too.

I was running from drugs, pain, violence, myself, everything. I never asked to be a part of any of this, and sometimes it's all too much. When I look back on everything, I don't see where I could have made choices. My life ran like a crude machine lurching forward with no change in direction. There were choices, of course, but they were obscured from me at the time. There was only survival, doing the next thing. Alternative options were there, but so what? By the time we get here, we are already what we are, so what's the use in looking back?

Before I started running, I'd spent months floundering around in AA meetings. My old friend Joey, from kindergarten in Boston, the one I had met in the time-out box, told me he was moving out to San Diego. He'd begun running in college; since then, he'd competed in several marathons and triathlons. I've always admired him. He never used drugs or drank much alcohol and has been one of the happiest and most successful people I've ever known. When I was out in the streets, I missed him dearly.

It was a moment of pure desperation when I decided to start running. I was educated but unmotivated to do anything but ingest alcohol and drugs. I was unemployable. I hated authority figures, and even worse, I hated myself and anyone having to do with me, including the people I loved. My politics of youth—the fierce antiracism, the militant stand against neo-Nazi skinheads—was all but gone, replaced by an eternal chemical cloud. I became sickly, my skin yellowish white and my brain sizzling with anger. My suicidal thoughts were uncontrollable, and I wanted to die. I was becoming an expatriate of my own self, and I was worse off than when I had lived in an Oak Park recording studio that doubled as a heroin den.

I didn't start running to be like my friend Joe, but to get a taste of what he had. I wanted to experience joy without the effects of drugs. I wanted to be happy and creative without having to rely on chemicals. After all, how could I claim a piece of writing as my own if it was the splendor of drugs that had created it?

I started running on a treadmill. I smoked cigarettes, so I could only go for about two minutes at a time. When I ran, I felt a layer of fat jiggling up and down and up and down, so I joined the YMCA to get in shape, and each week I'd increase my time by a few minutes. Soon I was running for fifteen minutes. Then I increased it to twenty, then to forty-five, and so on. Pretty soon I'd stopped going to AA meetings altogether. Instead, I went to the gym. I quit smoking, and even though I thought about it every day, I didn't drink.

Occasionally I caught an unfamiliar glimpse into a future not shrouded by misery. So I started running longer distances. When you get accustomed to running long distances, your breathing becomes different as your body exerts the energy it takes to maintain your stride; your mind is focused but free to wander. It's a euphoric feeling that lasts as long as you're running. When you stop, that feeling is replaced by another feeling—accomplishment, followed by strength and confidence. And when you're an addict, at home that night eating dinner, you begin to crave another run. Sometimes it takes all your wits not to skip dessert and slip out into the night for a run along the river.

On August 3, the morning of the San Francisco Marathon, I could barely contain myself; I felt as if my entire body would explode in anticipation. I had stayed with Crystal, my girlfriend then, in a hotel downtown the night before, where I'd slept for a fitful three hours. I'd spent most of the night tossing around the bed in a cold sweat, wondering what it would be like to run my first marathon. I got up thirty minutes before my alarm went off, because I couldn't take the restlessness anymore. When I got to the Embarcadero, it was shortly after 5 a.m., and a crowd of runners loitered at the start line. I had gone the wrong way, so a large fence separated me from the other entrants. A cop stood in the street telling people they had to go around, but I didn't have time. I pretended not to hear the officer and jumped over the fence when he looked away. "Hey, you!" he said. "You need to go around." I ran into the crowd so he couldn't catch me. I had so much practice running from cops that it wasn't a problem.

When I stood in the sea of several thousand runners, a surge of energy surrounded me, like standing in the middle of an electrical storm. Everyone was jittery and couldn't stop moving. I couldn't stop smiling. My knees trembled from the nerves and the cold. Before I knew it, we were running along the wharf at a good pace past Pier 39, shoes patting around me like thousands of fingers typing on keyboards. It was like nothing I'd ever heard; my mind began firing rapidly. I could barely contain my thoughts. The city glowed orange under the streetlights, and thousands of runners moved forward together in the dark. I'd never felt so connected to the earth, my feet touching down so intently upon the road, soaking up the energy of the other runners, as a unified spirit pushed us forward.

The wind felt good against my face. When cars passed on the other side of the street, they honked and waved at the pack of runners keeping a steady pace as we passed by Ghirardelli Square. Just past the buildings and through a thicket of trees, the Golden Gate Bridge sat on a hill in a bed of fog like a majestic kingdom.

I was crying. I didn't understand it at first, but it felt good. I didn't wipe away the tears, because they were supposed to be there. I stayed in the moment, letting the tears stream down my face. I wasn't sad at all. It was the happiest moment of my life.

I can't escape my addictions. Even during the San Francisco Marathon, a prankster dressed up as a devil offered runners glasses of cold beer instead of water. I took the water but seriously considered the beer. On mile 16, I felt surprisingly good with no aches and my breathing still regular. We ran over the Golden Gate Bridge, through the Outer Richmond, and up the winding trails of Golden Gate Park, where Joe's wife, Keely, was there to take pictures and ride her bike along the course to cheer me on. She followed me through Haight-Ashbury and waved goodbye as I ran through mile 19. By mile 20, I felt the wrath of the road. My legs, I realized, were more tired than they'd ever been for the entirety of my life. Just ten minutes prior, I'd been smiling and feeling fine. I managed to run two more miles and realized that I had hit the dreaded "wall" you often hear about in marathon stories. It seemed like every incline was a 90 percent grade, every pebble in the road a sworn enemy, every crack in the ground put there to trip me. People on the streets cheered, and all I wanted was for them to stop.

"Nice tattoos," a lady on the sidewalk yelled as she waved and gave me the thumbs-up sign.

"Fuck you!" I wanted to yell back, but I was too tired even for that.

I passed through the Mission and looked around at some of the other runners. They all looked as bad or worse than I did, giving me a little hope. I kept running through the torture, maybe just to see if I would die. The thought of me splayed out on the street, dead from running, made me giggle. But the joy didn't last long.

Someway, somehow, I didn't stop. On mile 25, we ended up by the ballpark, so close to the finish line that I could smell the hot dog stand at the end. Vomit gurgled up in my stomach, and my legs were no longer in charge. If I were a religious man, I'd say that God was powering them, but I'm not; like many of the phenomena attributed to a higher power, my strength came from pride and stubbornness.

The Bay Bridge poked up in the distance, and just a little bit farther was the end of my first marathon. When I saw the finish line within reach, I ran as fast as possible, which was comically slow. In the distance, my mom, my stepdad, and Crystal cheered by the sidelines. I crossed the finish line and looked at my time: three hours, forty-four minutes, and forty seconds. I took a medal, grabbed a banana, and collapsed onto the ground.

Most nights I still dream about smoking meth or drinking. I have this recurring dream where I go into a neighborhood like a war zone—groups of thugs wander around, picking fights with everyone—so I hide behind trees until I find the apartment I want. It's upstairs, and the door is broken. When I knock, a man with a shaved head and goatee peeps through a crack in the door. He opens at the sight of me and produces a plastic bag full of narcotics: ecstasy, crack, cocaine, and meth. The guy hands me the drugs, and I run to the park to do them as fast as I can. Only in my dream, I can't feel the high. I always wake up with a feeling of extreme disappointment.

Not a day goes by when I wouldn't rather be drinking or doing drugs. I love them like they were my own family. Drugs are more fun than running. They are instantaneous. Running is hard and torturous. It's not easy for me to fight the boredom of life. From birth, I was plagued with restlessness and a desire to feel more than the dullness of day-to-day life, the nervous unease with the world. These are my demons. Sometimes I think these ghosts follow me in karmic retribution for all the people I've hurt with my selfishness, and sometimes I think that my past is following me, nipping at my back, simply to get me moving, to keep me on the run.

HOW MANY INTERVIEWS CAN I FAIL?

I'm at the last college I applied to, impatient and hopeless, ready to return to working in retail or robbery. It's my fourth interview in the district, and I'm pissed. Each interview ends with a little spark of hope, but a week later, the same email shows up:

We're sorry, but . . .

Now that Ezra is a little older and doesn't require a parent catering to his every mood at all hours of the day, I need a steady income, a full-time teaching gig. I'm unsure how long I can sustain a life as an adjunct professor, piecing together the scraps of classes leftover from the tenured professors at community colleges. Maybe I'm too desperate. It probably shows on my face, the mug of a man who would do anything for some good health care.

I did pretty well at the previous interviews, considering I'm not great at interviews. I practiced my teaching demonstration in front of my computer's webcam and played it back, trying not to cringe at the sight of my unnecessary vocal inflections and exaggerated facial expressions.

At my first interview, eight stoic-faced professors were crowded around a conference table. I learned later that they were all told not to smile for any of the candidates, which is why it looked like they were gathered to inform me that the cancer had spread to my brain.

"Tell us what you might do to foster a diverse classroom," said a pudgy white guy with glasses. I think he was a poet.

Well, I'm a fucking Mexican who grew up in Boston and was ushered away from Mexican culture because my mother believed in assimilation. We moved from suburb to suburb, away from the lure of gangs, lowriders, and anything spicier than a packet of Taco Bell hot sauce. But over the past several years, I've been reclaiming my culture. I've been fighting the constraints of

white supremacy etched onto my DNA. I've been digging into my skin with
an obsidian blade, extracting chunks of crackerishness lodged into my body
through the years. When I'm done with that, I'll focus on what's outside—the
banks, the police stations, the courts of law, and I won't stop until it's all in
flames, even this very institution, where I hope you'll give me a job.

That's what I would have said if I had any guts.

But I answered how I knew they wanted the answer, the way I was told
in my Faculty Diversity Internship Program: with a personal anecdote that
shows you dealing with a diverse population of students. I told them about
my student Lakeisha, who struggled through my college composition
course. When she showed up, she was the life of the party. She sat up front
and never put her hand down. Sometimes she didn't show up, because she
worked at McDonald's and her hours were unpredictable. Halfway through
the semester, she told me she didn't have a computer, so she couldn't turn
some of the essays in on time. I knew a lot of people who could raise money.
I had met most of them through journalism when I wrote for publications
about music and culture. Liberals with disposable incomes. They wanted
to do activism but didn't have the time, so they donated to causes. Within
four hours of posting a GoFundMe on social media, they'd raised $2,500—
enough for a fancy laptop and a printer. Before class, I took Lakeisha into
the faculty lounge and gave her the Apple bag.

"It's for you," I said.

She took the bag and peeked inside.

"What?" she said.

"It's yours," I said. "My friends raised money for you."

Lakeisha started crying, and I cried too. We stood in the faculty
lounge crying together for a second.

"Thank you, Professor," she said.

"You deserve it."

The faculty listened intently to my story and nodded their heads.

"Wow," said a lady with glasses.

"I mean, I don't do that for all my students," I said.

The group chuckled.

A couple of years later, Lakeisha contacted me. She had moved to
Washington for a job. She hadn't finished school, but she was making
good money, so she didn't see the point. It was a smart move, I told her. I
was glad she had contacted me. Glad she was happy.

I'm proud of you, I wrote.

I didn't get a second interview. I knew I wouldn't. The community college's English faculty consists of white dudes pretending they're distinguished professors from Yale. They write bad poetry and publish each other in their little jackoff presses to create an illusion of prestige. I didn't fit in that world, and I'm not sure I wanted to.

The next interview was at the community college down the street from my house. It's where I met Crystal, where we sat underneath the oak tree, cherry blossoms picking up in the slight breeze. I held her hand and begged her to come and eat with me. She did, hesitantly, where we ate burritos and talked about punk music and got into that little argument about the band Operation Ivy and she didn't know I was old enough to have seen them when I was a kid, and I didn't tell her. We chewed and had a stilted conversation until she drove back to the campus and we went our separate ways. It was awkward, but there was something. When I asked her later about that first date, if she remembered it, she said, "Yeah, of course," and she had thought I was a bore.

The interview went well. We sat in a large brick auditorium and had a relaxed conversation about pedagogy, a fancy word for *shit you do in class*. I plagiarized Paulo Freire's idea about examining power structures as a means toward liberation. I told some bullshit story I heard on NPR that morning about a rich school on the East Coast switching classrooms with a poor school as some kind of experiment. I don't remember the point, but the interview committee enjoyed it.

The following interview phase was a live teaching demonstration where the panel recruited a classroom of actual students as my audience. This might have freaked some people out, but I love students. I love being with them, even in an artificially prepared situation. I can see the mischief in their eyes, and they can see it in mine.

"Hey, kids!" I said.

"We're not kids!" a lady in the front row fired back.

"We're kids until we die," I said.

She laughed.

Sometimes it's easy to win them over.

I launched into a compact lesson about using quotes in essays, which went well. I nailed the interview. I felt good about it. I got a call later that day that I had made it to the second round. It was between another candidate and me. We'd each meet with the college president, and she'd determine who got the job. The other candidate, it turned out, was my friend Dawna, an energetic white lady who came up in the same kind of punk scene as I did. She'd also been teaching part-time for a while and was probably just as desperate for a full-time gig as I was.

I met with the college president, a large woman with the grace of a queen. She wore a flowy dress with a beautiful African print. It wrapped around her whole body like she was peeking out of a kaleidoscope. It was hard for me to focus on anything but her wardrobe, so I probably appeared a little shifty. I answered her questions and left her office, feeling okay about the interview.

Later that day, I got a text in all caps from Dawna:

YOU GOT THE JOB. I CRIED DURING MY INTERVIEW.

That's one thing I heard constantly from people. Whatever you do, don't cry during your interview. I guess it indicated to the interviewers you couldn't handle a classroom of community college students. I never had the urge to cry during an interview. Punch the interviewer in the teeth, maybe, but never cry.

Dawna ended up getting the job.

I don't know what happened. I used to think that powerful Black women didn't like me very much. They could sense weakness in me. Maybe they imagined me as their son. More likely, to them, I was a shifty asshole with all the advantages in the world who still chose to fuck everything up, squander everything away like an idiot. I don't know. I told Dawna congratulations and started preparing for my last interview in the district.

And now I'm here, a Chicano at the whitest, richest community college in the area.

And I'm showing up to this interview carrying a Venti light roast coffee and a blade of anger.

I drive to Folsom early and stop at Starbucks. I don't want to drink a coffee, because caffeine makes me pee too much, but that's the only place I think to go, so I wait in line in front of a couple having a loud conversation.

"Why don't they just," the old man says, then whispers, "*go back?*"

"Exactly, right," the old woman says. "Go back to where they came from if they don't like it here."

"I mean, these people are so unhappy here, right?"

I feel my blade shimmering under the dim Starbucks lighting. I'm tempted to turn around, look them in the eye, and say, "We're here to fuck all your kids and turn this cracker town beige." I could turn around and stab each of them in the face. Or I could probably jump a little, and that alone would give them heart attacks.

But instead, I wait patiently for their increasingly common xenophobic Tea Party generation conversation to fizzle out. Then I order my drink and drive to the campus, where I enter the conference room to a table of faculty interviewing me with my rage still sizzling in my head.

I didn't prepare for this interview. I answer their questions and do my teaching demonstration and tell them the story about the racist octogenarians in Starbucks and say that's what education is for—to eradicate that kind of thinking so that we don't have any more crusty old white people left to ruin the lives of the Brown kids we're trying to protect.

When I leave the interview, I'm sure I didn't get the job. I'm too angry. Too nonchalant. I stand out in Folsom, the town of salmon-colored shopping malls and Lexus SUVs that look like they were built a week ago.

The following week, I'm sitting around at a coffee shop near my house, and I get a call from the vice president of instruction, the same lady who would orchestrate my firing.

"We'd like to offer you the job," she says, excited.

"Really?"

"Really."

It's like all my troubles are over. A salary. Benefits. A tenure track. A weight is lifted off my chest, and I can finally breathe.

On my first day, one of the professors from the interview panel pulls me aside.

"I'm not supposed to tell you this," she says, "but you were a wild card."

"What do you mean?"

"We weren't sure about you," she says. "It could've gone either way."

I wasn't sure what to do with that information at the time, but apparently, it was a warning.

The Long, Long Distance

Almost sixty miles into the one-hundred-mile San Diego 100 race, my body began to break down as the sun set under the Cuyamaca mountain range, painting a sky layered in deep pink and purple hues.

"It looks like the Patagonia logo," I said, pointing to the psychedelic sky, breathless and delirious after running for more than eleven hours.

"It does," Dave agreed, probably humoring me.

I had met Dave through a mutual friend. Dave was a vegan who was only eating fruit at the time. A *fruitarian*, he called it. When he showed up the day before, he met my mom, Lauren, Joe, Crystal, and me at a restaurant, where we were going to plan the next day's hundred-mile race. My mom and Lauren were my crew. They'd be waiting at various checkpoints throughout the race to feed me snacks and make sure I wasn't dying. Joe, my childhood friend who I had known at that point for thirty-five years, would pace me from mile 91 to 100 if I made it that far.

When it came time to order dinner, Dave told the waitress he didn't want anything and pulled out a Tupperware of cantaloupe chunks. My mom gave him a look but didn't say anything.

Lauren and Dave got into an argument. Dave had shown up without a place to stay, and Lauren thought it was irresponsible. They bickered. She called Dave an asshole. My mom started clearing her throat and changed the subject.

Dave was a perpetually happy man, one of the most positive people I'd ever met. He was a former alcoholic who'd lost a lot of weight after he had stopped drinking and eating meat. He loved being a vegan and running. He'd narrowed his life down into a thing of simplicity.

"Your mom and sister should be at the bottom of this mountain," Dave said, running behind me.

"Okay," I said.

"You can see the lights down below."

I looked toward the bottom of the mountain and saw a string of lights at the Cibbets Flat aid station. They looked so far away.

We continued running switchbacks until my body and mind became a formless slop. One of the most uncomfortable feelings one can experience is running to the point of fatigue. You're thirsty but can't drink. Hungry but can't eat. You want to stop running but can't, because it's a race.

By the time we reached the bottom of the mountain, it was pitch black, aside from the Christmas lights decorating the aid station. My mom and sister huddled up in blankets on their lawn chairs. They greeted me, standing up, and my mom asked me what I needed as she handed me a peanut butter and jelly sandwich.

"How are you feeling?" my mom asked.

"I don't know," I said. "I'm tired." It was hard to talk, as if my body knew that speaking would take up the energy I'd need for the last thirty-five miles of the race.

"You're amazing," Lauren said, handing me a beverage.

Seeing my mom and my sister there made me cry. My stepdad didn't make the trip, because he didn't think running a hundred miles was a good idea. He was a safe man, not a risk-taker. This kind of activity didn't fit within the constraints of a healthy lifestyle, so he didn't want any part in it. But my mom wanted to be there for me, even if she agreed with my stepdad. Even if I was doing something risky. Even if I might get injured or die. It was love. All I wanted was love, despite my and my parents' philosophical differences, despite the fact that I was covered in tattoos from head to toe, despite the fact that I liked to run until my body collapsed. I thrived on unconditional love.

"We shouldn't stay here too long," Dave said, repeating the advice I had heard over and over since I'd signed up for the race: *Don't stay at Cibbets Flat for too long, or you won't want to leave.* They were right. I could already feel my body settling into the comfort of not moving.

"Let's go," Dave said, pointing up.

The mountain we just ran down, we had to run back up. It seemed impossible.

When we reached the top of the mountain, I couldn't breathe. My mind was operating in a dream state. Nothing seemed real. Dave, who was now in front of me, leading the way, didn't stop talking for the entirety of our journey, a skill that makes a great pacer. He was trying to entertain me. I had no idea what he was talking about, and I was too tired to tell him to shut the fuck up, so I tried to listen, now and then muttering, "Fuck me."

At some point, I looked up and a black panther was standing in front of us on the path. He was curled back, ready to pounce, but when I blinked, he was behind a tree. We kept running on the side of a cliff. I thought about the panther. Had Dave seen it? If so, why hadn't he said anything? I wanted to see the panther again. I hoped the panther would leap out and send me flying off the cliff. I wanted to die. Anything to let me finish the run without quitting.

The next aid station was at Dale's Kitchen, named after a guy named Dale who made soup for runners. I sat down on an uncomfortable chair and felt the greatest discomfort of my life. Worse than being beaten up.

Worse than going to jail. Worse than a speed hangover. Like every nerve in my body was being wrung out by a vengeful god. *Maybe this is karma*, I thought. *Maybe this is what I deserve.* I sat on the chair for an hour, dozing in and out of consciousness.

"Let's go," Dave said. "We can't stay for too long."

I learned later that Dave was doing exactly what a pacer was supposed to do: get the runner back on their feet no matter how shitty they felt. One of my friends ran the race too, but his pacer wasn't as skilled. Once my friend got sleepy, his pacer asked him if he wanted to drop out of the race and get brunch, and that was it. I would've dropped out in a heartbeat if Dave had asked me the same question.

"Let's go," he said.

I got up reluctantly and followed him in the dark, our headlamps casting creepy shadows in our paths.

By the time we got to mile 84, I was freezing. Dave had given me hand warmers that kept my palms toasty, but the rest of my body was shivering so hard that my back was starting to give out. All I could think about was Crystal, my beautiful wife who had stood by me for all those years; my son, Ezra, the cutest boy in the world, who would be waiting for me at the finish line; and our little girl, Luna, growing in Crystal's belly. I cried and cried and tried to muffle it so Dave couldn't hear me. He was still talking, trying to keep me occupied. At the aid station, I sat down with the other runners, who were in various stages of pain. A man next to me was lying on a beach chair groaning. A man huddled up next to a firepit rocked back and forth moaning. It reminded me of a zombie movie, surrounded by the undead. A volunteer, a young man with a mustache, approached me.

"You can't stay here," he said.

"What the fuck," I said.

"Look," he said. "You hate me now, but I swear to God, if you get up from here, you'll start walking—just walk. Then you'll run a little bit, and it'll be light soon, and once the sun comes up, you'll be a new man. You'll be fresh. It will be like you haven't been running at all."

"What the fuck," I said. "I can't go on."

Dave looked at me. It was the first time he hadn't smiled the whole run. "Are your legs broken?" he said.

"No."

"Then let's go."

I tried to get out of my chair, but my legs weren't working. Maybe they were broken. I hoped they were. I wanted nothing more than an honorable discharge from the race. But Dave pulled me up, and we set out toward the final aid station, where Joe would be waiting to relieve Dave of his pacing duties to help me run the last nine miles.

Nothing in the world can explain ultrarunning other than to say that it is a practice of running straight into the worst situation imaginable. There is no benefit. There is no redeeming aspect to putting your body through physical and mental torture other than to say, *You know what? I did something stupid as fuck.* These were the thoughts that got me to the next aid station. And the next.

Risk is rewarding. I know it. My bones know it. This is why I am at odds with my stepdad. His goal is safety. Until he knows he's safe, he cannot live a life worth living. I understand it. I've processed it, and I can see how I or anyone else might abide by that philosophy's principles, but I don't. I don't feel alive unless there's a chance of dying. This was why I spent years as a drug addict. This is why I push my body to its limit. This is why I get home from work to organize for the community. This is why I will confront a white supremacist. This is why I have children. It's not because I want to die. It's the opposite. I want to figure out the boundaries of life before I die. I want to make the world better by making myself uncomfortable. I don't enjoy running. I don't enjoy fighting. I do them both because I want to test the limits of what I thought I was capable of. I want to run head-on into the things that are considered bad ideas. This is the only growth.

By the time I reached mile 91.5, the sky had lightened. The mustachioed man at the aid station had been right: I felt like I hadn't run even a mile. My body felt light. I wasn't sleepy. I looked for my crew. Joe stood with my mom and Lauren. They all give me a big hug.

"You only have nine miles left," Joe said. I remember us swinging our legs in the time-out box in kindergarten, how fun it was to be in trouble. Here we were, forty years later, still dumber than ever.

Nine miles might as well have been another hundred. The morning was already creeping up into the eighties. We took off running before the sun had a chance to reach its peak.

The desert hadn't been a hard run. It was bland and rocky, but my legs still worked for it. Every few minutes, my body lost momentum and I needed to walk. Joe stayed next to me, asking me about the race. I tried to talk but was too delirious to make any sense. We ran like that for a couple of hours until we passed a horse stable I recognized from the start of the race. We followed a trail into an open marsh, and suddenly there was the finish line, complete with cheesy rock 'n' roll blaring from the speakers. My legs held a steady pace, and I ran toward the finish line with Joe by my side.

Dave, my mom, and my sister were there to hug me. Tears poured from my face as I clung to my sister.

"I am so proud of you," she said, crying.

Crystal and Ezra walked up holding hands. Ezra had no idea what had just happened, but he was laughing, excited to see me. I hugged Crystal and caught a whiff of myself, a deep stink that prompted a gag reflex.

I approached my mom, who looked tired but was smiling as she congratulated me. We hugged hard, and for a moment I was wrapped in her smile, wrapped in her embrace, the strength of her arms holding my entire childhood, its joy, its uncertainty, its worry.

HOW TO MAKE A DEAL WITH THE DEVIL

It's almost 1 p.m., so I put on my jacket to pick up Luna from day care. The crisp January air in California is always surprising and annoying, pinching my cheeks like a drunken auntie. Maybe it was living in frigid Boston for so long, but the cold has never appealed to me—the layers of clothing, the clods of snow seeping into your pants, the stinging red face—and I especially hate being cold in California. It seems like such a waste. I escape to my car and crank up the heater.

The phone rings. It's Chad, the HR director. Over the past year of this investigation, I've endured several meetings with Chad, a tall, average man in his sixties, always smiling and tan with a Titleist golf hat perched on his head like a crown of the upper middle class. He's a perfectly mediocre administrator who seems to like me well enough. He once gave me a chance to travel around California to recruit other professors in different cities—an opportunity I jumped on immediately, if only for my love of eating out at restaurants and staying in fancy hotels. I always appreciated the trust he'd given me then, but he's an administrator for a large district, and his generosity doesn't extend past the electrified fence of the institution.

My Prius stops silently at the light at the park by my house. A man is crossing the street, walking a comically large dog and having an animated conversation on his phone. Chad sounds nervous on the other end. "I've been, um, well, um, well . . . the college has authorized or directed me to give you a call," he says in a timid, echoey voice, like he's calling from the bottom of a well.

"What do you mean, the college?" I say, trying to sound surprised. But the truth is that I know what he means and what the call is about. Robert warned me that the HR guy would be calling today and explained everything that would happen. But I play along with him just to see what he's going to say.

I want to hear him squirm.

"The college wants to come up with a potential settlement agreement," he says. "Or, in other words, a payout or a buyout."

I can hear Robert in the back of my mind. *Whatever you do, don't accept the offer.*

"I'm confused," I say.

"Okay, so—" Chad says, trying to catch up.

"I was under the impression that my tenure depended on the outcome of this investigation," I say. "But I don't have the results of the investigation yet."

"Right, right," he says, taking several strained breaths, like he's being forced to make this phone call at gunpoint. In a way, he is. The institution is a brutish thief, taking what it can, using your job like a gun barrel to smash against the back of your head. This pathetic man is under duress, but I love listening to him flail on the other end. "I mean, I wouldn't say your tenure depends on the results of this investigation—"

"But that's exactly what I was told."

The freeway is clear at this time of day. The growing downtown skyline reaches toward the endless gray clouds. I love driving. I prefer the second to slowest lane, the lane that says, *I'm cruising, so leave me the fuck alone*, where I can take my time and not be bothered by tailgaters.

"I mean, well, ugh, you know, I think there was ... concern that you had potentially engaged in or solicited students to engage in potentially dangerous activities and—"

"Right," I say. "But that's why this investigation would be helpful, because I didn't do any of that."

I take the J Street exit. At the stoplight, a man holds a tattered cardboard sign that doesn't say anything. I wonder if he knows it doesn't say anything. Maybe he found the cardboard but didn't have a pen and thought, *Eh, good enough. They'll get it.* He's sitting beside a wall where someone has graffitied *Amy Tan is my favorite author* with a Sharpie. The light turns green, and I drive into the mouth of the city toward Luna's day care.

"Again, I have been directed to call you and engage in this conversation just as an option, nothing you have to accept or not accept."

I round the corner and find a parking spot right in front of the day care. I park but leave the engine on to run the heater at full blast. "Who's directing this?"

"Well, it would be the management."

"But who is that? I don't know who that is."

I want names. I want him to say the names of the people turning my life into a courtroom drama.

"Well, management is all your vice presidents, your president, um, and then, you know, the management," he says, gearing up for his pitch. "Here's the option: discontinue the investigation, discontinue the evaluation, see if we can reach an agreement on a cash payment—and you resign."

A bribe. They're bribing me to leave them alone.

They want me to quit my job so I will go away.

These administrators want to continue discussing equity and diversity in broad terms that sound good, but they don't want to change anything about racism in a meaningful way, except fire the loud person making them look bad. I get it. I'm annoying. I've known that since I served time in Mrs. Clark's time-out box. But if you're going to preach, you also need to take action. When it comes to racism, the action isn't always pretty. They're constantly talking about equity, but I don't think they actually understand what that means. It's not equality. Equity will require that you snatch something away from a white person and give it to a Brown person. Are they ready to do that? That would mean hurting white people's feelings, and our chancellor is white. And the vice chancellor is white. The institution is white. And we can't go around tearing down white-ass institutions, can we? They thought they were hiring a writer whose byline would get students in classes, and they did. But they also got the guy who split open a bonehead's face with a can of Coke. A two-for-one.

"Okay, no. I'm not doing that."

"Do you want to discuss an initial cash offer?"

I know that if I tell him right now to fuck off, I'll be the coolest motherfucker he's ever dealt with.

"What is it?" I ask, my curiosity winning out over my desire to appear disinterested.

"I have the ability to negotiate, and certainly you'd want to talk to Robert, but, you know, initially we're talking, uh, low fifteen thousands."

I can't hold my laughter. I laugh and laugh until I realize that people on the sidewalk can hear me. A couple walking toward me peers into my car.

"That's a ridiculous offer," I say. If he'd offered me $300,000 I would have taken it, no questions asked. "No thanks."

"I'll let the campus know we engaged in a conversation."

"Sure, that's fine, but I'm interested to see what this investigation yields, since I was told everything hinges upon it. I'd like to see what happens with that."

I laugh again at the ridiculousness of this man, a tinny-voiced spokesman for a soulless institution that crushes anything it deems a threat. I lock my car and head toward the day care, my breath billowing in between the buildings, the scent of human shit baked into every sidewalk crevice. The main jail is directly across the street, and a person who's just been let out stands on the ledge out front. His beltless pants sag low on his hips, and he's carrying a large plastic bag with his belongings—probably a belt, a watch, shoelaces, and some cash if he's lucky. We lock eyes for a second, and I give him an awkward nod that he doesn't return. He doesn't have time for me, probably wondering if anyone's going to pick him up and bring him back home.

Luna's day care resides in a building that reminds me of Korea—drab and utilitarian, with no particular purpose but to house any business that will sign a lease. A liquor store, a salon, and an old folks' home occupy the upstairs. I enter the door code, and the drabness turns to chaos; screaming babies and kids run in all directions.

Luna's teacher sees me and pulls me aside. "We wanted to talk to you."

"We?"

"Me and Luna's other teacher," she says with a serious tone.

"Oh, okay," I say. "What's up?"

"Luna hasn't been listening," she says, pausing to see what I say.

At first I don't know what to say. I'm not even sure we're obliged to listen to everything people say. Most of it is garbage. Then I wonder if I'm projecting my experience with teachers onto Luna's teacher, so I feel bad.

"I'll see what I can do." I find Luna and take her soft little hand in mine, two motherfucking renegades, and we swing our connected arms in unison back to the car.

MY NEW JOB

My favorite student is a baseball player, a kind and gentle boy who's always sleepy, his head permanently resting on his palms. I'm trying to teach him how to write, but he hates writing. He just wants to pass the class.

"Write about what you know," I tell him, so he writes about baseball—what a mistake. Baseball is the most boring shit ever. Maybe that's why he's so sleepy all the time.

When he first started my class, he kept falling asleep at his desk and missed an entire week of school. Once, he fell asleep in class, and I let him snore until everyone got up to leave, and he awoke, crying in a panic. One day, out of nowhere, he left me a note that said, "Thanks." I don't know what for, just "Thanks." Another day, his mother sent me an email that said, "Please take care of my boy," and I forgot to respond.

He wrote about baseball as a metaphor:

If you can hit a baseball, you understand the meaning of life. You don't have to hit hard, but you have to understand who's throwing the ball, where on the bat to connect, and when to run.

Once, he fell asleep leaning on his steering wheel while a semitruck careened toward him like a meteor in the early morning. He was nineteen years old when he flew through the windshield of his tiny car; his body twisted in the street like a nightmare.

I'm sitting in my dark office underneath a poster that says Joy Division, and I flip open the newspaper. His obituary is there. It's too short. There's something crass about the entirety of someone's life wrapped up in an inch of newsprint. Underneath the announcement is an ad for mattresses. I think of my classroom with an empty seat, what I'll say to the other students, if I say anything at all. I think of a real professor, who would say something profound and moving, but unattached, like it was part of their lecture. Then I think of me, staring at the blank space in my classroom, eyes shaking with misery and rage, unable to move my lips to form a sentence, and I feel wholly unprepared for this, like an imposter pretending to be a regular person.

A RESCUE

It's 4:45 a.m. Crystal is asleep in the bed, and the kids are fast asleep in their rooms. I'm fumbling around the room, trying not to wake anyone. I can't find a good pair of socks in my drawer, so I tussle around, the light from my cell phone casting dramatic shadows in the closet. I grab some old socks with a hole forming in the left toe, slide them on, and then slink into the living room for my running shoes before heading into the darkness of the early morning.

It's summertime and already warm. I've grown to appreciate the early mornings; I relish the moonlight and the cool air before the sun heats the city into a miserable oven. Sweat has already soaked through my shirt as I run along the park. I head toward the freeway overpass that leads to the levee along the American River, the thirty-mile stretch of water that runs from the Sierra Nevada to its confluence with the Sacramento River in downtown Sacramento.

The first time I ran along the levee, I didn't bring a headlamp, and in the pitch black I came within an inch of running face-first into a homeless dude standing still in the middle of the bike path. I nearly jumped out of my skin with fright. But this morning my headlamp lights the way directly in front of me; the broken yellow lines against the black concrete are the only details I can make out, but I know the river is on my left, and the freeway, now empty, is on my right.

It's an eight-mile loop from my house down the bike path, through downtown, then back home. I've been doing the route several times a week for a few years. For someone who's led a life of chaos and destruction, there's something to be said for routine. The predictability of repetition acts as a security blanket.

The bike path ends, spilling into a parking lot for the boat docks. Miller Regional Park is one of the sketchier parks in Sacramento. The park is downtown and on the water, which makes it a perfect place for people to make illicit money while taking in the pleasant scenery. I've been there to buy cocaine on several occasions from my dealer, a malnourished Italian with a shiny gold tooth, always leaning against a tree looking relaxed.

I turn the corner into the part of the parking lot that spans for a half mile and turns into Broadway in the old, run-down section of Sacramento. As I turn, I see two sets of eyes glowing under the light of my headlamp. I stop running and the eyes get closer. Two dogs are approaching, and one of them is growling. I back up slowly, and they're both growling, getting closer. I reach in my pocket for something, anything, that might distract them. I find an energy gel and toss it as far as possible, and the dogs go after it. I head straight toward a parked car with its lights on.

"Hey man, can you get me out of this parking lot?" I ask. "I just have to get away from those dogs."

The driver is slender with a goatee, and he's wearing glasses. He looks me up and down, then rolls up his window.

Miller Park is a popular spot for cruising, which may answer why a man is idling a car here at 5:15 in the morning, so I'm a little offended that he doesn't find me attractive enough to assist. I walk back toward where I started, hoping I can creep back to the bike path without the dogs seeing me. As I cross the lot, they run in my direction and stop when they reach me, crouching low and barking. I sprint toward a giant electrical box and hop on top of it while the barking dogs jump up and down, trying to get to me. I never bring my phone on runs, but today, for some reason, I did.

I call my stepdad, and he answers, his voice croaking with sleep. "Hey, Josh," he says.

I know what he's thinking: *What kind of bullshit did this idiot get into this time?*

"Hey, Dad," I say. "I need your help."

"What is it, Josh?" He's up now.

"I went out running, and now I'm surrounded by dogs," I say. "I'm on top of an electrical box."

"Be right there," he says.

I think I can hear the relief in his voice that I'm not in jail or an alley, beaten and bloody. I hang up the phone. The dogs still surround me, waiting for me to jump down so they can rip my limbs from their sockets.

The headlights from my stepdad's car are enough to make the dogs scatter, each one going in a different direction. I jump from the box and hop in his car.

"Nice do-rag," he says, joking about the buff on my head that catches sweat. Then he says, "That could've been bad."

"Yeah," I say. "Thanks."

"Of course."

We take Broadway back to my house, the moon still shining above, homeless people still tucked into the doorways of businesses, sleeping. The sun peeks above the horizon, graying the once-black sky, and my stepdad turns on the radio to NPR, where the nasal host runs down the week's news. Even after forty years, we don't have much to say to each other. We were crafted of different materials. My stepdad is solid wood, stained like the shelves at an old library, while I'm a flimsy box of rusted metal stuffed with frayed wires and broken circuits.

A homeless man tweaks out on the corner, yelling and dancing, his face streaked with grease, like stage makeup, as the curtain of sun rises above the city.

HOW TO PRETEND

Crystal and Ezra sit in a triangle of light, reading. At this very moment, there's nothing wrong with the world. Everything is in its place. I've come to appreciate these moments, and they're arriving more often now, the moments with no tension, the ones where I can be present with what I've helped create or nurture, the panic of life so far away that I briefly know the feeling of perfection.

I'm not going to think about the red-faced principal taunting me to hit him until I finally balled up a fist and socked him in the face. I'm not going to think about the way my brain spins in my skull in the midst of a panic attack. I'm not going to think about the pit of fire in my stomach when I sense a threat, and the way my soul escapes my body just long enough for me to do the things that seem to always land me in jail.

Not today, at least.

In the back of my mind, the threat of the school administrators lurking in the shadows with rusted shanks behind their backs is ever present, but I've learned to push them back, like my dad taught me to do with the FBI agents who came to take us away.

"When they come, kick them," I can hear him saying in his Mexican surfer voice.

I've crafted this life with the luck of avoiding a million disasters, the love of my family, the care for my people, and if I think about it too much, my breath will quicken. The lightheaded feeling will emerge from the depths of my belly, and I'll have to leave the room and pull the blankets over my head. But for now, everything is fine.

I LIVE IN AN ETERNALLY FRENZIED STATE

I'm at the sink rinsing a glass and setting it gently into the dishwasher and I know a panic attack is coming on when everything starts to annoy me. *Fuck you* to the shine of the water spouting from the nozzle. *Fuck you* to the dishes piled randomly in the sink. *Fuck you* to the hardened cheese clinging to a ceramic plate. And *fuck you* to the sound of my kids stomping through the kitchen behind me. I hunch over the sink and rest my elbows on the ledge. My breathing grows heavy, then shallow and short. My head spins. I think I'll pass out for a second, so I put my head in my hands. But it doesn't pass. It never does. Crystal is doing a load of laundry and asks me a question, but I can't hear her. I pretend I don't notice she's talking to me, but she asks me again.

"I don't know," I say, annoyed.

She told our therapist that I'm short with her sometimes, and this is why—the panic attacks. I'm too embarrassed to tell her. She knows I'm fucked up, but not this fucked up.

"Think of a code word for your panic attacks," the therapist said, "and say it when you feel one coming on."

It sounds good in therapy, but I can never do it. The thought makes me cringe. The panic sets in to my soul and petrifies me. I can only focus on my breath. My demise. Panic attacks are like being able to see your death from a near distance, like a car without brakes headed full speed toward a wall.

Crystal huffs away into the back of the house, but I really don't know what she's saying. It's not a lie. I only know the windstorm blowing around my head. Words don't make sense to me. I don't know how to explain it to her. It's the feeling of being ten years old and coming home from school knowing you're in trouble, the feeling that swirls around your stomach and into your head, a whirlwind of every trauma you've ever inflicted on yourself and every trauma you've inflicted on others spinning like a cyclone around your skull and into your lungs. The sensation of fear and humiliation when standing in front of your parents as they scream at you—your mother's face twisted into a configuration of rage. You know your mother will take you into the basement to spank you, so you brace yourself. It's not going to hurt so much; it's more about all that anger. Directed at you. Your mother hates you. The wish that you were anyone else but yourself ... I clutch the edge of the sink and breathe. I try the breathing technique we practiced in therapy. Count backward. "1000, 999, 998, 997 ..."

I run into the bedroom, shut the door behind me, and crawl under the blankets. I'm so scared. Maybe this is the bomb going off. The explosion. Every horrible thing I've ever done, all the drugs, the violence, the deception, the theft, the trickery, each wire of negativity touching the correlating circuit to cause a brilliant explosion that disintegrates my body and mind into a clumsy plume of smoke.

Crystal comes in, and I pretend to be asleep. She turns off the light, leaving me to drown under the tiny waves of short breaths. I want her to be in bed next to me, but at the same time I need her to be as far away as she can get. I want to scream at her and give her a gentle kiss on her forehead. I'm paralyzed, afraid to move even slightly, for fear any movement will send another wave of explosions through my body. At some point, I fall asleep. It's never as hard as I think. My body just gives up after a certain point, too weak to hold the panic.

When I wake up from a dreamless sleep, I'm in the same position, with no pillow, clutching a clump of sweat-drenched sheets like a lover. Crystal is also in bed, and Ezra and Luna are in between us, watching shows on their tablets with the volume up too loud.

Luna is watching a YouTube show where a strange voice yells, *"It's baby Joshua!"*

"Oh, hi, Dad," Luna says, showing me her tablet. "Look, *you're* baby Joshua."

"Okay," I say.

"Hey, Dad," Ezra says.

They're so big now. Ezra cracks self-deprecating jokes and reads comic books until the early hours of the morning. Luna, who once clung to her mother, bashful with the world, now walks up to strangers so she can pet their dogs.

Crystal is on her side, still sleeping.

It's morning and the blinds are shut, but the room is filled with light. My breath is regular again. The storm in my head is clear. I wonder for a second if everyone hates me and if they want a refund for their broken father, who breaks down in panic at the sight of a sink full of dishes. I know they don't, but I wait anxiously for Crystal to wake up to make sure.

PRESENT DAY

HUGE LIBERAL FAGGOT

Wayne walks into my college composition class holding a foil-wrapped burrito in one hand and a miniature bong in the other.

"'Sup," he says, and sits near the back of the classroom. He's wearing one of those American flag Punisher shirts with a thin blue line running down the center of its face.

"'Sup," I say back.

The fact that Wayne hates me is no secret. I caught him muttering a few times that I was a piece of shit, a pansy, a boring liberal asshole, and so on. The insults are endless and entertaining. I don't mind them. I hated most of my teachers too. Teacher versus student is a good tradition that I honor. I remember Mrs. Tieman from fourth grade, a curly-haired white lady with huge glasses that rested on her face like a couple of fried eggs. Everyone called her Terrible Tieman, even the parents. Any slight sign that students weren't paying attention—a whisper or a wayward glance— would work her into a frenzy, subjecting the class to one of her severe tantrums, where she'd storm around the room yelling and throwing whatever object she could find. One time she threw a stapler across the room, which landed in the goldfish bowl with a plop. Our laughter only made her more furious. It's like she never understood that we were in the fourth grade and it was in our DNA to laugh at everything and pay attention to nothing. Once, before class, I found a thumbtack on the floor. I rushed to her chair at the front of the classroom and set it on her seat. When she walked into class, she gave us a scowl, put her coffee mug on the desk, and sat, immediately letting out a yowl so fierce that Mr. Jones next door came running in to see what the problem was. Mrs. Tieman rolled around on the carpet and clutched her huge ass in pain. When the principal asked what happened, I raised my hand, not to confess but to offer a theory: perhaps the thumbtack had fallen onto her seat accidentally. It seemed a sufficient answer for the principal, who probably called her Terrible Tieman too. She was not pleased. The rest of the year was like being in a corrections facility, with constant humiliation from Mrs. Tieman, the most hateful warden of the fourth grade.

But Wayne hates me not because I am mean, but because he perceives me as a liberal, the kind they talk about on Breitbart, a whining vegetarian too lazy to work, which I guess is partially true, so I don't blame him for his scorn. One time, when we were discussing ways to flush our ingrained methods of colonized thinking, a student told the class how women in her tribe would receive mentorship months before their menstruation began. Once it arrived, they were swept away by the women in the tribe and given a beautiful ceremony of celebration, which, as my student put it, was a stark contrast to the American tradition of letting girls be taken by surprise by their period, sometimes spending several frightful hours weeping in an elementary school bathroom. The women in the class came alive at that story, some sharing their menstruation horror stories, but Wayne, in the back corner of the room, snickered and said, "You people are fucking gross."

But today, Wayne is noncombative. He puts his feet up on the desk, peels the foil from his burrito, and takes a cartoonish bite.

"Is that a fucking bong?" I ask, prodding him a little.

"Yeah."

"And a burrito?"

He nods while chewing, and I hate to admit it, but I kind of admire his brazen rejection of me. We start the lesson with a discussion about transitions between paragraphs. The class is at the stage of writing papers where they write a paragraph and then move on to a completely different idea with no finesse. They don't see any art in writing essays, only page counts and grades at the end of the class.

"Think of it like a conversation you'd have in real life," I say. "You don't start talking about Keanu Reeves, then bring up mathematics in the next breath. You need to provide a transition between the two ideas."

Sienna raises her hand.

"You don't need to raise your hand," I say. "Just blurt it out."

The students know I've banished hand-raising, but Sienna's hand-raise is likely a knee-jerk remnant from tradition. I don't want students to raise their hands, not out of lust for chaotic disruption or *Dead Poets Society* cosplay, but because I want to take as many walls away from inspiration as possible. Often, students have ideas, then think about raising their hand, then raise their hand, becoming increasingly more self-conscious as time passes until they decide not to ask their question. It happened to me all the time in college. Learning is supposed to be fun—at least that's what we've been told, despite all evidence suggesting otherwise—and I don't want my students to rehash the five stages of grief every time they want to answer a question, so I tell them to shout out answers and to yell when they need to yell.

"Who's Keanu Reeves?" Sienna says.

"Goddammit," I say. "Do you really not know who Keanu Reeves is?"

"Fat black dude?" Alex asks in earnest.

"Jesus fucking Christ," I say. "What the fuck are you learning in high school? You've never seen *The Matrix*?"

"Ohhh," the class says in unison.

Even Wayne joins in. "Why didn't you say that in the first place?"

I shoot him an expertly crafted look that says, *Fuck you, dickhead.*

These informal moments in which the students unite in a common, playful annoyance for their professor support the class by taking away the prefabricated structure hastily built by the hands of the empire—like a tornado might uproot a gated community, leaving behind only earth and making room for something beautiful to grow. These students, like me, were indoctrinated into a system of strict tradition, a Eurocentric model of learning where respect for the authority figure—the teacher in front of the class wagging his white finger at everyone until the room falls silent—is paramount. Laughter is underrated. Silliness is not appreciated. Strict rigidity is worshipped like an unmovable stone god. The Terrible Tiemans of the world made me despise school, which is why it's important to clear that mindset, to burn down the institutions of the mind—the churches and their priests, the schools and their schoolmasters, the Fortune 500 companies and their CEOs—that stand in the way of our wild human spirit.

I look to see if Wayne is still following along. He's staring at his half-eaten burrito in bliss, probably in a food coma, stoned out of his gourd, daydreaming of his own rebellion: crouched and camouflaged behind a rock with a sniper rifle strapped to his back, his poorly crafted crucifix tattoo peeling under the sun.

After I was expelled from junior high for my fight with the principal, the only place willing to let me in was Christian Brothers, a private high school where everybody knew each other from attending the same religious schools their whole lives. The place was slithering with priests and buzzing with an alpha male energy, sturdily calcifying my position as an outcast.

Everyone had to take a religion class taught by Father Joseph, a four-hundred-pound priest whose vestment made him look like a killer whale. He often sat behind his desk taking sips from a flask when he thought we weren't looking. One day, he made us play a game of telephone to illustrate how man's intervention changes biblical verse, and he whispered the phrase "If you believe, you will receive whatever you ask for in prayer" into the first student's ear. By the time it got three-quarters around the circle to me, the phrase was still intact, so I changed it to "Satan is the only God." The last student was a bony kid with greasy blond hair. He blurted out my phrase and sent the classroom into a frenzy of maniacal laughter. Father Joseph sat wide-eyed with a face of true horror, his jowls shaking in disappointment. He ordered us to sit there until one of us confessed, but when the bell rang, we all ran out of the classroom knowing he wouldn't catch up to us until the next class period, and by then he'd likely have forgotten the whole thing.

During my time at Christian Brothers, I was kicked out of gym class for fighting, kicked out of creative writing for writing homosexual poems, and sent to the principal's office for drawing horny cartoons of sexy nuns. There was no way a Christian school was going to take my rebellion. In fact, the puritanical finger-wagging only made my angst stronger. By the time I left, I hated everyone and everything, especially religion.

I understand Wayne more than he cares to admit. But when he finally drops my class in the face of a dismally low F, he manages to find me online and he sends a Facebook message:

I don't give a fuck about your class.

I know, I respond. *But I hope you do well.*

I will do well. I joined the Marines to protect all you liberal faggots.

I can't help but imagine Wayne, of frail frame and with a face full of acne, in the middle of Afghanistan with a bullet belt wrapped Rambo-style around his shirtless, zitty chest, taking a single shot to the head in the name of all the liberal faggots at home who weren't alpha enough to fight.

I write him back: *I'm not a liberal, by the way. I'm something much worse.*

I punctuate the sentence with a little winking smiley face for effect. That's the last I hear from Wayne, but definitely not the last of his kind. I see them now and then—the little Waynes, protesting at the state capitol building with their bright yellow DON'T TREAD ON ME banners, wrapping their pot bellies in American flags, dozens of them forming sloppy skirmish lines like a league of unloved man-children lashing out at their lack of hugs, running toward the police once the actual violence starts.

GOING TO PRISON

I start taking every opportunity offered at my work. Overworking. Joining committees, work groups—maybe to prove that I'm not a piece of shit. Maybe to be annoyingly visible, as if to say, *I'm still here, motherfuckers. You can't fire me.*

When I find out our school contracts with the local prisons to teach inmates, I jump at the chance. I begin teaching part of my load at a men's facility that houses almost four thousand prisoners, a sprawling concrete institution in the middle of California farmland.

On my first day, I show the guard at the front gate my ID and find a spot to park in the sea of Ford trucks coated with hunting stickers. Each tree in the lot is decorated with a blue ribbon. One of the employees at the prison later tells me the ribbons are a memorial for the three corrections officers who killed themselves that month. Suicide is not uncommon among the guards. She also tells me that corrections officers are like twelve-year-old boys—crude and dumb—so watch out for them. They roam around the prison, keys jangling, wearing their anger like chain mail. The break area where they eat their packed lunches with their feet up on the desks is decorated with Trump and other right-wing stickers, a constant reminder of their brazen politics. Whenever I walk through the yard, the guards study me like scientists who study a virus. I can feel them scanning my build, my tattoos, the black roses on my neck, the three arrows that point southwest. If they're in groups, they whisper, laugh, and point in my direction. Sometimes they try to stare me down as a means of intimidation. Although the prison has been host to many high-profile serial killers, kidnappers, molesters, and necrophiles, it's not the inmates who scare me. It's the guards—their lack of sophistication, their rage, the way they wield their power like warlords. The only thing scarier than a murderer is a dumb murderer who makes a lot of money. They know I'm a different species, so they keep their eyes on me.

The classrooms are tucked in the corner of the overpacked C Yard. The first time I walk in, one of the inmates, a leader of the Nazi Low Riders, gasps and says, "You look like one of us," which is the first time anyone has said that to me. When I walk into meetings on my campus, administrators shuffle papers, clear their throats, and barely manage their fake smiles.

Kel, the small, tattooed man at the back of the classroom, is sitting still but vibrates with energy, as if at any moment smoke will pour from his ears, his ass will light on fire, and he'll lift into the atmosphere like a model rocket. He looks like every Nazi skinhead I've ever fought or bought drugs from during my childhood: the little soul patch under his smirking bottom lip, the bald head shining like an evil sun, and the dim glow of madness twinkling in his crystal-blue eyes. He scares me the way many people have scared me throughout my life, not because he's mean or angry—he's quite the opposite, always jovial, smiling and raising his hand to answer a question—but because underneath his enthusiastic personality, something sinister can surface at any moment. It's not something everyone possesses, but it's a trait that I can see in others and especially in myself.

I'm not sure what to think about everyone else, like Jeremy, a member of the Aryan Nations gang who has murdered people outside of prison, as well as inside. He's a straight A student who lifted his shirt on my first day to show me his gigantic swastika tattoo. There's James, a carjacker and polite dark-skinned man with braids who uses words like *unequivocally* in casual conversation, and Jerry, the eighty-something-year-old Silicon Valley marketing executive who, along with his wife, adopted Russian children and molested them. And of course, there's Ricky, the lunkheaded former MMA fighter who laughs at all my jokes. On my first day, I told them that the only rule in the class is you're not allowed to stab me to death, and he's been my pal ever since. He sits right up front and center. "You're my spirit animal!" he declared, which made me feel good until I made the mistake of typing his name into Google to learn what had landed him in prison.

One night he and his sparring partner drank mushroom tea and became entangled in a paranoid, drug-hazed fantasy war between God and the devil. As the night wore on, he attacked his friend, dismembered him, and removed his still-beating heart, which the police found cooking on the stovetop when they arrived.

But, still, Ricky's right. I'm his spirit animal. We're all spirit animals. All of us. Everywhere. Not in the yoga-mom-going-to-pick-her-kids-up-from-soccer-practice sense. We're spirit animals in the same sense as the Ojibwe people would say "Ode," or heart. We're all of the same heart. From the depraved and sick lowlifes slithering in the world's sewage to the weasel-faced warden in his Sears suit two sizes too big—all connected by the make of our flimsy skin and the murky air we breathe. That's why I love working in this horrible and cold place crawling with cops and murderers and molesters. There's heart here in this prison, a different kind of heart, the kind that's born out of desperation. When a good thing happens in prison, this heart beats loud against its miserable backdrop.

Kel's waving his hand like a victory flag. "Can you come read this?" he says, slightly embarrassed. He pulled me aside early in the class to tell me he wasn't used to a classroom full of students, that he didn't know how to act in an educational setting. I said not to worry, that none of us know how to act and that we're all pretending anyway. He laughed, but I wasn't kidding.

I walk through the rows of desks, the inmates working on the paragraphs I instructed them to write: start with a bold sentence to outline their idea, write an explanation adding to the idea, then get specific with some evidence, then write about the evidence in your own words, then wrap it up.

"Think of the paragraph as the home where your idea lives," I say. "The more we look into the home, the more we understand the idea."

The class musters a mass look of confusion.

"What did your childhood home look like?" I ask the class.

Petro raises his hand. "It looked like shit," he says.

The class laughs.

"Why?"

"It was a trailer," he says, "not a house."

"If I walked in, what kind of stuff would I find?"

"Drugs."

"What kind?"

"All of them."

"Was there anything good in there?"

"Food," he says, closing his eyes. "We always had good food."

"You described the trailer as shitty, but it wasn't all shitty. There was good food in there, right?"

"Yeah, I guess."

"So that's the complexity of something that is labeled shitty. It's not all shitty. There can be good shit too."

The class laughs again.

"I'm not following," Petro says.

"If I want to examine your personality, I can look into your childhood home. I'd find a lot of shitty stuff, some good stuff, and some boring shit too."

"Yup."

"So your childhood home is one piece of you," I say. "Examining that place is a good way of finding out who you are, but is that everything?"

"No."

"What if I looked into your home right now?"

"My cell."

"Your cell," I repeat. "Another paragraph. Does that tell me anything about you?"

"That I'm a fucking degenerate."

The class laughs.

"Is that all you are?"

"That's how they see me," he says, pointing to the outside.

I tell the class that when we step inside a paragraph, we see what's in there and who lives there by examining its sentences and evidence. Each paragraph is its own house; each set of houses is a neighborhood, or an essay. Some are gated communities, some are slums, and some are prisons.

Kel's handwriting is messy, but I can still make it out. He's written about his youth, a tragic cycle of drugs and fighting and neglect punctuated intermittently by his grandfather, the only person who showed care toward him. He wrote about hugging his grandpa and the feeling of warmth he received from the embrace. The essay is an acutely self-aware argument about what it takes to end up in a penitentiary and how it can be avoided. It's better than anything I've read from any other student. I have to fight back tears while reading. His paragraphs are structured, each one its own house, including this one, a filthy squat, a dim, piss-soaked shithole filled with rats and drugs, but one that produces a desperate and soulful art. It's perfect.

"You got it," I say, raising my shoulders, signaling that I have nothing else to say.

"Really?" he says, looking confused, as if nobody has ever told him that. "Do you have any advice?"

"Keep doing it." I head back toward the front of the classroom. I can feel his smile burning my back all the way there.

This is not uncommon in prison: the human mind's uncaged brilliance, the unrefined writing skill, and the ability to weave a story onto a page. It seems like a waste to lock this up in the middle of the California farmland.

One day, after class, Kel tells me he's getting out in August, which is only a few months away.

"Try not to murder anyone in the meantime," I joke.

"No promises," he says, shrugging.

I've never seen him so excited. He's getting an A in the class. He's helping the other students, who don't understand the concepts. He's writing brilliant arguments and defending them with evidence. I have hope for him. I tell him to look me up when he gets out so we can grab a meal and see some black metal shows. He nods and says, "Fuck yes."

I'm trying to get some grading done a couple of weeks later at my desk when I type Kel's name into my Google search bar to see if anything comes up. An Instagram page with Kel wearing a fedora. His bio says he's looking for porn, his eyes glazed with a meth stare. A picture of his mug shot pops up. Then a photo still from a surveillance video camera on a bus. It's fuzzy, but I can make out his face. He looks angry, his features distorted like a demon, and he's clutching something in his hand. I click on the image, and an article pops up. Kel was released and made his way to Colorado. In Leadville, he was on a public bus when he got into an altercation. He attacked another passenger from behind with a knife and tried to kill him. I read some of the comments. *He looks like a psycho. What a piece of shit. A thug. A nightmare. Lock him away forever.*

If only they knew what I knew.

I open my email and find a message from a student on the main campus, a rich girl who's a constant pain in my ass. She complains about everything in the classroom—the lighting, the books, the essays we read, the other students. She's angry about her grade and explains that she can't have less than an A because she needs to get into a "nice college." She hasn't turned anything in. No homework. No essays. I imagine she grew up in Folsom, in the hills where the mansions overlook the valley below. Her parents are probably doctors or lawyers. Or maybe they're marketing executives, like Jerry, the molester. She's probably not used to hearing the word *no*. I want to tell her to fuck off, that I know a neo-Nazi serial murderer who's managed to turn in all his assignments, but instead, I send a message that says she can make up any work she wants and still get an A, that it's just going to take some work. She says she's going to write on the internet about me and tell the dean that I'm a horrible teacher, which I encourage. Get on Rate My Professor. Go to the dean. Use whatever power you have to do whatever you're going to do. It doesn't fucking matter.

It's after 3 a.m., and I am lost in a YouTube vortex, watching video after video of fistfights in the street. I know I should be sleeping, but I can't. I'm too caught up in watching other people make horrible mistakes. I open a new tab to a YouTube video of a civilian getting arrested for pretending to be a cop. He drives around on a motorcycle pulling people over, yelling at them to comply. I'm fascinated by these videos. I watch them until early morning, hours of footage of fake cops being confronted by real cops. Of all the things to pretend to be, why a cop? Why not a firefighter or a mermaid? People never cease to amaze me—their brilliance, their mind-boggling idiocy, their pathetic desperation.

I understand. I'm all these things too. Some see me as a good man, so I remind them I am not. Some see me as evil, so I show them why they are wrong. I am the sum of my life, little hands tinkering away to make me better, my own hands fixing their work as I go.

SMASH THE CITY TO BITS

The streets are alive with righteous anger that rings through the city like church bells. People search for places to convene, shaken back into a state of rage since the last murder at the hands of police—Joseph Mann, Breonna Taylor, Stephon Clark, and now George Floyd and Daunte Wright, and the inevitable murders to come next by the hands of police. Protesters flood into César Chávez Plaza, gathering near the stage, standing in groups, shuffling nervously as a man with dreads sets up the microphones, everyone waiting for something profound to happen.

Our self-defense collective was asked to provide security for the event, a loosely billed anti–police violence protest where people would speak and march and form community around our collective strife. We've been doing security for protests, asylum seekers events, and antiracist marches for the past year, so we know what to expect. Within the crowd of protesters, like wolves in a flock of sheep, undercover cops, alt-right YouTubers, Proud Boys, and neo-Nazi provocateurs will blend in and slink around, looking to inflict damage on anyone and everyone.

The crowd fills the park, probably three hundred people sectioned off into groups. The same aging people who've made it their life's work to upset the system are all there, some recognizable even under their black masks. But there are hundreds of younger faces, high school kids, too hyper to sit through a line of middle-aged speakers. Their youthful rage is ready for a war. They want action, not just passive listening. Our collective splits into groups of two and walks the park perimeter.

Jose and I are used to doing security together. The first time I met Jose was at a Black Lives Matter march a couple of years earlier, after the Sacramento Police Department murdered unarmed Stephon Clark when they mistook his cell phone for a gun, and then I ran into him again at an MLK march where a bunch of right-wing YouTubers showed up and tried to provoke some unsuspecting marchers. Jose and I hung at the back of the crowd and tried to pick off the right-wingers. A couple of them were trying to film the protesters slyly with their cell phones. One thing I've learned about YouTubers is they know how to talk. Often, they'll use their gift of gab to get out of dicey situations. Sometimes it's better to get your point across quickly and not cause a scene.

I spotted one who'd strayed from his group, cornered him against the door of a bodega. "Get out of here," I said, shooting a quick elbow to his ribs.

"Okay, okay," he said, clutching his side. He ran off just in time for his friend to deal with Jose, who was in the middle of the street with his hands up, ready to fight. His friend was a beefy ginger who wore sunglasses and a newsboy cap, like an old-school Irish boxer. I could see him standing in front of Jose, weighing his options. Jose is small like I am, but he looks like he could be insane. He grew up in Los Angeles, in the punk scene that intersected with gang culture, which showed in every motion he made. He wore long hair and a bushy beard, often mistaken for a homeless person. The ginger wasn't going to fight. The way he stood, shoulders slumped, body pointing the opposite direction as his head, as if he was positioning himself to flee while still trying to look badass, gave away his cowardice. After a minute of uninspired posturing, he ran.

After that, I knew I would be friends with Jose. Our energies matched. The way our anger manifested in violence toward white supremacists could be just what these actions needed, a level of protection against the growing number of fascists brave enough to agitate a crowd. Having people looking out for protesters simply trying to walk down the street was probably a good idea, and it was something I knew we could handle. Or it could lead to our collective demise. Whatever it was, it drew us toward each other.

Jose and I scan the crowd, as we have done dozens of times before, pointing out suspicious characters, creeps wearing cop shoes, and people pointing their cell phones at faces—a telltale sign of a right-winger trying to get clear pictures of activists for their doxing campaigns, flooding Twitter with images of "Antifa thugs," with names and home addresses if they can find them.

Nothing looks out of place until I see a group of medics handing out water bottles. I don't recognize any of them. There are only two medic teams in town, and this isn't either of them. They mill about the crowd, smiling and handing out water bottles, but they're wearing Hawaiian shirts, flak jackets, and army helmets. I motion to Jose, and we circle slowly toward them.

The largest of their group does all the talking, a jolly oaf of a man who seems to take pride in handing out water. I walk up to him, and he offers me a water. "Thanks," I say, taking one. A closer look at his jacket shows a morale patch of Pepe, the little cartoon frog co-opted by the far right as a symbol used to identify each other online. Next to the patch is another patch that reads *Boogaloo*. Boogaloo Boys, an online group of extremely far-right agents of chaos who refer to themselves as accelerationists, meaning their sole purpose is to usher in a civil war by any means necessary, even if it means cuddling up with neo-Nazis or handing out water bottles at a BLM rally. One of their tactics is to latch on to left-wing protests to gain allies in their struggle, an agenda that includes a race war, killing cops, and general pandemonium in the name of liberty and freedom.

Until this point, Boogaloo Boys had only existed for me online. I had never seen one in the wild. I turn to Jose. "Boogaloo Boys," I say.

He doesn't seem to understand what I'm saying, so I repeat it, and he shrugs his shoulders.

"Let's follow them," I say, and Jose nods.

We follow them around the park until they run out of water. There are four of them, three men and a woman. As we tail them out of the park, I try to assess the outcome if things get physical. Jose and I are both small, but we're trained to fight, which usually gives us pretty good odds. But despite what most people think, when you're outnumbered, you're outnumbered. It doesn't take much to beat the shit out of trained fighters if you have enough people willing to pounce.

We follow them to a white truck. In its bed are pallets of water bottles. Before they reach in for them, I put my hand on the big guy's shoulder.

"Hey, man," I say. I have to look up to meet his eyes. I'm wearing all black with black gloves and a black ski mask.

He looks surprised to see me standing there. "Hey," he says with a wide smile.

"You gotta get the fuck out of here," I say.

He looks confused. His friends stand next to him, also confused. "Why?"

Out of the corner of my eye, I can see Jose sliding into a fighting stance, just nimble enough that he can punch and kick, but casual enough that he doesn't look like Karate Kid gearing up for a crane kick.

"You're a Boogaloo," I say. "Get the fuck out."

"Can I just explain to you what we're—"

"No," I say, this time more firmly. "Get the fuck out of here." I move toward him, close enough that I could lick his face if I wanted. Jose also moves in, taking a few steps forward. "Look, man," I say, "I don't want to hear your bullshit story. I'm going to allow you to leave, and if you don't, you and your friends are going to get fucked up."

"I'm not going anywhere," he says. His lips tremble when he talks.

"I'm telling you right now that we're trained to fight," I say, offering a fair warning. "And you're going to get fucked up."

Jose talks this time. "I'm going to count to thirty ..."

Thirty? I think. *That's a lot of fucking seconds.*

Jose starts counting. "One ... two ... three ..."

The wait is excruciating. I'm so close to the Boogaloo that it quickly becomes too awkward. I give Jose a glance after he reaches five seconds.

A right cross is launched into the Boogaloo's chin. The punch is a little too high, more toward his cheek. His fat face devours the fist. Then the Boogaloo absorbs a kick to the stomach, and he flies backward into the white truck with a huge *bang*. His friends scream and point at us. I lunge toward one of them, and he takes off running down the street. The other runs into the middle of the road, begging people in cars for help.

The woman they are with yells frantically at Jose and me. "They're medics! Why are you beating up the medics?!" It's the worst thing she could've said, because a crowd forms around us, and a shirtless protester screams, "Who's beating up medics?"

"Them!" the lady points toward us, and a group of large men move closer.

"They wouldn't even talk to me," says the Boogaloo, trying to garner sympathy and turn the crowd against us. They're so good at victimizing themselves. He's bleeding from his nose and mouth, which gives his case a little extra flair.

Jose shoots toward the bloody Boogaloo, but instead of hitting him, he rips the patch off his vest, holds it up to our would-be attackers, and says, "Look! It's Pepe!" and the crowd gasps in unison, just as they do in the movies. That one quick action saved us from an ass-beating by the people we were trying to protect. Jose is smarter than us all.

The shirtless man sees the patch and yells, "Pepe!" and the crowd immediately understands what is happening, the cartoon frog turned fascist signifier beautifully betraying itself. The crowd shifts its focus from Jose and me and chases the Boogaloo back into his truck, and we all watch him skid off down the street, leaving his other friends to find their way home.

The following week, protesters flood the park once again, their anger growing like a boil on the city's skin, so agitated that the only thing left to do is explode. Hundreds of people leave the park under the cloak of night with baseball bats and sticks and rebar and take to the streets, smashing everything that can be smashed. Every store and every office building is a feasible target to be broken and looted for all of its contents; Sacramento is bright with the orange glow of fires in the trash cans and buildings. Everything is smoking or on fire or dented to high hell. Even the cars. Even our car. We walk through the hordes of youth breaking and fighting and throwing rocks at the police, and when we arrive at our parked car, its windows are bashed in, the car's contents strewn about the sidewalk.

As we stand among the wreckage, a kid passes by with a group of friends. They carry baseball bats. One of them turns to us and says, "Ah fuck, that's your car?"

"Yeah," TJ says, shaking her head. TJ is a fierce fighter who will do anything—absolutely anything—to spark a revolution.

"I'm sorry," he says.

"No," she says, laughing at the streets covered in broken glass. Packs of youth roam them with makeshift weapons, bashing everything in their way. The city is burning into its own unintentional rebirth. Police fill the air with tear gas but park their patrol cars away from the major streets, afraid to engage. The streets are ours tonight. "It's going to be okay," she assures the bat-wielding youth.

Yes. TJ is right. Everything *is* going to be okay.

HOW TO TEACH A CLASS

One week passes since my call with the HR director, and still nothing from the district office. At this point, my tenure review process is completely stalled as everybody awaits the investigation results. It's been a year of this—365 days of spiritual unrest to add to my other forty-plus years of spiritual unrest. My colleagues and superiors are avoiding me. My dean only answers the occasional email from the union about the tenure evaluation timeline laid out in our contract, which the district has exceeded by three months now. He sends these brief messages:

Just waiting for some additional info. Thank you for being patient!

But we're not being patient—quite the opposite. Robert and James are frothing at the mouth. They'll take down the entire institution if they have to. I'm convinced of it. If this were an action movie, we'd be at the climax, right before Robert turns to James and says, "This is what the union was made for, buddy," before biting the pin off a grenade and lobbing it into the school. Not only have the administrators destroyed my evaluation timeline, but they've violated the contract probably a dozen times since my investigation began.

I am at work, trying to sit still in my office chair, slowly breathing in and out, as if one false move and a wire will trip, and my body will explode into a billion bloody pieces. It's been this way for the entire year while under the administrative microscope, short of breath, bracing for incineration.

On my desk in front of me is a piece of paper stuck to my door while I was teaching—no note, just a cutout of a cartoon from the conservative cartoonist Ben Garrison that depicts a KKK member standing next to a man in all black with the words *Berkeley Antifa* next to him. The man in black is holding a rope hanging over a tree branch with the Statue of Liberty choking in a noose on the other end. The KKK member says, "Need help with yer lynchin'?" and the Antifa says, "We call it virtue signaling." It's one of those weak jokes that conservatives are famous for—not funny, but topical enough that the slack-jaws nod enthusiastically in approval. His point is that if you say you're antifascist or antiracist, then you are virtue signaling. Claiming antifascist is akin to the days when white men would hang Black people from trees. Maybe a few months ago I would have been appalled at the nerve of this cartoonist and this student's gall, taping a humorless comic strip to my door. But this process of watching my liberal colleagues, the ones who hold antiracist book clubs and diversity and equity seminars, scramble to get me fired for organizing under the antifascist banner is right on brand with the political cowardice of those who operate in institutions. Whether they vote red or blue, they're vying for a spot at the top, speed bumps be damned.

I am a speed bump. I'm sick of buzzwords. I'm sick of sitting though meetings where saying the right combination of phrases will get you a gold star from the diversity overlords. I want to stop the momentum of the superficially woke and rattle the engine free from the undercarriage.

I've known this since I was little, skipping school, rolling spices in Bible pages, fighting football players in the local pizza joint, and robbing hipsters in Midtown. I'm under no illusion that my sole purpose is to slow down the functioning world, disrupt momentum, and annoy the important man at the wheel. I get it. If there is a God, he was playing a little joke. *"Try this one!"* God roared, giggling as he hurled me toward the earth, a messy ball of blood, brains, and fire.

Every now and then, a concerned colleague will pop their head into my office.

"You okay?" they'll ask.

I'll lie and tell them, "Yeah, I'm fine."

Some of them will offer solidarity. They'll offer up a lawyer or to write a letter to the editor.

"Let's fuck this place up!" said another professor.

I love it. All of it. Any form of solidarity gives my heart a little extra pump of blood.

But I don't want anyone to do anything. I know what I am and what I have done.

It's not worth it, I think. *Save your effort for a saint. I ain't it.*

I pack up my shit and head downstairs to the classroom. I'm never late to class. I love being there a few minutes early to break the awkward silence that sits in the room like a layer of pond scum. I like to ask my students what kind of shit they're up to. Professors who care about their lives freak them out, and I enjoy watching them squirm. Their answers are always achingly dull. They're working. They're studying. They're taking care of their siblings. One of the first surprising things I learned about teaching is that I'm always the most fucked-up one in the room.

My class seems extra crowded today; all the spaces are full, some students jammed four to a table that's supposed to sit three. I forgot my syllabus and my lesson plan, so I put my backpack down on the table in the front of the class and stare at them. I think of my colleague who has dated students, wondering what he sees in them. I like them, sure. I love them, even, but when I look at the kids in my class, eighteen-year-olds, some of them seventeen, staring at me googly-eyed, what stands out is how completely oblivious they are to the fact that life is about to creep around the corner, hit them in the face with a brick, and take them for all they've got. That kind of ignorance is unattractive to me. I can't imagine being trapped in a room alone with someone so unaware of their own impending demise.

"Professor, are we doing anything important today?" Jenny asks, not looking up from her phone. She's a beautiful Korean girl who wears so much makeup that she looks like an Instagram profile picture. She hasn't repeated an outfit once since the semester began thirteen weeks ago.

"No, Jenny, we're just going to stare at each other and drool for an hour and twenty minutes because I get paid anyway, so fuck it," I say, annoyed by her question. Jenny rolls her eyes. People who say there are no stupid questions have never taught in a community college. I don't know why that question annoys me so much. Maybe it's that I spend large chunks of my life creating lesson plans, toiling over each class, hoping that I can transmit my love of writing into their eager heads. Or maybe I've just run out of patience. Maybe the administrators are right: maybe I have no place teaching in a classroom.

"You look tired," Alex says. He's right. I am tired. I haven't slept in almost a year, since this investigation began. On the other hand, Alex is on the baseball team and never looks tired. He sits in the back of the class, shoulders slanted toward the front of the classroom, like he's waiting for me to say something profound.

"*You* look tired," I say, a lazy retort. I'm lying and not profound.

The class laughs, for some reason, maybe out of kindness, and we begin.

"Soooooo," I say. "What the fuck are y'all up to?"

"My boss is going to kill me," Katie chimes in immediately. Her red hair is pulled back so tight into a ponytail that it gives me a headache to look at it. "Like, really going to kill me."

"Why?"

"Because, well, he's a fucking psycho, but also because some money came up missing from the till, and I'm getting blamed. And I don't know what to do."

"Did you do it?" yells Alex. The class laughs.

"Don't answer that," I say. "It doesn't matter if you did it."

"Yes, it does," Abdi chimes in.

"No," I say. "Katie, just lie. You'll be fine."

"What do you mean, lie?" Abdi says with a look of horror on his face.

"You've never lied, Abdi?" I say.

"That's her boss," he says, not answering my question. "You can't lie to your boss."

"Bosses are a class of people you're supposed to lie to," I say. "Don't you know anything about life?"

"Who else can you lie to?" Eddie asks from the back of the room.

"I don't know. Bosses, your parents, cops, and college professors."

The class laughs, but I'm not joking.

They break into stories about their jobs—fast-food supervisors who spit in the food, racist coworkers, sex with managers . . . maybe I'm *not* the most fucked-up one in the room. They just weren't giving me the good shit.

I tell them about when I worked at Macy's in San Francisco, right in the middle of Union Square. I worked in the young men's section, where loud techno music blasted from morning until night. I spent my time avoiding customers and folding shirts, watching all the wealthy Japanese businessmen grab as many stacks of Levi's as they could carry, balancing the tower of denim from the shelves to the checkout counters. I wasn't on commission, so nobody cared if I didn't help anyone. The associates who worked for commission took as many customers as possible and rang them up, leaving me to do whatever I wanted. Sometimes I'd clock in at the beginning of my shift, sneak out of the store and go skateboarding until my shift was over, then clock out and do it again the next day. It wasn't long until I started stealing from the register. Every morning, right after the till was counted, I'd ring up a customer and crunch up a twenty in my palm to slide it into the cuff of my long-sleeve shirt. It took months for management to notice. They called us one by one into the office to be grilled.

"Have you been taking money from the register?" one of the suits from corporate asked. She was in her late thirties, a serious-looking woman who probably took pride in her job as a bigwig retailer.

"No," I said.

"Do you know who's been stealing?"

"I don't," I said. "I'll let you know if I hear anything." That last part was extra. I don't think they believed me. But they clearly didn't have anything on the surveillance cameras, so I wasn't worried. They expected to catch the thief with good, old-fashioned detective work, but I wasn't going to crack. I went downstairs and finished my shift in bliss, knowing I would keep my job.

A few months later, I moved to San Diego and transferred to Macy's in La Jolla with a promotion as a Nautica rep. I got my own section of the store to manage and decorate. It only took a week or two for me to start stealing.

One time, I caught a guy using a fake receipt to try to scam the store. I recognized him because he had tried the same shit in San Francisco.

"You're that guy who got chased out of Union Square by security!" I yelled.

He must have been in his fifties, with long gray hair and a sunken heroin face. He looked like he had seen a ghost. "Wasn't me, motherfucker. Now process my refund, asshole," he said.

I would've hooked him up if he hadn't been such a dick.

I told him to fuck off, followed him outside, and beat him up in the parking lot. After that, I became the hero of the store. I was untouchable. Nobody would ever try to fire me.

We end up spending the entire class trading stories about our jobs, and I feel bad because Jenny was right: we didn't do anything important today. She could've gone home. We wasted an entire class pouring out our feelings, sharing stories of debauchery and shame. We laughed for an hour and thirteen minutes straight. Maybe that's the most important thing we could have done in an Introduction to College Composition course.

It's the last seven minutes of class, and it dawns on me that we were supposed to discuss conclusions today—how to end an essay. I try to think of something profound to say about the process of writing a composition, the rules of writing an essay, and the most efficient and effective way to signal the end of your paper. But really, I mean, what is there to say? You're done. Just end the fucking thing.

I ask the students to picture a bird.

"What kind of bird?"

"Any kind of bird," I say. "Got it?"

"Got it."

"Now, what does it represent?"

"Freedom."

"Okay, what else?"

"Traveling."

"Good. Anything else?"

"Shitting on people?"

"Nice," I say. "Now, who is right?"

"We're all right," Alex says.

"Exactly," I say. "You're all right."

BLACKING OUT

The shop is empty. Ezra is in the tattoo chair next to me playing on his Nintendo Switch, and Luna is watching her tablet while Andre blasts into my arm with his new tattoo gun. A mix of ink and blood gently pools in the fresh wound he's creating. The pain is dull and annoying but not unbearable.

Andre is tattooing my entire arm black, covering over years of colorful tattoos: a rose, a sloppy sugar skull, a wilted tulip, and some other shit I've already forgotten. He's going to go over the black with white designs, but I want a blackened arm for now. I want to look at my arm in the mirror and know a portion of my life is done and a new one is beginning. I also want to scare old white people, who seem horrified by my body full of tattoos. I might as well give them a show. I want to look a certain way and deprive myself of the people I don't need to be around anyway—strip away the shitty parts of the world, so all that's left are the people I love.

I see these videos on YouTube of brutal tattooing, where the artist digs into the skin so hard with black ink that it's a form of torture. It's supposed to be like sadomasochism, a form of release for the artist and the canvas. I'm too cowardly for that kind of shit, but I understand it completely. Humans need pain to feel more connected to death, so when the day comes, it won't be unfamiliar. We'll have dabbled a bit.

I started getting tattoos when I was seventeen: a cowardly lion on the side of my calf, then a band of stars, then a Francis Bacon self-portrait. I always felt uneven, so I kept getting more and more until my body was covered.

People ask me what all these tattoos are about, and I don't know what to tell them. Some of them I don't even remember getting. One day I woke up with a hangover, and there was a spider with a skull on its belly tattooed on my shoulder.

At some point, I'd wake up from a blackout to find my tattoos had started getting satanic: an upside-down cross, a pentagram, a goat on my chest, the word *LUCIFER* in calligraphy across my belly. My dad would literally try to murder me if he saw those, but he won't. He's gone for good. Not dead, I don't think. Men like him never seem to die in a timely way.

Maybe I get tattoos to ward off the things I don't want, like shitty jobs (they'll never hire me at Walmart) and God (I won't make it past the first waiting room of heaven with this back tattoo of a veiled Mary taking a bite of Jesus's bloody heart).

One of my favorites is on the side of my knee. One of my students, a Mexican punk who drew pictures throughout the semester, told me she was trying to be a tattoo artist. I said I'd let her practice on me, so one day she came over and tattooed some Black Flag bars with the word *SICK* in plain letters.

After three hours my arm is almost entirely black, except for the tattoo of a typewriter on the center of my forearm. My sister Lauren got it for me for my birthday one year. We sat for hours in a shop on Telegraph Avenue in Oakland while the artist toiled, sweat dripping from his forehead until the image was a perfect replica of an old Monarch typewriter. I don't have the heart to cover it over.

Andre is done for the day. We're both tired and hungry. Our stomachs are growling, and I'm feeling lightheaded.

"Does Ezra want to tattoo?" he says.

"Does he want a tattoo?" I'm still delirious from hours under the needles.

"No, does he want to do a tattoo on you?"

I look over at Ezra, who is sprawled out on the tattoo chair across the room, staring into the face of his Nintendo Switch.

"Yo, Ezra," I say. "You want to tattoo me?"

"Sure," he says.

"Luna, what about you?" I say.

She shakes her head no, but gets out of her chair to watch the show.

Ezra puts down his Switch and takes a seat next to Andre. Luna follows.

"Sit here and hold it like this," Andre says, placing the tattoo gun gently in Ezra's hand.

Andre's a father too, and it shows. The way he talks softly. The way he gives slow, step-by-step directions. The way he doesn't make a big deal out of something that is kind of a big deal. All the traits of a thoughtful father. I think of my dad, how he would have shoved the machine in my hand and told me to get to work, his sickly eyes staring right through me, into a distant universe.

"Now draw on his skin," Andre says.

Ezra points toward a tattoo of a heart on my arm and fills it in with black ink. I can barely feel it.

Ezra holds the machine like a pen and squints in concentration. His hand is steady, like a little surgeon performing a lifesaving operation. I flinch a little bit at the thought of my life being in his hands, the boy who laughs so hard he slobbers on his shirt.

"Good," Andre says. "Keep going."

Ezra fills in the heart until it's scribbled in black, and he hands the machine back to Andre. Luna looks at her brother with wide eyes and Ezra is smiling ear to ear.

"Good job," Andre says, stretching his arms toward the ceiling.

I pack the kids in the car and take notice of my black arm, all the years of tattoos I've covered up in three hours. I hardly remember what it looked like before. We head back toward home, through Citrus Heights, a bombed-out part of town where skinny white people ride stolen BMX bikes into the gas station parking lots and congregate behind dumpsters. I wonder if I would have ended up like that.

Crystal is at home making dinner. The house smells of sauteed onions and roasting broccoli. The kids rush to tell her about their day in the tattoo shop, how they played video games while Andre worked on me, how Ezra sat next to Andre and filled in a bit of my arm.

"You did?!" Crystal says, feigning surprise. She's not actually surprised by anything anymore. Since she's known me, our lives are controlled chaos. Nothing is boring. Our lives are stable, but open to intrigue.

I kiss Crystal on the forehead while she stirs the browning onions around the pan, sizzling with butter. She looks tired, her eyes showing the beginning of bags underneath. *I wonder if I did that to her*, I think. Maybe I should chill out, go to work, come back, talk about the weather, turn on the baseball game, pass out clutching a Coors Light.

"Dinnertime, kids," I say in my best impression of a dad.

The kids run to the table.

"What are you laughing at, Dad?" Luna says.

"I don't know," I say. I can't help but to chuckle at the thought of me as a normal person.

WE'RE ALL GHOSTS HERE

My stepdad calls and says he's going to drop off some gardening tools for the garden I'll never plant, so I plop on the couch to wait for him while I scroll through my phone.

Crystal is at the sink washing vegetables, running a carrot under a stream of water for an abnormally long time, drowning it. Her phone is tucked under her cheek, resting on her shoulder, and she's yelling in Chinese, arguing with her mom again. I can't tell what they're saying, but it's heated.

Every now and then, she'll break into English—"Okay, Mom, fine"— and then she'll turn to me and I'll hold up my fist in solidarity.

The kids are off in their rooms, Luna watching a mind-numbing show on her tablet and Ezra on his bunk bed flipping through a comic book. I don't know when or how he learned to read, but one day he came home with a stack of books under his shoulder and read it and everything else in the house. He's voracious, lost in a world of language, just like his dad, which worries me a little, but maybe that's one of the good parts, maybe I can configure him toward literature and away from everything that turned my life into a time bomb, the drugs and violence. Or maybe too much configuration, too many fingers fumbling with the wires, is what set the detonator to explode.

"Ayooooo, Mom!" Crystal yells from the sink. She puts the phone down on the countertop in defeat and lets her mom yell into the abyss.

Crystal shoots me a look, and I shrug my shoulders. Sometimes I'm afraid that we're only united by trauma and pain, that our relationship now is a sounding board for our problems, but that can't be the truth. Our therapist says we're doing okay, and I believe her. She cured me of my body dysmorphia. It was mostly latent trauma that she fixed by making me lie on the couch while contending with my inner child. It seemed creepy at the time, to conjure up that upside-down little guy, but maybe it was out of the sheer desire to never experience that awkward form of therapy ever again that I was cured.

While Crystal and her mom yell back and forth on the phone, I remember when I was eight years old, Ezra's age, still wearing sweaters my mom picked out at Filene's, and my stepdad strapped my bike to the roof of the car, a booger-green VW bug so old that you could see the road from little rusted holes in the footwells, and the whole family, my mom, my stepdad, Sunshine, and me, drove to Plymouth, Massachusetts, the spot where pilgrims landed—and depending on which history you believe, they broke bread with the Native people or unleashed a genocidal bloodbath upon my ancestors.

It was gray and windy when we parked at the top of a grassy hill that reached the ocean, little whitecaps on the waves jumping in the distance. It was only an hour drive from Brookline to Plymouth, but it seemed like a different planet, the ghosts of dead Europeans still chipping away at the gray cobblestone. My mom and sister stood at the top of the hill, shivering in the frigid air and taking in the scenery while my stepdad set my BMX on the grass and straddled its little frame. It made me laugh, like watching a giant on a toy bike.

He told me to get on the handlebars.

"The handlebars?" I said, wondering if it was a good idea.

"Let's go for a ride," he assured me.

"I don't know, Dad," I said, measuring the steepness of the hill, our slim chances of survival.

My stepdad motioned for me to sit.

I got on the handlebars reluctantly, the bike pointing down the slope, my hands rolling around the bars underneath me, frantically seeking the sturdiest grip.

"Ready?" he yelled.

"Yup," I said, my legs dangling in front.

He picked up his feet, the bike balancing momentarily in perfect harmony with the world until we lunged forward with his first pedal stroke.

These moments are rare, when time ceases to exist, when our world is replaced with another world, one where common measurement no longer matters, like the summer I spent working with my best friend Joey at his uncle's restaurant in Manhattan. One evening after work, a group of kids surrounded us only a couple blocks from our apartment. We both had pepper spray and skateboards, and the kids weren't that big, a bunch of rich assholes pretending to be tough. Joey looked at me as if to say, "You ready?" but I couldn't move. Everything had stopped. I stood there, unable to reach into my pocket to spray them, unable to swing my board at their faces. It was like one of those horrible dreams where you're fighting in slow motion, everything underwater, except I didn't even get to the fighting part. It's not that I felt scared. Or angry. I felt nothing, as if I existed before I was born, waiting for the big birthing moment, but you're never born, just suspended in the womb. I only awoke to the motion of large men with badges on their necklaces lunging at the kids, sending them scattering away. "NYPD!" they shouted. The kids ran in all directions, leaving Joey and me standing there, our skateboards hanging from our hands like dead flowers.

"Why didn't you do anything?" one of the men yelled in a thick, angry New York accent.

"You had skateboards!" the other one chimed in.

"Next time that happens, swing those motherfuckers!"

The men left as quickly as they came. I stood there with Joey, replaying the situation in my mind.

"I was about to kill those kids," I lied.

"Me too," Joey said.

I was supposed to be the tough one.

My stepdad grunted as he pushed the pedals, the bike picking up speed until the world was out of control, the bumps lofting me momentarily into the atmosphere, my ass somehow landing perfectly back on the handlebars, my knuckles white from gripping too hard.

The closer we got to the ocean, the more afraid I became.

I wonder if this was how my ancestors felt, the overwhelming sense of connection to the earth, its beauty and magnificence sprawling out before you in its wonder, riding fast toward the edge of something unknown, unaware of whether it was a new horizon of beauty or imminent death.

The bike lunged forward until the speed was beyond our control.

It would take too long to brake if we needed to stop right away, so we both screamed at the top of our lungs, as if we had both given in to the possibility of death.

I think we both saw it at the same time, a drop, maybe ten feet down, that led to a park below us. The way the hill slanted, the drop was invisible from the top, like an optical illusion.

If we didn't stop, we'd both plummet to our deaths or at least break a dozen bones apiece.

"Fuck!" my stepdad yelled, his feet digging into the grass.

I swallowed my innards up into my stomach, but I was already resigned to the afterlife. There was nothing left to do but wait.

I closed my eyes, thinking I would rather die in blindness.

The sound of my stepdad's feet digging into the earth, the dull dragging of his shoes tearing up fresh grass, was worse than watching my own demise, so I opened my eyes again.

The wall was a few feet in front of us when we finally slowed to a stop, the front wheel of the BMX finally hanging over the edge, like the scene in every action movie where the truck tilts precariously on the edge of the cliff, my stepdad's hand grabbing the collar of my sweater.

We fell onto the ground laughing, clutching our stomachs in exhilaration and pain.

Cheaters of death.

Settlers on a settled land, conniving our way out of an arrangement with fate.

I wished the pilgrims could have seen us then. A little Mexican boy and his Irish stepfather. Two mismatched scoundrels, tempting fate on a land taken from Wampanoag by sleight of hand, the Irishman tearing up their stolen lawn with his heels.

It is one of my favorite memories from childhood.

Crystal is still on the phone with her mom when my stepdad shows up. I'm still on the couch, dreaming of the past. I get up and shuffle to the door.

The door opens with a thud, and we say polite hellos.

My stepdad looks exhausted. I can tell his smile is forced.

"Can I tell you this memory?" I say.

He stands in the doorway while I recount the death-defying story of Plymouth, Mass., to hear his perspective.

"Do you remember that day?" I say, hands in the praying position, as if his answer will spiritually unify us.

I want to know if he was as afraid and exhilarated as I was. I wonder if he felt the same exhilaration as I, if there was even a little part of him that felt alive at the gates of death. I want him to tell me it was a test to see if I was a real man, his real son.

"It never happened," he says.

"What?"

"That never happened." His eyes are twisted in confusion.

"None of it?"

"No," he says, assuredly. "None of it."

"So I just made it up?"

"Well . . ."

I stand there, gobsmacked, amazed at my capacity to lie—or at his capacity to forget.

Did I ever go to Plymouth? Did I live in Boston? Are my knuckles all broken from fistfights? Was there an investigation into my political activities? Do I even have a goddamn job? Or is this all a fever dream, some blurry mental hellscape where you wake up shivering in wet blankets, covered with sweat, gasping for a clean slice of air? Who the fuck am I? Who made me? What am I made of? Am I going to be okay? Has my brain finally short-circuited?

All these questions run through my mind as my stepdad waits there, confused, the porch lights glowing around us like a couple of ghosts who have been traveling through centuries to haunt the living shit out of everyone.

HOW TO SAY "FUCK YOU"

I'm at home trying to grade essays when I get an email from my union's executive director that says:

> Hello again, here's some exciting bedtime reading. The investigation report is 33 pages, and there are 103 pages of exhibits.

This is it.

My entire future is in a plain email with a PDF attachment.

Right after being hired to teach full-time, I wandered all over downtown Sacramento. It was a good day. The air whispered with the slight breeze of a fading spring. Families milled about, soaking up the sunshine. I passed a simple flyer pasted to an electrical box. Underneath a crude cartoon of a man in a black mask crushing a swastika, the words *No Nazis in Sac* were written in bold letters. The advertised date was June 26 at the state capitol building, just a few weeks away.

I showed up at the capitol on June 26 by myself. I rode my skateboard over with the plan to roll to the park afterward, where my stepdad was celebrating his birthday. Hundreds of people were gathered in front of the capitol, most dressed in black, with black bandannas covering their faces. Black flags waved in the wind. A group arrived with a gigantic banner reading *THE ONLY GOOD FASCIST IS A DEAD ONE*.

Memories of ten kids stuffed into Aragorn's apartment, the beginnings of Sacramento's chapter of Anti-Racist Action, filled my throat until I nearly choked. The punk shows in tiny venues, the skinheads stomping in, the fists to the face and neck, the baseball bats, the groups of kids who had had enough. It was all there, again, thirty years later. Nothing had changed.

My friend Aragorn, the old SHARP, came to visit recently, and we sat in an expensive coffee shop in downtown Sacramento. He wasn't a skinhead anymore. He had gained a hundred pounds and dressed like a schlub. Many people hated him. He was a natural antagonist, an anarchist with a long history of publishing and podcasting, mostly critiquing leftist movements, specifically any movement he wasn't a part of. If he caught on to the fact that he was being agreeable, he'd change course, which would sometimes land him in treacherous waters. In a world of nihilists, egoists, and anarcho-nationalists—people disagreeable to most—Aragorn seemed all too pleased to grill them on his podcast, like a Joe Rogan of the anarchist world. At some point, Aragorn changed his name to add an exclamation point—Aragorn!—like a fucking psychopath. But that kind of shit reminded me of something my dad would do, so I played along.

"You're wasting your time," he said, with his characteristic shit-eating grin.

"What do you mean?"

"The Antifa shit," he said. "Waste of time."

Despite him not being there, he went on to document his secondhand version of the rest of that day at the capitol, describing what a shitshow it was, how disorganized and chaotic it became, how the Nazis were more willing to fight and die than we were, how they didn't hesitate to start stabbing people, how the antifascists were outsmarted at every turn by a bunch of prison Nazis.

But he wasn't there.

He didn't see what had happened.

There were kids barely out of high school standing in the path of giants twice their size, doing whatever it took not to let them through the line. Old women locked hands and chanted antifascist songs while a scuffle broke out on the east side. A group of three Antifas clad in black chased a skinhead on foot until they caught up with him and left him bleeding in the street. Trying to run toward a scuffle between an Antifa and three Nazis with knives, I tripped over a gun lying in the grass. An old Native man caught a couple of Golden State Skinheads in a corner and broke their heads with a stick until a cop on a horse escorted them to safety.

Nobody wants violence, but nobody wants Nazis to roam free, either. If Antifa is a waste of time, then everything else is a waste of time.

I open the PDF attachment and brace myself. It's even worse than I imagined, a hundred pages of jumbled-up legalese complete with numbered lists and bullet points, a labyrinth of confusion. I'm not sure what I was expecting, maybe just a big *GUILTY* written in Comic Sans.

I get a text from my old friend Joe. It's a picture of him with a handlebar mustache. Now and then he'll send a picture of him wearing a different mustache. He was a hacker by the time he was a teenager. He joined a collective called L0pht, a bunch of awkward nerds who testified in front of the US Senate that they could shut down the internet within thirty minutes.

Joe's a jolly troublemaker, an antiauthoritarian, and a lover of counterculture, so we have always stayed in touch, even though our paths have diverged more than once. He has more money than I'll ever make in my life and hasn't changed since we were kids sitting in the time-out box, telling jokes while greasy-faced Mrs. Clark wagged her skeleton finger at the rest of the class.

I once went back to Boston to visit Joe.

"Let's go see Tony," he said. "I need a haircut."

We walked the familiar path down the tree-lined hills of Brookline, past the modest houses that had become million-dollar properties, the same giant cracks in the sidewalk that existed when I was seven.

Our childhood barber, Tony, was an old Italian man who kept *Playboy* magazines in the lobby. We stole them, and he pretended not to notice. I asked him to give me a fucked-up haircut, and he was delighted to oblige. My parents flipped out when they saw their only boy with a gigantic mohawk perched on top of his head like an exotic bird. Their punishment was almost worth the horrified looks on their faces.

"Josh!" Tony said in his thick Italian accent. "Is that you?"

"Tony!" I called.

Tony stopped cutting a man's hair and gave me a giant hug, his spicy cologne clogging my nose.

"It's so good to see you," Tony said.

The man sitting in Tony's barber chair turned to me. He was a fat Russian with a shaved head.

"Josh," he said. "Do you remember me?"

I didn't recognize him.

"It's Sasha," he said.

Sasha. The Russian bully. The one I kicked in the face and ran away from all those years ago. I'd managed to escape him for twenty-five years.

"Sasha?"

"Look. You did this to me!" he said, and he smiled, pointing to a gold tooth on the left side of his mouth.

I scanned the document from the investigator for a few minutes until I finally found the criteria of the investigation:

1. Whether Mr. Fernandez asked, encouraged, or pressured students to participate in meetings regarding an Antifa or Antifascist group.
2. Whether Mr. Fernandez stated or implied to students that the meetings of the Antifa or Antifascist group, or the group itself, were sponsored by the District.
3. What type of activities occurred at meetings of the Antifa or Antifascist group and self-defense classes led by Mr. Fernandez and held at his home?
4. What was the purpose for which Mr. Fernandez and students attended certain Antifa/Antifascist protests?
5. What occurred during the protests to which Mr. Fernandez took students, including but not limited to:
   a. Student activities during the protests;
   b. Mr. Fernandez's activities during the protest;
   c. Whether students or Mr. Fernandez engaged in any violence during the protests;
   d. What the students wore to the protests;
   e. Whether the students carried weapons;
   f. Whether the students covered their faces; and
   g. Whether the students brought signs and, if so, the text on the signs.
6. Whether Mr. Fernandez has communicated with the students regarding the Antifa or Antifascist group since he claimed he stopped doing so via social media, in class, or any other communication method.
7. Whether Mr. Fernandez encouraged students to place flyers around the Campus on December 6, 2018.
   a. If this allegation is sustained, whether students felt pressured to put the signs up by Mr. Fernandez.
8. Whether any action taken by Mr. Fernandez constituted a violation of District or College policy.

I scroll frantically to the end, past the Witnesses, past the Credibility Determinations, past the Standard of Proof, past the documents review to the allegations. I don't care about any of that shit.

Each allegation would either have been unfounded or sustained, in bold.

There it was, in bold:

Unfounded.

The lawyer concluded, not in bold, almost as an afterthought:

None of the conduct of Mr. Fernandez rises to the level of any violation of policy.

The district was wrong.

They couldn't have been more wrong.

Even the investigator they had hired couldn't prove their claims.

Even though I talked too much, even when my union reps told me to shut the fuck up, the administrators couldn't catch me in an inconsistency.

Someone asked me later if I felt relieved, and the answer was no. Not at all. Sure, my breath left me for a moment. I felt weightless, lightheaded maybe. But I was not relieved. I felt angry. Angry at the system that had put me in the position where I had to defend myself. Angry at my dean, who had smiled to my face and orchestrated my demise with his superiors. Angry at the district that had treated me like a time bomb.

Although maybe they had a point.

HILLBILLIES NEED HUGS

It takes an hour to get to work now. I started teaching a few classes at the satellite campus in Placerville, a rural town outside of Sacramento. It's like a little taste of Tennessee in California. Cowboy boots. Star-spangled T-shirts. White trucks with NRA stickers tailgating Prius drivers until they pull off to the side of the road.

I'm driving the windy country road past the farms and steep driveways, and it reminds me of being a kid. Not the farms, but the smell of earth and trees. My stepdad used to drive us every birthday to New Hampshire to Canobie Lake Park, where lucky kids would have their birthdays with pizza, ice cream, and roller coasters. I sat in the front seat, and two friends sat in the back. My nerves started taking hold a half hour into the drive. I used to worry then, too, about everything, even though I was seven and didn't have to worry about anything. I twisted the car upholstery in between my fingers.

"Ouch!" my stepdad yelled. I didn't realize I'd been twisting his leg hairs.

"Sorry," I said, slumped in my seat, waiting for the car ride to end. Maybe the roller coasters would crush my worries.

I didn't know what to say to him. Not just then, but ever. I was shy around him for most of my life. Part of it was intimidation. He scared me a little, even though he had no violence in him. I was more afraid of his demeanor, how he cut through a room and analyzed each situation, calculating the most efficient way to complete a task. I was afraid of his success. In the back of my mind, I knew I would never amount to anything worthy. I had no ambition or dreams. Sometimes I'd tell him I wanted to be homeless just to get under his skin. A little game I played. He didn't like games the way I liked them. I'd go all in just to watch his face turn sour. I didn't realize how much power my words had. He would try to play it cool.

"I'm going to be a hobo," I said in the car. "I'll live outside."

"Well, Josh," he said, using the measured tone I imagined he used with his patients. "I'm not sure that's a good plan."

"So, I don't need school," I said, "because I'm going to be homeless anyway." I held my breath as his rigid eyes sliced into me. I'd become accustomed to finding the danger spot and running face-first into it.

He shook his head in disgust and turned up the radio. "Unbelievable," he muttered under his breath.

The satellite campus is located near the edge of a couple of gigantic farm properties out in the middle of nowhere. When I park, I notice all kinds of white students milling around the parking lot. A group of them stand in front of an empty parking spot and stop talking when I approach. When I pass, they laugh. I'm used to this. Here, I am a spectacle. A heavily tattooed Mexican professor from the city. If I wasn't in charge of their grades, I'm sure one of them would consider attacking me. I love it. It's an exciting job.

When I get to class, most students are waiting in the hallway for me to unlock the door. The building reminds me of a cabin made of concrete and dark wood. It smells like a truck stop in the mountains.

The classroom is unremarkable. Some of the fluorescent lights work. There are no decorations besides a fire safety poster barely clinging to the wall. My students look tired. It's the tenth week of the semester. I'm tired too. They're all supposed to have picked the topics for their research paper, an essay where they have to use academic research to explore a hypothesis. I want them to rely only on scholarly evidence. This is torture for some students. Many of them want to spew their views without any discretion. Last semester, a student turned in a screed about how liberals are whiny bitches. Not that I disagreed with the thesis, but there wasn't any research, only a few references to dodgy websites and a couple of Fox News articles.

"Professor, do you want to hear about my topic?" a student asks. He plays in a rap-rock band.

"No," I say.

The class laughs, but I'm not joking. I don't want to hear his topic. I figure if he plays in a rap-rock band, probably nothing he does will be any good.

We go in order so I can hear their topics without skipping anyone. It's usually the standard array of issues: marijuana, sports, mental health, abortion, etc. Nothing too jarring until I get to Tony, a skinny, quiet kid who's failing my class because he hasn't turned much in. He sits in the back and fumes whenever I say anything.

"My paper is about how Black people need to stop bitching about slavery," he blurts out. A few people in my class laugh and clap.

I know I'm in the middle of the countryside, surrounded by farms and the hillbillies who run them, but I'm still caught off guard, as if a college campus acts as some sort of force field for bad ideas. I'm almost angrier that he got a round of applause than I am at his statement.

"Hold up," I say. "We're going to have to stop everything right here. We're done with what we were doing, and now we're doing this."

Tony sits up in his chair, invigorated by his fan club. He thinks I'll yell or scold him for his opinion, but I'm not going to do that. I'm going to do something much worse. We're going to spend the rest of the class learning about the origins of modern racism. We're going to share our ideas about that statement and why it might be harmful. We're going to dig deep and express ourselves, something I've found that frothing right-wingers hate. They hate vulnerability, something I used to hate too. I'd cringe at the thought of expressing emotion when I was younger, especially fear. Maybe it was the by-product of growing up in a family that only dealt with the superficial. Since then I've figured out that the more open I am, the more I attract better people and the more they trust me—the real me, the one with the sketchy past.

If there's one thing I've learned, for better or worse, it's that in these uncomfortable situations, it's best not to turn your back on them. Run face-first into them. If anything, it'll be a good story later.

I glance over at Faisal, a Muslim student who never holds back his opinion. He's visibly upset and shaking.

"I'm a Muslim," he says, crying now. "I can't understand why you would say that."

"Okay," I say, stalling, trying to find a way to start the conversation we're about to have. "Tony, do you understand why what you said might be offensive to people?"

"It's not like that," he said, striking a defensive pose.

"Nope," I say. "Let's just trace this back to its origin."

Tony looks defeated, slumping in his chair. It's not my intent to defeat him, but as long as he shuts the fuck up for a minute, I'll take it. We start at chattel slavery, not as a history lesson but to put Tony's paper topic into a framework. "When you say you wish Black people would shut up about slavery, it seems like you may not understand the horrifying aspects of humans owning other humans as property."

"But we have civil rights now," Tony says. "And Africans sold slaves too. Why is it that white people get blamed?"

I think about the Polish skinhead who used to sell me drugs. I don't think he was even that racist. He was dumb, sure. And confused. And he loved the Nazi skinhead aesthetic. But at his core, he was an abandoned child stuck, through self-isolation, in his most ignorant moment, where he would probably remain until he died. Or my imprisoned students, like Jeremy, the Aryan with SS bolts tattooed under his eye. Also a straight A student whose honest and powerful writing would move you to tears every time, a man of misplaced wires that would short-circuit and self-destruct now and again, but salvageable, maybe, with the right hands to set the electronics straight. In every horrible person, I see myself. Even Tony, slumped in his chair, mad at a world he probably feels is tilting against him.

Class is over, and nothing's better. Tony storms out of the room, and the rest of the class looks entertained by the drama, probably glad we got no work done today. Sometimes in situations like this, when the class goes awry, there's no cinematic *Stand and Deliver* moment where the class learns a lesson and we all go home better people. Sometimes it's like a slow, silent fart that smells up the room, the lingering stench sometimes lasting for days. Teaching is hard. And gross.

The next time the class meets, a couple of students bring a box of churros to share. They're peace churros. Unity churros. We each grab a churro and try to remember where we left off.

Tony doesn't show up for class. He's failing the class anyway. He probably figured, *Fuck it, what's the point?* Tony is a casualty. There is nothing I can do. He'll go off and live his own life, explode when he needs to explode. I hope he'll remember this class before he does. Maybe it'll make him pause for a fraction of a second.

TROUBLE AGAIN

I get a text on the encrypted messaging app on my phone:

Did you fucking see this?

I'm looking at a screenshot of a conversation on Telegram about a group trying to organize a White Lives Matter rally in Sacramento, which isn't a surprise. Since about 2015, white nationalist groups like the Aryan Renaissance Society have been mobilizing against Black Lives Matter to pack racists from different affinity groups into one large tent, like clowns at the world's dumbest circus. They've been trying to organize a national movement, leaving their WLM stickers around downtown under cover of night for the past few weeks, like they're testing the waters, trying to gauge interest in their movement in a city with 70 percent nonwhite residents.

The message indicates that the rally is today at a park, but it doesn't say which park. I send the screenshot to a group I've been organizing with for years. I get messages back immediately.

Where? texts TJ.

I don't know.

Capitol? Jose asks.

Don't know, but maybe at Fremont Park? I'm going to roll around and see.

I run into my room and search through my drawer to find the right clothes. Half of an antifascist's work seems to be finding the perfect outfit. Are you trying to be nondescript? All black so you can blend in with a crowd? Will you be running? Do you need steel-toed boots?

The three arrows tattooed on my neck make it hard to be discreet, so I pull on some dark blue jeans and a Fred Perry bomber jacket to put on over the shirt I'm already wearing. I lace up my black Adidas and try to figure out what I'm going to say to my family.

The kids are playing in their rooms, and Crystal is in the bathroom doing her makeup.

"I have to go to the park."

"What's happening?"

"They're trying to have a White Lives Matter rally."

"Who?"

"I don't know," I say. "White people."

"Where?"

"I don't know. It's probably nothing. I'm just going to go check it out."

"Who are you going with?"

"I'm going by myself," I say. "I'm just going to check it out. Nothing's going to happen."

Crystal gives me a look that says, *You just endured a yearlong investigation, and you have tenure now. Don't fuck this up, you dumbfuck.*

On the way to Fremont Park, I get another message:

They're going to McKinley Park

That's a surprise. It's a park in an upscale neighborhood in East Sacramento. A few years ago, there was another white nationalist rally at the same park, hosted by the now-defunct Identity Evropa, one of the first neo-Nazi groups to try to polish up their image by promoting clean living and tan chinos, a bunch of *Sieg heil*ing whiteboys dressed like Ivy League scholars. At that rally, a group of antifascists ended up surrounding the park and stabbing everyone's tires, some getting caught and spending a few days in jail. Shortly after that, the Nazi group briefly changed its name to American Identity Movement, then disbanded after Antifa groups targeted them in relentless online doxing campaigns. Here's the thing about Antifa that people don't seem to understand: most of the work is online. Sure, there are videos of antifascists in the street giving (but mostly taking) beatings, but the real success is the relentless nature of the antifascists who don't stop until the white nationalist is left jobless, broke, paranoid, and frightened for their life. These campaigns—calling their jobs nonstop and harassing their employers, filling their neighborhoods with flyers, plastering social media with their images—make up the majority of Antifa. Ultimately, it wasn't the televised and highly memed punch to the face that left Richard Spencer jobless, moneyless, wifeless, and rotting in a dungeon of obscurity, it was the relentless online campaigns from antifascists.

I park my car across the street from the park and walk toward the playground, a sprawling structure filled with more children than I would've thought, given that we're in a global pandemic. None are wearing masks; they're just playing without a care.

I get another message:

Where are you? We can be there soon with signs.

It's from a woman who's part of a group of elderly socialists from San Francisco, mostly retired college professors and old hippies. I don't want them to show up, but they're insistent. They want to do a counterdemo with banners and bullhorns, but I kind of just want to shove my foot up a Nazi's ass.

We're going to handle them in our own way, OK? I text.

Sounds good, she replies.

I give her the directions reluctantly and size up the park for anyone who looks like they might be extra white. It's a beautiful April day in Sacramento, the sun sitting high in the sky like royalty, warming the air just enough to even out the morning chill. There are some families with picnic blankets over by the duck pond. A group of people practices fencing in the distance, their silver foils flashing under the sunlight.

Just ahead is a lone guy sitting on a bench wearing a white bandanna over his face. His legs bounce up and down nervously. He's staring at his phone, so he doesn't notice me. I walk closer and feel him tensing up, so I pass and lean against a tree directly behind him. He looks up, scans the park, and hunches back down into his phone.

I think I found one, I type to my group.

We're on our way, someone says.

The guy suddenly gets up and walks toward a concrete path that leads out of the park, so I follow him, spacing myself a few steps away. He's a kid, probably in his early twenties, scrawny and nervous. He looks back and sees me following him, so he speeds up. I speed up with him, and he breaks into a run. I don't chase after him but see him get into a car up the street, so I approach. I take a picture of his license plate. He's sitting there in his car, wildly texting. A police car rolls slowly up the street, and

I head back into the park to wait for my friends and the old socialists who are probably arriving.

I sit on some bleachers, and when I see Jose and TJ walking up, I fill them in. A couple more people arrive by the duck pond, these ones more obviously fascists, a beefy man in fatigues with a close-cropped hairdo and messy beard, and a tall woman with the sides of her head shaved like a white samurai. I recognize her from her YouTube channel. She bills herself as an unbiased journalist but reports strictly from right-wing and Proud Boys rallies, clutching her pearls every time she gets an antifascist on camera. She recently filmed herself taking a Proud Boys oath at a local anti–vaccine mandate rally at the state capitol, yet she still tries to maintain a guise of objectivity.

The kid in the white bandanna walks back into the park and toward the couple by the duck pond. The three Nazis begin talking as a group of ten cops on bicycles surrounds them. The socialists show up with banners and signs and set up as close to the white nationalists as they can, about fifty feet from the cops on bikes. People in the park begin to notice the scene, and they pick up their blankets and move away. The police are having a conversation with the Nazis, and it seems like they're trying to convince them to leave. I walk over to the kid with the bandanna and say, "Hey, is this the White Lives Matter rally?"

He pulls his white bandanna over his nose. His hands are shaking. "I don't know what you're talking about."

"You're about to get real fucked up," I whisper.

"*Help!*" he yells. "Help! Police!"

The police surround him, pushing me away, and escort him toward his car. My friends surround the police, and the socialists start chanting antifascist slogans at the few white nationalists who bothered to show up.

I spot the Proud Boy journalist couple slinking away in the other direction, so I follow them. They end up under a tree, the woman pointing her phone camera at the man. They're doing a live stream. I wave for my friends to join me, but I'm unsure if they see me. I approach the couple, and they say hi.

"Were you guys just at the White Lives Matter rally?" I ask.

"We're journalists," the woman says defensively.

"Journalists? For who?"

"We're independent journalists."

"You weren't here to attend the White Lives Matter rally?"

"We not with anybody," she says. "We go to Antifa rallies, these rallies
. . ."

"Right," I say.

"That's what you need to keep clear," the man says, an angry baritone
coloring his voice. "We're not with anybody." He paces back and forth,
lips trembling as he talks.

I recently read a book that claims how we breathe—long, slow breaths
through our noses—is the most important part of human health, so I have
become intentional with how I breathe now. I take a long breath in through
my nose and a long breath out. I'm not sure if it's working.

My friends TJ and Jose find us underneath the tree, and I can tell
they're surveying the scene.

"You look nervous right now," I say to the couple.

"No, dude, because we've been approached by BLM, Antifa, and Proud
Boys," the woman says. It's her way of saying, *We're neutral, man*, leaving
out the parts about how she runs with fascist groups and damns antifascism in many of her YouTube videos with dismal viewership.

I remember now she goes by something like crazygurl on Twitch.
She's probably in her forties—too old to be a "gurl" but still has the same
sense of humor as someone who never evolved past high school. She
drinks a lot and is wasted in every one of her live streams.

"Why are you here?" the man says.

"Because you have beautiful eyes, sir," Jose says, joking.

Jose is funny and I love him. He's like a brother to me; I wish everyone knew him. He's what humans are supposed to be: unafraid, loyal,
smart, curious, hardworking, and hilarious. But people are judgmental,
especially leftists, who don't say it aloud but treat college as a spiritual
awakening rather than a means to an end.

"I understand who you are and what you are," the man says.

"At least I'm honest, right?" I say. It's all I had at the time, but when I
think back on it, I wish I'd asked his opinion on who he thought I was, like
the real me. What am I? Who am I? I'm not quite sure myself.

"Oh, I'm completely honest," he says.

"Do you like to box?" I ask.

"What the fuck is this," the man says. He reaches in his pockets. "Turn
your camera on," he says to the woman.

She nods her head. "It's on. We're live streaming."

"This is fight-starter karaoke," he says. He's bracing for something.

Instead of trying to be light on his feet, he plants himself, another sign that he's not the badass fighter he pretends to be. "Don't walk up on me," the man says. "This is not something you want to do."

I know this tension well. It often happens—the awkward emotions before a fight. "I'm not walking up on you," I say. "My hands are down."

Here's the thing: I am not an online person when it comes to antifascism. I don't start doxing campaigns. I don't call people's workplaces. I don't flyer neighborhoods. When I was younger I was full of rage, when I grew up I was full of rage, and now here I am, full of rage. I never understood how to use that rage, so I started training to fight. I practiced with people a hundred times tougher than I, who understood the slight movements, the twist of the hips that generate power, the breathing that turns fear into focus. It's the only way to channel rage into something less destructive, by turning it toward the people who wish to destroy me. These are the actions I associate with antiracism, a way to break free of the academic theorizing of liberation, to utilize the body as a means to freedom.

This tension and the formalities before the fight are all too familiar. "Do you like Mexicans?" I ask the man, who is shifting around suspiciously with his hands in his pockets.

"I love Mexicans," he says, the telltale phrase of white people who despise anyone browner than a Saltine cracker.

"But you don't like when they cross the border," Jose says.

"Show me who the true racists are," the man says, pointing wildly at Jose, who decides to lean in to the racist label.

"*Matando Güeros!* Kill whitey, homie!" Jose says, laughing. "White genocide 2021, homie!"

"This is exactly what we're talking about," the man says, missing the comedy of the statement, taking Jose's jokes as proof that he has found the holy grail of reverse racism: the Mexicans who hate white people. Trump's "bad hombres" in real life. The man jumps around in victory as if he were an old-timer panning for gold and found a gleaming nugget.

At this exact moment, I don't know what happens. I zone. Lock up. Suddenly, I'm in a barrage of fists, and I'm not sure whose fists are whose. I jump back to get a better view, and the man is covering his head, screaming. The woman is also screaming. The man jumps back, reaches in his pocket, and fumbles for a second.

The next thing I know, I see the flashing of a knife. I notice the beauty of the handle: gold, or maybe copper. It looks golden under the light, like the ancient weapon of a Greek warrior. Or like the knife of the man who robbed my house all those years ago. It looks like the same exact knife. Is this some coincidence of the universe? Is this what people feel when they believe in a higher power dictating the fate of the world? The man is lofting the blade wildly over his head, the most predictable maneuver from someone who doesn't know how to use a knife. When someone does that, it's a little gift for people who are going to use knife defense. People who don't know how to attack with knives are easier to defend against. They telegraph their movement in a cartoonish way, so the defender can anticipate their swing. But I choose to use my favorite, safest knife defense, which is to run away screaming.

"Cowards!" the man yells, waving his golden knife. "You are cowards!"

The woman is screaming now. "Help! *Help!* We're being attacked by *racists!*"

I look around to see who she's talking about until I realize she's talking about me.

"Call the cops!" the man orders.

I fast-walk past the fencers, who have stopped practicing to watch the scenario, their jaws wide open, foils hanging limp at their sides.

"Fuck you, Nazis," I say loud enough for everyone to hear, hoping that the fencers will understand that we were fighting with fascists, not actual people. Maybe they'd feel inspired to point their foils at the Nazis and lop off their heads.

I wonder what my students in prison would think—Jeremy especially, with his giant swastika tattoo covering the span of his chest. I think he'd be proud that his professor—the man who taught him to tame his wild sentences into the tight structure of a paragraph, into the beautiful house of an essay—flings his fists in the name of making the world a better place and ridding the streets of racists who are too cowardly to call themselves racists. At least Jeremy knew who he was.

I look behind me, and the bike cops are following about ten feet behind.

"What happened?" one calls behind me.

"Nothing," I say. "We're fine."

"Stop," another says.

"No thanks," I say. "We're good."

"Stop now," he commands.

I stop and turn around. Jose and TJ are by my side. The bike cops surround us.

"What happened?" says a tall cop with a goofy bike helmet sitting on his head.

"Nothing," I say.

"We just want to talk," says another cop, a short Asian man. "You're not in any trouble."

That's when I know we're going to jail. I use my phone to send out messages to every network I know:

We need jail support.

We don't say anything to the cops, even when they poke Jose about his ACAB tattoo. We just wait. And wait. A cop squats on the ground and watches the lady's live stream, trying to collect evidence. Another cop talks to a woman who saw the whole thing. Another cop takes my cell phone. A patrol car pulls up, and another cop tells us to look directly at the car so the victims can identify us. I flip the car the bird.

The cops shove Jose and me into the back of one car and TJ into another, and they take us downtown to booking. On the way there, we pass through Midtown, rows of old Victorian buildings with colorful paint jobs, the place I spent drugged out and poor in my twenties, the streets where I robbed hipsters for dollar bills and snorted cocaine in alleyways. Now I'm a college professor with a wife, a house, a car, and two beautiful children who are probably playing in the backyard on the trampoline, totally oblivious to the fact that their dad is in the back of a police SUV, a pair of ice-cold handcuffs digging mercilessly into his wrist bones.

SACRAMENTO COUNTY JAIL

The SUV pulls into the carport that leads into the guts of the Sacramento County Jail. I've been in there a few times before. A fistfight. A few for public drunkenness. Nothing too serious, except when I went to court thinking I had to deal with some tickets and the judge slapped me with an outstanding warrant. That time, the bailiff handed me a stack of clothes and a towel and escorted me to a cell, where I stayed for a couple of weeks wondering what the fuck just happened.

The cop driving us to the jail is a pudgy thirtysomething with dark brown hair styled into a razor-sharp side part, like he walked into a barber shop and asked for "The Hitler." He parks, gets out, places his palm gently on my head, and pulls me out of the SUV. Then he does the same to Jose. We go through a set of double doors, and he asks about my watch, a Garmin that I've just paid more than a thousand dollars for.

"It's a running watch," I say.

"You run a lot?" he says.

"Yeah."

"Like how much?"

"I ran a hundred miles this week," I say. "I would have ran more, but you caught me."

He doesn't laugh at my joke.

The people I organize with tell me I talk to cops too much. They're right. I shouldn't say anything, even meaningless shit. Cops are vile, and they'll use any piece of information against me to expedite my legal damnation. But I can't help it. I love talking to people. My weakness is anyone asking a question. I would be a horrible superhero.

"What are you training for?"

I'm training for the Moab 240, a 240-mile race through Utah that should take about four days to complete. The idea is to run until you're too tired to run anymore. Then you take a little trail nap, and when you wake up, you run some more. It's a challenge of endurance and mental grit. The people who finish are the ones who can hold their pain in the palms of their hands and change it into something else, like magicians of suffering.

I remember, though, that I should probably shut the fuck up. "I'm not training for anything," I say to appease my activist friends.

The cop leads us to a booking room bustling with chaotic energy. We're herded around and told to sit on various benches as we wait to have our photos taken. I can see a side conversation between the cops, speaking in hushed tones. Occasionally, one of them points at me.

A steady flow of fresh prisoners streams into the room, all with horrible trauma written on their faces. I wonder if I look sad and beaten too. It's weird, I think, that when humans do something bad, and we're caught, we're put in a cage for a certain amount of time. It's kind of funny when you think about it. Or maybe it's just sad.

Finally, a beautiful Asian cop with CSI on her uniform tells me to stand in front of a wall and take off my shirt. I can't help but notice how her boxy uniform is no match for her beauty. It's ridiculous to lust over a cop, especially one who is documenting all your tattoos so they can slap you with a gang enhancement, but goddamn if she doesn't look like a model. She uses the large camera hanging around her neck to snap photos of each of my tattoos—the one that says *LUCIFER* across my stomach, the image of Satan burning down a church on my forearm, the one of a burning cop car on my calf, the black flag on my neck, and the giant tattoo of two crossed obsidian knives with 161 and an Antifa flag under the handles. It takes a half hour to get through all my tattoos while a crowd of cops stops to gawk like they've never seen a guy with tattoos before.

After an hour, they lead Jose and me to the men's holding tank and drag TJ to the women's section. They take my Anti-Fascist Action shirt as evidence, so I only have my bomber jacket on with nothing underneath. Jose is shirtless, because they took his Brujeria's *Matando Güeros* shirt as evidence of him being a racist against white people. When we get to the holding tank, a dude looks at Jose and says, "Oh shit, you in here lookin' like Brown Jesus!" and laughter rings out in the filthy, smelly cell. That's the weird thing about jail cells: some of the best comedy is created there. Probably something to do with the bleakness of the situation—the confines, the bars, the lack of freedom—that demands light among the darkness. One thing I've learned in jail is that some of the funniest people are also some of most criminally mischievous.

A few hours later, an officer opens the door and calls out our names, handing us a slip of paper with our charges: felony conspiracy, felony robbery, battery, and a misdemeanor hate crime, the bail listed at $100,000. I can't understand how they'd give a hate crime charge to Brown people for smacking up a couple of neo-Nazis. It seems like behavior that should win a community engagement award.

I sit on the cold bench reading the sheet over again to see if I made a mistake, but all the charges are still there, so I panic a little and use the phone to call Crystal, and to my surprise, she answers. Her voice is calm. I can hear the kids in the background asking questions. A deep, sinking feeling in my heart settles into my soul. *I want to go home*, I think.

"I called Lilliana, and they're working on it," she says. "I love you."

"I love you," I say, and hang up the phone. I want to cry because I love her so much.

I wonder if Lilliana, our friend who runs an organization that bails activists and refugees out of detention, will help us. I wouldn't bail me out if I were her. The bail amount is a hundred grand, but you only need 10 percent of it to get out. But $10,000 for three of us is a shitload of cash.

I stand at the phone booth watching a buff Russian dude nodding out next to me. Jose is sitting on the bench trying to keep warm by hugging himself. All of this would be so hilarious—the soggy bread and spaghetti thrown by an agitated gangster across the tank in disgust, the piss I just took that lasted five whole minutes, Jose in the corner shirtless and shivering like a Brown Jesus caught in a snowstorm—but despite how funny this is, it's hard to laugh in such a filthy shithole.

After several hours, a bored cop hands us our bright orange jail scrubs, some towels, soap, and toothbrushes and ushers us into another room, where they say it'll be a while until we go upstairs to our cells. We all stake out spots on the benches to sleep, the heroin addicts getting the last dibs because they're so fucking slow and confused. I sprawl out and close my eyes, trying to drift off under the bright lights and sounds of various screams bouncing along the walls.

I wake up with a kink in my neck to the sound of an officer telling us that we're going upstairs. It must be around midnight. We all get up, shake off the sleep, and follow him in a line to the elevator. Every now and then someone gets yelled at for stepping in the wrong area. "Stay behind the fucking line!" the cop yells with the boredom of someone who has to repeat the same thing a thousand times a day.

A whiteboy next to me with dirty blond hair and a sun-reddened face seems to be coming off a heroin high; he's groaning and itching and holding his stomach. He looks miserable, like he's about to vomit and then die. A tattoo on his forearm reads 14/88, a symbol for the fourteen words "We must secure the existence of our people and a future for white children," with the 88 standing for "Heil Hitler." Part of me hopes he drops dead right there so I can spit on his corpse.

"Is that an Antifa tattoo?" a voice behind me calls as the elevator jerks upward.

A shiver runs through my spine. I pretend not to hear.

"Is that an Antifa tattoo," the voice says again. I look back. It's the cop, our shepherd into the prison, a goofy-ass redhead with jowls.

I raise my shoulders to indicate that I don't know what he's talking about.

"Yup," he says, showing me his phone. He shoves the phone in my face so that I can see the Wikipedia page for Antifa, a picture of the flag tattooed on my head with the description: *Symbol commonly used by Antifa depicting an anarchist flag overlaying a socialist flag, based on the logo of the German Antifa movement.*

"It *is* Antifa," he says proudly, like a fisherman who just caught a largemouth bass.

This explains the extra attention at intake, the photos, the gawking. They finally caught one.

We exit the elevator in a line and walk into the pod, where some flimsy blue mattresses are stacked in the corner. The cop tells us to grab a bed when he calls out pairs of names. The person he calls will be our cellmate. He calls most of the names until he gets to Jose, who grabs a mattress and then heads to the door to wait for his cellmate. The next person called will be Jose's celly.

The cop looks up from his list of names. "So, like, do you think *I'm* a fascist?"

"I don't know," I say. "Do you have a picture of Hitler hanging above your fireplace?"

The cop laughs and shakes his head, then calls my name.

I catch up to Jose and tell him we're cellies, and we laugh like we've just arrived at the worst summer camp in the history of the world.

It's pitch-black now, except for the lights of the construction site down below. Our cell looks over the north end of Sacramento, where unfinished high-rise buildings jut into the sky in an incomprehensible network of scaffolding, ropes, and wires. I wonder how anyone makes sense of assembling a skyscraper. The toilet paper holder in our house has been broken for months, and all I can do is stare at it, wondering if I have the skills to engineer its recovery. Construction workers don't get enough credit.

I sit on the top bunk watching Jose cleaning the cell, wiping down the metal table, sweeping the floor with a makeshift broom he crafted from a paper bag. He works as a janitor at a shopping mall, and it shows. He's very good at his job.

"Why did they put us together?" I wonder. "Do they know we got arrested together?"

"I don't know," he says, scooping up a pile of dirt into the little trash can.

"They're probably too stupid to notice," I say.

"I gotta take a shit," Jose says. "But we don't have any toilet paper."

We were supposed to take a roll of toilet paper from the pod, but we both forgot, so we ring the emergency bell for the cop. Nobody answers. Jose pounds on the door, but it's the middle of the night, and we're probably starting to annoy the other people in their cells. Jose will have to use the brown paper bag as toilet paper. He tears off a little square and takes a shit, wipes, then crumples the soiled paper into the rest of the paper bag. I have to shit now too, so I do the same thing, and our paper bag fills with shitty paper bag pieces. We roll it up and throw it in the trash. When I finally lay on my bunk, all I can smell is shit in our little grime-covered cell, shit and a trash can full of shit chunks. I pull the blanket over my head and start laughing like a little boy.

"What?" Jose says.

"We're in fucking jail," I say. "And we're covered in shit."

And we laugh uncontrollably.

In the morning, I watch the workers taking the lift up and down the side of the structure, taking a break at the top of the building to eat sandwiches from their lunch boxes, the blazing sun getting hotter by the second. I have to break my vegan diet to eat some breakfast: rubbery eggs, flavorless oatmeal, canned fruit, and a puck of sausage. It's not the worst thing I've eaten, and there's something about it I enjoy, a meal I don't have to cook myself. I don't have to do any dishes. When I'm done, I just slide the tray through the metal slot in my door, and a fat cop takes it away.

It's boring, though. The jail is on lockdown because of the pandemic, so we're left to entertain ourselves all day and night in our cell. Jose and I do a workout, some pull-ups, push-ups, and squats. We talk and fall asleep a few times until I hear "Fernandez" over the speaker in our cell.

It must be my lawyer, I think.

The door buzzes and I get out of the cell, but I don't know where to go. Jail is weird, because everyone expects you to know what to do, but it's like setting foot onto a new planet where everything is different and nothing makes sense. Add to that the fear of getting your ass beat by a cop, and you turn into a bumbling idiot.

I ask a tall skinhead sweeping up the pod what I'm supposed to do, and he tells me to get out of the pod and go up to see my lawyer. I leave the pod and see a door that says ENTER, so I try to open it. Immediately a booming voice tells me to go around the corner. I go around the corner to find a red-faced corrections officer in an office. He's unreasonably fat and out of breath when he yells at me.

"You are the stupidest motherfucker I've ever seen," he screams. The more he looks at me, the angrier he gets. I'm pretty sure he wants to tear my face off with his teeth, but he's too fat to get out of his chair and walk down the small flight of stairs from his booth to get to me.

"Why? What did I do?"

"You don't ever try to open that door," he screams, pointing to the door I tried to open, the one that says ENTER in giant block letters.

"Oh," I say. "I wasn't sure where to go."

"You want to get shot?" he yells.

"No."

"You want to get killed?"

"No."

"I should break your fucking ribs."

"I'm just trying to figure out where to find my lawyer."

"She's up there, you stupid motherfucker," he says, pointing to a row of windows up a flight of stairs.

I mean, yeah, it seems obvious when he points it out. I walk up the stairs and open a glass door and sit at the visiting window where my lawyer,

Amy, sits on the other end of the glass. She's an attorney for the National Lawyers Guild. They represent activists who get caught up in the legal system.

"Are you okay?" she asks.

"Yeah," I say. "I'm fine. I think that cop down there wants to kill me."

"They're assholes," she says, waving him off. She tells me that I'll probably be in jail for a few days as Lilliana gets the bail money together, or if the DA drops the charges, which she thinks he might. She gives me some affirming words and tells me not to worry. I can't help it, though, because I'm already worried. I don't tell her that, though. I want to seem tough. I say goodbye, get up, and go back downstairs through the large metal door into our pod. The skinhead is still there sweeping.

"How did it go?" he asks.

"Not great," I say.

"You're staying here awhile?" he asks.

"Nah," I say. "Not that. The guard said he was going to murder me."

"Oh," he says. "Yeah." He continues sweeping.

He's not doing it right. George, the owner of the apartment building who taught me how to sweep, would have disapproved and maybe even yelled at him and snatched the broom, but I don't have the courage to say anything, so I continue up the stairs to our cell, where Jose is doing pull-ups on the bottom bunk. I climb to the top bunk and watch the construction workers from the window. I imagine myself as one of them, standing on a plank seven stories up with a tool belt strapped to my waist, chugging an energy drink to stay alert enough not to plummet to my death, eyeing the clock for my lunch break. I can't tell which is worse—that life or this one. I decide life is whatever hell you make of it and curl up in my blanket.

"Fernandez," the loudspeaker buzzes, cutting my daydream in half. "Pack up. Downstairs."

Downstairs? I think. Isn't that where the violent offenders, gang members, and pedophiles go?

"What the fuck," I say to Jose.

He shrugs his shoulders. "I don't know."

GANG UNIT

The door to my new pod opens, and the cop leads me toward a cell on the first floor. I wonder who my new cellmate will be. I half think the pig is transferring me downstairs just to shack me up with a Nazi skinhead so he and his mustachioed buddies can watch the drama unfold, watch me leave the world the same way I entered it: bloody and crying. Throughout my years entering jails, both unwillingly and now willingly as a teacher, I've grown to understand one thing. For people who work in a prison, the spectacle of the incarcerated, the psychology of herding the shackled, and the gleeful breaking of our collective spirit is nothing more than a soap opera for the dumb and violent—the guards slump forward on their couches and watch the show unfold for years as they wait for their retirement date to approach. I can't blame them, I guess. Entertainment is entertainment. And who wouldn't want a fat-ass pension?

The guard points to my new bed like a bellboy showing me into the worst zero-star hotel room.

"No tip for you," I joke.

He doesn't laugh. Or smile. He simply shuts the door behind me with a traumatic *clang*.

To my surprise, the cell is empty. The hastily scribbled graffiti. The perpetually dripping faucet. The cold metal toilet. The off-white wall streaked with boogers and dried blood. It's all mine.

I shuffle in, carrying my sleeping mat on my head like a giant blue hat. The pod, much louder than the last one and still locked down from the pandemic, echoes with screams, punctuated by inmates banging on their cell windows with their fists. I set my mat on the bottom bunk and peek at my new view out of the thick, blurry windows.

The street is closer now, and it's easier to people-watch from down here;

the sidewalks are bustling with weekday workers. Across the street, a man and a woman face the jail, each with balloons that say *Happy Birthday!* The woman holds a homemade sign saying *We love you, Johnny!* and waves it at the jail with a gigantic smile plastered to her face. A woman trying to leave the state building is trapped behind the couple, because they're blocking the exit. I can see her trying to move around the couple, then saying something, but they're oblivious, waving the balloons and sign in the general direction of the jail. The woman, probably trying to go on her break, waits patiently for the couple to move. She takes out her phone and starts scrolling. I fall asleep, wondering what Johnny is in for. Hopefully, it was for something righteous, like robbing a bank or punching a cop in the face.

I wake up in the morning to an officer shoving a breakfast tray in my cell. Breakfasts are always the worst, an array of mushy tan foods, applesauce and oatmeal. I push the tray back and look outside, half expecting the couple with the balloons to still be out there trapping the worker, who'd still be doomscrolling through her phone. But they're gone, and it's still dark outside. The morning traffic won't begin for at least an hour. The city gurgles along under yellow streetlights like it's drowning at the bottom of a poorly maintained urinal. I drift back asleep for what feels like an instant and wake up again to piercing sunlight and my name sputtering over the intercom.

"*Fernandez kwaahhh.*"

I ring the emergency bell, and an annoyed voice picks up. "What."

"What did they say over the intercom?"

"Fernandez *kwah.*"

"What does that mean?"

"Stupid?" the crackled voice says.

"Maybe," I say. "What does 'Fernandez kwah' mean?"

"Fernandez *cwa.*"

I think for a minute, then ring the bell again.

"Oh, court? You're saying court?"

"Yes."

"When?"

"*Waddlebladdu.*"

"Okay, thanks," I say.

After a long flight of gray stairs, an officer points to a door at the end of the hall. "Wait until the door opens," he says. "You're next."

"Okay," I say, and continue down the bright hallway. The fluorescent lights glow so powerfully that the gauzy corridor radiates a heavenly white. Everything feels like a dream. Like a movie where I'm in purgatory.

The door opens, and a man with tight cornrows holds the door for me. I nod a quick *thanks* and enter a plexiglass box in a courtroom so drastically different from the jail that I lose my breath for a second. The dark-stained wood and white people in suits take me by surprise, and I can't stop looking around, as if I've finally made it into God's chambers, a sacred place we've only heard about in fables.

"Fernandez? Sir? Are you here?"

I immediately snap to reality and face the judge. "I am so sorry," I say.

"It's okay," the judge says. "Did you hear what I said?"

"No, I apologize," I say. "I was distracted."

"No need to apologize," he says again, his voice low and dripping with honey, a sharp contrast to the acrid bark of the guards. I can feel tears forming under my eyes. "I said I'm letting you go on OR."

"Thank you!" I say like a kid who's just gotten a PlayStation 5 for Christmas. OR is Own Recognizance, which my lawyer told me might happen. It's one of the best possibilities that at court the judge will drop the felonies, and then we'd only have the misdemeanor to contend with later down the line.

I shuffle back through the door and hold it for the next guy. I recognize him. I spent some time with him in the holding cell, a dirty white guy with long, greasy hair and blackened fingertips who kept blowing his snotty nose into his bare palms.

"How did it go?" a voice yells from a cell upstairs.

"You goin' home?" yells another voice.

"Fuck yeah!" I say. "I'm getting the fuck out of here."

"Make better choices," another voice rings, "and don't come back."

What the fuck? I think. *What is this, a self-help pod?* I'm still happy with my goddamn choice to tenderize the head of a Nazi. If I could do it a hundred more times, I would.

I take the blue mat off my bunk and shove it against the cell door so I can watch whatever's on the TV. It's a movie about a former Olympian who crashes a bomber plane and is captured by Japanese soldiers and taken to a POW camp where he's beaten mercilessly by a Japanese corporal. It's a horrible movie, but I can't stop watching it. There's nothing else to do. Jail is so dull that a propaganda film about American heroism is a perfectly entertaining option. Every now and then, the guard comes around and shines his flashlight in my eyes. I wave, but he ignores me. Someone in the cell next to mine is having a crisis, screaming at the top of his lungs. He puts a bunch of wet toilet paper over his window so the guards can't see in. A river of water flows from his cell into the pod, and a giant lake forms in front of the television. It reminds me of reading the Bible in my dad's old, cramped apartment in Boston. The flood, Genesis maybe:

> *The Lord saw how great the wickedness of the human race had become on the earth, and that every inclination of the thoughts of the human heart was only evil all the time. The Lord regretted that he had made human beings on the earth, and his heart was deeply troubled. So the Lord said, "I will wipe from the face of the earth the human race I have created—and with them the animals, the birds and the creatures that move along the ground—for I regret that I have made them." But Noah found favor in the eyes of the Lord.*

I can't for the life of me remember how that verse ends or what happens to Noah and all those animals. I bet my dad knows, wherever he might be. As the lake in the middle of the pod grows, ten guards rush in and drag a skinny old Black dude kicking and screaming out of his cell, then out of the pod. His screams fade into the distance. A trustee rolls a mop toward the cell and starts to clean up as slowly as he can.

"Fernandez *plabub*," someone says over the speaker.

I'm not sure, but I think he's telling me to pack up and get out. I pick up my blue mat, place it on my head, and wait for the *clang* of the door and for the guard on the other end to take me the fuck out of here.

CLOTHING AND FOOD FOR EVERYONE

I'm looking at this man's fingers and trying not to vomit. They're streaked brown with wet chunks of shit clumped in the crevices. The nail of his fore-finger is wedged up from the skin, and the space is filled with sandy mud.

He reaches out for a pair of socks in the sock bin.

"Oop," I say. "I'll grab it."

His hand hovers over the socks, so I quickly grab a pair and hold them in his hand until I can feel it clenching.

"Thank you," he says. "Bless you."

"You too," I say.

The woman behind him is leaning against her shopping cart, staring into the unknown.

"Next up," I say.

She snaps to and gives me a gigantic smile, showing her rotted mouth.

I've been serving the homeless in César Chávez Plaza for a couple of years. It's an aid program set up by my friend Armando, who's been out there running this volunteer operation every Sunday, rain or shine, for twelve years, serving hot meals, clothes, and toiletries to whoever is in need. Every Sunday, a line of houseless people looking for the bare necessities stretches around the block.

I hear a scuffle behind me.

A man on a bike is yelling at a woman. The woman lifts her hands over her head. In each hand is a knife. The man recoils, but he's on a bike, so he almost tips over, barely catching himself.

I run behind the woman to grab her arms, but she doesn't follow through. One of the volunteers, a friendly, overtalkative white woman, runs over to a cop cruising by and tells him what happened.

The cop approaches.

"We don't need you here," I say. "It's over."

The white woman points to the knife-wielding lady, who's already across the street making an escape.

"Stop talking to that cop, please," I say.

"She can talk to whoever she wants," says the cop, a fit man in his thirties with a blond mustache.

"Fuck you, pig," I say. "I wasn't talking to you."

"You have a nice day, sir," he says.

"Go fuck yourself, coward," I return.

"Excuse me?" he says.

It happens every time. Their facade breaks down. A challenge to their authority is one thing. A challenge to their manhood is something different. It's war.

The story goes like this: The cop prowls the streets. The cop forms a bond with the well-meaning white woman. The well-meaning white woman snitches to the cop. The cop confronts the criminal. The criminal argues their innocence and the cop calls it resisting. There is no recourse. They drag the criminal to jail with the other criminals. The criminal gets out of jail with no money in their pocket, so they slip a steak down their pants. The white woman runs to the security guard. The criminal dies in an alleyway with shit on their fingers while the white lady pats herself on the back for a job well done. Then, when confronted, she cries a river of white-lady tears hoping we all drown to death in the current. I'm not falling for it this time.

Everything calms down, and we start the line again, person after person, until all the people have been served. When we're done packing up, I run home, a six-mile trek along the river levee. I turn the corner and pass one of the men who took some hygiene and socks.

"Going back home after your good deed?" he asks, grinning.

"Ah, man," I say.

I want to stop running and tell him my story, how I barely escaped, how I keep fucking up, how it's only a matter of time until I'm on the other side of the table of toiletries and socks, but I don't say anything. I run a little faster until I can see the river that acts as a border of the city, rich people floating by the riverbank dotted with flimsy tents.

MY STEPDAD CAN'T TAKE IT ANYMORE

My stepdad picks out a table for two at his favorite coffee place, a hip little café where the baristas have tattoos and freakishly good posture. A regular cup of coffee costs $4.60.

Maybe it's that I haven't sat face-to-face with my stepdad in years, but I don't remember him being this old, his face sectioned off by deep wrinkles. He's thin and pale, and he looks weak. Old pictures show him with his medical school friends on the basketball court, shirtless with muscles and long hair. I always saw him as a basketball player. A man's man. When I was a kid in Brookline, I thought he was the strongest man on earth.

I could never get a read on him. I still can't. Sometimes he's an intense man, his face fixed with an underpinning of anger, as if he's carrying around the frustration of a thousand men—which makes sense, considering he's been a psychiatrist for most of his life. But today I know my stepdad as a mostly sweet and joyful man, the man I never gave a fair chance, one of my greatest regrets in the world. How different things would've been if I'd followed even one of his directions. I may have finished high school, or at least stayed out of jail. But he wasn't my real dad, the psychotic alcoholic, and nobody could ever match up to him.

I can tell my stepdad is going to say something I don't like. He wouldn't have met me for coffee otherwise.

"You know, you got where you are in life because of your ability to make human connections," he says. "Not because you tell people to fuck off."

He's right. Telling people to fuck off is extremely euphoric, with a long-lasting pleasure effect, like snorting a line of speed and then smoking a bowl of speed to wash it down. It's gratifying but probably not good for you or others.

My stepdad doesn't understand any of this, of course. He's an Irish man who grew up in the suburbs of Philadelphia in a large family with a successful mom, a successful dad, two successful brothers, and three successful sisters. Their parents expected excellence, and that's what they got.

My stepdad expected excellence, and he got me.

When I was growing up, he was so focused on my grades that I got nervous and failed almost every class I ever took. In the third grade, I had this teacher with curly white hair and a round face with little black hairs coming out of her chin. It was too much for me. I'd always been sensitive to aesthetics and couldn't learn like that. Her name was Mrs. Concannon, and she meant well. We took a test called the Mad Minute where she'd put a sheet of math problems in front of us and then start a timer for a minute, and we were to solve as many problems as possible. Looking back, it probably wasn't a big deal. Nobody seemed to give a shit about that test but me. Whenever she started the timer, I'd have a mini heart attack. I couldn't take it. I'd sit with my hand hovering over the paper, my body stuck in cardiac arrest. Because of my poor performance on that test, she put me in the math class for slow kids.

On my first day of slow-kid class, I was so mad that I sharpened my pencil extra hard until the point was as fine as I could make it. I told myself that the first person to make fun of me would get that deadly-sharp pencil plunged into a critical area of their body.

The class was down the hall from the regular classroom in a little converted broom closet. When it was time to go, I grabbed my extra-sharp pencil and ran toward the room, thinking, *I don't belong with all these slow kids.*

When I reached for the door and tried to twist the handle, my pencil lodged itself into the palm of my hand so hard that a quarter of it disappeared into my flesh, like I'd been crucified. I pulled the pencil out and blood squirted all over the wall and carpet. My teacher rushed me to the nurse, who patched me up and called my mom to tell her what had happened. To this day, I have a circular mark, like a little tattoo, to remind me of my place among the slow kids.

These are the wires that make the bomb—the skipping school to watch pornos with my friends and drink their dads' alcohol, the fights, the chasing of girls and fucking them in weird broom closets full of spiders, the hatred of school, the hatred of authority, the hatred of cops, the hatred of everything, all of it, third grade, Mrs. Concannon, the Mad Minute, the slow-kid class, my bloody hand of shame—a single event isn't enough to do anything. But there they are, colorful wires, fuses touching charges and placed in a deadly configuration, stuffed into a tiny box with an unruly timer.

That's when things explode.

I listen to my stepdad talk as I run my forefinger over the lead mark in my hand. I try to figure out how many years I've had it, but I can't, because I'm still bad at math.

"I mean, I don't hate all cops," I say sheepishly, lying.

"You have a poster of a police officer as a pig hanging in your living room," he says.

He's right again. They were giving them out for free at Hasta Muerte Coffee in Oakland, a little co-op run by anarchists who refuse to serve cops. It's a beautiful print that we hung right over the couch.

He's worried my kids will one day run around damning the police to hell, which they already do.

"Not all police are bad," he says, a sentiment I've heard from liberals and Republicans and many of my colleagues, all of whom have told me to tone it down in various forms throughout the years.

"But they work for a bad institution," I say. "It's not about the individual cops. I'm sure there are some nice people. But as long as the institution remains, I will be against it."

That kind of thing scares him. He likes to believe that the establishment is not necessarily right, but *safe*. I get it. His family had success. That success came from respecting the confines of choices that wouldn't put anyone in any danger. His family respects authority, an authority that in return grants them a key to unlock a special door where there's a room with another set of doors. Show more respect, and you get another key. For each set of rooms, there's another set of doors. If you choose all the right ones, the ones that are clearly marked with the green sign that says ENTER—like listening to your teachers, blind respect to authority, staying away from drugs—then you get to retire with a fortune at a decent age.

I tried to bypass all that shit by climbing headfirst into the sewer. Turns out, there's a system under there too. You can traverse the city just the same as the people who stay above ground, walking through all the right doors. But it's dark in the sewer system. And gnarly. There's rats and other creatures. And when you reach the end, you're a little fucked up. And smelly.

His eyes are getting red. He's crying. "Ezra is such a nice kid," he says, wiping a tear from his cheek.

I think my son is a genius, but everyone is scared to say it, because geniuses are just as fucked up as fuckups. Or at least I think he's a genius until he does some weird shit like falling out of his chair for no reason in the middle of dinner, bringing his plate of food with him to the floor. That's when I breathe a sigh of relief that he's as simple as his dad.

But I can see where this is going.

My stepdad thinks I'm going to fuck up my kids.

He thinks he fucked up his kids. We're all crazy. Addicted to drugs. Can't keep jobs. He thought I was going to get fired because everyone at my work thinks I'm a left-wing terrorist.

My stepdad looks up at the ceiling like he's searching for an answer in the rafters. I want to tell him to stop looking up there. To look at me. The answer to our fate is in our history. It's all there. But that is probably too painful to think about, the way I am constructed, the way each wire reaches back into our family history—my father the schizo, my mother the flower child, my dead sister, the drugs, the drinking—and the way all the wires lead to the same timer, the same trigger, the same fate.

He would rather let me go than enable my bad decisions. He'd rather live with a hole in his heart than stand there while I flip my own switch, both of us holding our breath, waiting for the explosion.

THERE'S A BRILLIANT LIGHT AFTER ALL THIS

The campus parking lot is nearly empty, multimillion-dollar homes resting on the skyline like judgmental gods snickering at the simple community college folk limping toward the idea of a meager existence. The pandemic ripped through the education system, leaving a ghost town in its wake. Nobody wants to waste money on school anymore. Nobody wants to waste time on work. It's almost as if COVID tore off our decorative gowns and left us in the nude. We're all covering our bodies, wondering if everyone else feels as awkward as we do, with our private parts slapping against our bodies in the wind.

If the modern campus with a sleek, angular design and drought-resistant landscaping was sad before, its current iteration—a barren and overgrown manifestation of our two-year isolated existence—is its suicidal cousin. A sense of dread sets in to my lungs and stomach as I walk across the lot toward the stairs that lead to my office. I wonder if my posters are still on the door or if a conservative student or the janitor who always looks at me sideways took a moment to rip them down in a fit of patriotic rage.

To my surprise, almost everything is still attached to my door—the large *Fighting Fascism Is Your Social Duty* poster, the *Antifascism Is Not a Crime* sticker, the infographic with the number to call if the police show up at your doorstep—with only a few blank spots where someone must have seized a golden opportunity to peel away a sticker or two. I don't even remember what was in the empty spots, but I have hundreds more stickers, each more offensive than the next to the Republican sensibility. I try my key a few times, but it doesn't budge. They must've changed the locks. I head to the business office to get a new key and see the conservative janitor. He used to stand outside my office door, reading my posters aloud in an angry tone. I sometimes thought I should open the door as fast as I could to scare the shit out of him, but I never did. I let him stand there, reading my posters to himself: "What to do when the police show up at your doorstep? *Pshht.*" Maybe he'd learn something. Probably not. Who gives a shit, really. But there he is, a gigantic man well over six feet, walking excitedly toward me as if I'm a long-lost relative.

"They'll be right with you!" he says.

"Thank you," I say. "How are you?"

"Eh, it's slow around here," he says.

Either he's forgotten who I am or doesn't care. Either way, I like this new relationship we have. Everything is different now. After George Floyd was suffocated by cops and the world erupted into riots that filled the streets with the flames of revolution, everything changed. Even our school went woke. The allegiance to the institution was replaced with an allegiance to "antiracism." The book circles about self-care and institutional effectiveness became antiracist book circles. The clip art of cartoon pens and books turned to email signatures calling for antiracist pedagogy. In official documents coming from our district, messages from higher-ups now suggest that faculty participate in "antiracist action" and "decolonization." What is survival for some is a fashion for them, a trend that will one day go away. Now that everything is upside down, I am right side up. The administrators who tried to fire me for being part of a group called Anti-Racist Action never apologized for accusing me of terrorism. They nod and smile politely in the hallways as if nothing happened, unaware that they're burning themselves alive in the flames of hypocrisy. I wonder if they think to themselves, *It's just business, just the nature of the institution.* I wonder if they know that's why we'll do our best to tear it all down and replace it with something better, something for actual people rather than just another conveyor belt full of bootlicking opportunists feeding the greedy mouth of the corporate world.

"We got new locks," the janitor says, as if he's trying to comfort me somehow, as if he's saying, *Don't worry, you still work here.* He points me to a room where I can pick up a new key.

I get my new office key and wander through the empty buildings, now and then passing a student with their head buried in their phone. There's a food truck in the quad with a few students milling around, but I decide to hit the vending machine for chips and a soda, but, to my surprise, it's out of service. The entire cafeteria is empty; what was once a bustling hub for student activity is now a sea of empty chairs and tables shining under the buzzing lights. It's like a postapocalyptic movie. I look around the room for something sharp to steal, but there's nothing I could use to bludgeon a zombie back to death.

I get to my classroom, and my students are lingering outside. It's the first time I've seen them in person, other than their shitty little profile pictures on our digital roster.

"Hey, y'all," I say, and open the door. They follow me sheepishly inside.

The classroom is just as I remember it after two years—drab tan walls with a brown carpet and unforgiving fluorescent lights where not a single blemish escapes scrutiny. I am visibly older now, the laugh lines deep enough to qualify as wrinkles. My hair, dyed half yellow, is scraggly but hidden under a dad hat. None of it seems to matter anymore. There's a sadness in my students' eyes. Probably in mine too.

This is where I'm supposed to be, I think to myself. A familiar warmth fills my body.

My parents haven't talked to me in two months. It was the argument stemming from my son's blue hair. My mom couldn't get over it. She met us one day to look at the ducks in the pond and had anger written all over her face like a manifesto before a mass murderer wires up a van with explosives. She wouldn't say anything, so my stepdad did all the talking. The conversation was forgettable. About the ducks. About the weather. My kids were annoyed and tired. They wanted to go home. Luna started crying and kicking. We called it early and went home.

The next day, I texted my stepdad, *Mom didn't look good. Is she OK?*

He replied, *She's fine, physically, but we should meet.*

We met up the day after that at the coffee shop, where my stepdad looked tense and concerned. I can still hear his voice as he looked up at the rafters. "You're setting him up for disaster," he said, taking a sip of his coffee from a large white mug.

They think his blue hair symbolizes hatred, a *fuck you* to society, a black flag in the eternal war of social mores and good manners. But it's none of that. We want our children to grow up in a world of expression and freedom, where their moods can dictate their style and their style can dictate how they choose to move throughout the world, hopefully with curiosity, kindness, love, and maybe even some well-placed rage. Their emotions will be theirs, and they won't be controlled, only nurtured and guided by parents who have made their fair share of mistakes but want a good world full of good people.

"Did you even notice if your kids said hello and goodbye to their grandparents?"

He was talking about the duck pond, when my mother wore the face of a madwoman and my stepdad's tension cut through the gloomy sky like a guillotine.

"Not really," I say. I don't notice these things. It's one of my weaknesses.

"You see?" he says, as if he's caught me once and for all in a final, unforgivable act of horrible parenting.

My kids, Ezra and Luna, children of energy and light and pure chaos, have emerged from a two-year pandemic just as lovely as they entered it, full of curiosity and wonder. We roll around the floor together, laughing until our throats are sore. We read under night-lights. We purr with our cats until we're all asleep under the glow of the television.

To my parents, I am a failure. A bad person. A loser. A madman. A savage. They watch my children as the prison guard watches the inmates with a cynical frown, knowing they're destined for damnation.

When I look at my students, I am filled with unbelievable joy. They're the reason I started teaching, not the emails from administrators or the dead homework discussion boards of the pandemic. We talk like old friends about our past two years and tell stories of our adventures. A student is talking about her grandma and holding back tears. We're here with each other like nothing ever happened.

"Should we go to the food truck?" I say.

"Can we?" a student asks.

"Yeah, why wouldn't we be able to?"

"I don't know," the student says. "Aren't we supposed to be working?"

"Yeah," I say. "But I didn't make a lesson plan."

They laugh, but it's not a joke. I didn't prepare for this day. I wanted to show up and see what happened. What if it was horrible? What if they were all boring? What if I had a panic attack? What if I ran to my car, skidded away, and never came back? Sometimes it's best to take things as they come with no preparation. Let the world hit you in the face if it needs to.

We leave the classroom and spread into the empty campus, filling it with life.

The student is right, I think. We are in school, and we should be working. But maybe this is the work. We're doing what this new world requires of us. First, we build the community. Find the people who have the skills.

The mass of people. To lift the heavy machinery. To untangle the mess of wires. To help you calm down. To help you focus on your breathing. To disassemble the technology. To pick the right wire. To tell you that it's going to be okay. To hand you the scissors. To craft a story to distract you as you snip the first wire, even if the story is not true, even if it's only to get you from one wire to the next. To wait for the explosion. To realize that all these wires, the ones others placed and the ones we placed ourselves, can be easily pulled out and redirected. To exhale a collective sigh of relief when there isn't an explosion, only a brilliant light that overtakes everything that we've ever known.

ABOUT THE AUTHOR

Josh Fernandez is an antiracist organizer, a father, a runner, a fighter, an English professor, and a writer whose stories have appeared in *Spin*, the *Sacramento Bee*, the *Hard Times*, and several alternative news weeklies. He lives in Sacramento, California.

ABOUT PM PRESS

PM Press is an independent, radical publisher of books and media to educate, entertain, and inspire. Founded in 2007 by a small group of people with decades of publishing, media, and organizing experience, PM Press amplifies the voices of radical authors, artists, and activists. Our aim is to deliver bold political ideas and vital stories to people from all walks of life and arm the dreamers to demand the impossible. We have sold millions of copies of our books, most often one at a time, face to face. We're old enough to know what we're doing and young enough to know what's at stake. Join us to create a better world.

PM Press
PO Box 23912
Oakland, CA 94623
www.pmpress.org

PM Press in Europe
europe@pmpress.org
www.pmpress.org.uk

FRIENDS OF PM PRESS

These are indisputably momentous times—the financial system is melting down globally and the Empire is stumbling. Now more than ever there is a vital need for radical ideas.

In the many years since its founding—and on a mere shoestring—PM Press has risen to the formidable challenge of publishing and distributing knowledge and entertainment for the struggles ahead. With hundreds of releases to date, we have published an impressive and stimulating array of literature, art, music, politics, and culture. Using every available medium, we've succeeded in connecting those hungry for ideas and information to those putting them into practice.

Friends of PM allows you to directly help impact, amplify, and revitalize the discourse and actions of radical writers, filmmakers, and artists. It provides us with a stable foundation from which we can build upon our early successes and provides a much-needed subsidy for the materials that can't necessarily pay their own way. You can help make that happen—and receive every new title automatically delivered to your door once a month—by joining as a Friend of PM Press. And, we'll throw in a free T-shirt when you sign up.

Here are your options:

- **$30 a month** Get all books and pamphlets plus a 50% discount on all webstore purchases

- **$40 a month** Get all PM Press releases (including CDs and DVDs) plus a 50% discount on all webstore purchases

- **$100 a month** Superstar—Everything plus PM merchandise, free downloads, and a 50% discount on all webstore purchases

For those who can't afford $30 or more a month, we have **Sustainer Rates** at $15, $10, and $5. Sustainers get a free PM Press T-shirt and a 50% discount on all purchases from our website.

Your Visa or Mastercard will be billed once a month, until you tell us to stop. Or until our efforts succeed in bringing the revolution around. Or the financial meltdown of Capital makes plastic redundant. Whichever comes first.

We Go Where They Go: The Story of Anti-Racist Action

Shannon Clay, Lady, Kristin Schwartz, and Michael Staudenmaier with a Foreword by Gord Hill

ISBN: 978-1-62963-972-7 (paperback)
       978-1-62963-977-2 (hardcover)
$24.95/$59.95   320 pages

What does it mean to risk all for your beliefs? How do you fight an enemy in your midst? *We Go Where They Go* recounts the thrilling story of a massive forgotten youth movement that set the stage for today's antifascist organizing in North America. When skinheads and punks in the late 1980s found their communities invaded by white supremacists and neo-nazis, they fought back. Influenced by anarchism, feminism, Black liberation, and Indigenous sovereignty, they created Anti-Racist Action. At ARA's height in the 1990s, thousands of dedicated activists in hundreds of chapters joined the fights—political and sometimes physical—against nazis, the Ku Klux Klan, anti-abortion fundamentalists, and racist police. Before media pundits, cynical politicians, and your uncle discovered "antifa," Anti-Racist Action was bringing it to the streets.

Based on extensive interviews with dozens of ARA participants, *We Go Where They Go* tells ARA's story from within, giving voice to those who risked their safety in their own defense and in solidarity with others. In reproducing the posters, zines, propaganda, and photos of the movement itself, this essential work of radical history illustrates how cultural scenes can become powerful forces for change. Here at last is the story of an organic yet highly organized movement, exploring both its triumphs and failures, and offering valuable lessons for today's generation of activists and rabble-rousers. *We Go Where They Go* is a page-turning history of grassroots anti-racism. More than just inspiration, it's a roadmap.

"I was a big supporter and it was an honor to work with the Anti-Racist Action movement. Their unapologetic and uncompromising opposition to racism and fascism in the streets, in the government, and in the mosh pit continues to be inspiring to this day."
—Tom Morello

"Antifa became a household word with Trump attempting and failing to designate it a domestic terrorist group, but Antifa's roots date back to the late 1980s when little attention was being paid to violent fascist groups that were flourishing under Reaganism, and Anti-Racist Action (ARA) was singular and effective in its brilliant offensive. This book tells the story of ARA in breathtaking prose accompanied by stunning photographs and images."
—Roxanne Dunbar-Ortiz, author of *Loaded: A Disarming History of the Second Amendment*

It Did Happen Here: An Antifascist People's History

Edited by Moe Bowstern, Mic Crenshaw, Alec Dunn, Celina Flores, Julie Perini, and Erin Yanke

ISBN: 978-1-62963-351-0
$21.95   304 pages

Portland, Oregon, 1988: the brutal murder of Ethiopian immigrant Mulugeta Seraw by racist skinheads shocked the city. In response disparate groups quickly came together to organize against white nationalist violence and right-wing organizing throughout the Rose City and the Pacific Northwest.

It Did Happen Here compiles interviews with dozens of people who worked together during the waning decades of the twentieth century to reveal an inspiring collaboration between groups of immigrants, civil rights activists, militant youth, and queer organizers. This oral history focuses on participants in three core groups: the Portland chapters of Anti-Racist Action and Skinheads Against Racial Prejudice, and the Coalition for Human Dignity.

Using a diversity of tactics—from out-and-out brawls on the streets and at punk shows, to behind-the-scenes intelligence gathering—brave antiracists unified on their home ground over and over, directly attacking right-wing fascists and exposing white nationalist organizations and neo-nazi skinheads. Embattled by police and unsupported by the city, these citizen activists eventually drove the boneheads out of the music scene and off the streets of Portland. This book shares their stories about what worked, what didn't, and ideas on how to continue the fight.

"By the time I moved my queer little family to Portland at the turn of the millennium, the city had a reputation as a homo-friendly bastion of progressive politics, so we were somewhat taken aback when my daughter's racially diverse sports team was met with a burning cross at a suburban game. So much progress had been made yet, at times, it felt like the past hadn't gone anywhere. If only we'd had It Did Happen Here. This documentary project tells the forgotten history of Portland's roots as a haven for white supremacists and recounts the ways anti-racists formed coalitions across subcultures to protect the vulnerable and fight the good fight against nazi boneheads and the bigoted right. Through the voices of lived experience, It Did Happen Here illuminates community dynamics and lays out ideas and inspiration for long-term and nonpolice solutions to poverty and hatred."
—Ariel Gore, author of *We Were Witches*

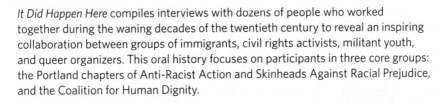

Insurgent Supremacists:
The U.S. Far Right's Challenge to
State and Empire

Matthew N. Lyons

ISBN: 978-162-963-511-8
$24.95   384 pages

A major study of movements that strive to overthrow the U.S. government, that often claim to be anti-imperialist and sometimes even anti-capitalist yet also consciously promote inequality, hierarchy, and domination, generally along explicitly racist, sexist, and homophobic lines. Revolutionaries of the far right: insurgent supremacists.

In this book, Matthew N. Lyons takes readers on a tour of neonazis and Christian theocrats, by way of the patriot movement, the LaRouchites, and the alt-right. Supplementing this, thematic sections explore specific dimensions of far-right politics, regarding gender, decentralism, and anti-imperialism.

Intervening directly in debates within left and antifascist movements, Lyons examines both the widespread use and abuse of the term "fascism," and the relationship between federal security forces and the paramilitary right. His final chapter offers a preliminary analysis of the Trump presidential administration relationship with far-right politics and the organized far right's shifting responses to it.

Both for its analysis and as a guide to our opponents, *Insurgent Supremacists* promises to be a powerful tool in organizing to resist the forces at the cutting edge of reaction today.

"Drawing on deep expertise and years of experience tracking the shifting constellations of the insurrectionist right, Matthew Lyons guides readers through the history, ideology, and agendas of these seemingly obscure but increasingly powerful political forces in America. If you want to understand them, you need to read this book."
—Mark Rupert, author of *Ideologies of Globalization: Contending Visions of a New World Order*

"A brilliant exploration of the U.S. far right today and its many different strains. In wonderfully clearheaded, deeply researched prose, Matthew N. Lyons provides a cogent and innovative analysis of far-right movements, using historical examination and his own contemporary reporting to expose surprising truths about the far right's base, motivations, and ambivalent relationship to capitalism. A vital resource for anyone who wants to fight the alt-right and other 'insurgent supremacists' in our midst."
—Donna Minkowitz, author of *Ferocious Romance: What My Encounters with the Right Taught Me about Sex, God, and Fury*

The Spitboy Rule: Tales of a Xicana in a Female Punk Band

Michelle Cruz Gonzales with a Foreword by Martín Sorrondeguy and Preface by Mimi Thi Nguyen

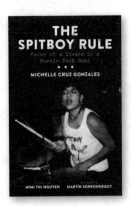

ISBN: 978-1-62963-140-0
$15.95   160 pages

Michelle Cruz Gonzales played drums and wrote lyrics in the influential 1990s female hardcore band Spitboy, and now she's written a book—a punk rock herstory. Though not a riot grrl band, Spitboy blazed trails for women musicians in the San Francisco Bay Area and beyond, but it wasn't easy. Misogyny, sexism, abusive fans, class and color blindness, and all-out racism were foes, especially for Gonzales, a Xicana and the only person of color in the band.

Unlike touring rock bands before them, the unapologetically feminist Spitboy preferred Scrabble games between shows rather than sex and drugs, and they were not the angry manhaters that many expected them to be. Serious about women's issues and being the band that they themselves wanted to hear, a band that rocked as hard as men but sounded like women, Spitboy released several records and toured internationally. The memoir details these travels while chronicling Spitboy's successes and failures, and for Gonzales, discovering her own identity along the way.

Fully illustrated with rare photos and flyers from the punk rock underground, this fast-paced, first-person recollection is populated by scenesters and musical allies from the time including Econochrist, Paxston Quiggly, Neurosis, Los Crudos, Aaron Cometbus, Pete the Roadie, Green Day, Fugazi, and Kamala and the Karnivores.

"The Spitboy Rule *is a compelling and insightful journey into the world of '90s punk as seen through the eyes of a Xicana drummer who goes by the nickname Todd. Todd stirs the pot by insisting that she plays hardcore punk, not Riot Grrrl music, and inviting males to share the dance floor with women in a respectful way. This drummer never misses a beat. Read it!"*
—Alice Bag, singer for the Bags, author of *Violence Girl: East L.A. Rage to Hollywood Stage, a Chicana Punk Story*

"*Incisive and inspiring, Michelle Cruz Gonzales's* The Spitboy Rule *brings the '90s punk world to life with equal parts heart and realism. Her story becomes a voyage of self-discovery, and Gonzales is the perfect guide—as she writes in rapidfire drum beats about epic road tours, female camaraderie, sexist fans, and getting accused of appropriating her own culture.*"
—Ariel Gore, *Hip Mama*

No Harmless Power: The Life and Times of the Ukrainian Anarchist Nestor Makhno

Charlie Allison
Illustrated by Kevin Matthews and
N.O. Bonzo

ISBN: 978-1-62963-471-5
$21.95   256 pages

Lively, incendiary, and inspiring, *No Harmless Power*
follows the life of Nestor Makhno, who organized a seven-million-strong anarchist polity during the Russian Civil War and developed Platformist anarchism during his exile in Paris as well as advising other anarchists like Durruti on tactics and propaganda. Both timely and timeless, this biography reveals Makhno's rapidly changing world and his place in it. He moved swiftly from peasant youth to prisoner to revolutionary anarchist leader, narrowly escaping Bolshevik Ukraine for Paris. This book also chronicles the friends and enemies he made along the way: Lenin, Trotsky, Kropotkin, Alexander Berkman, Emma Goldman, Ida Mett, and others.

No Harmless Power is the first text to fully delve into Makhno's sympathy for the downtrodden, the trap of personal heroism, his improbable victories, unlikely friendships, and his alarming lack of gun safety in meetings. Makhno and the movement he began are seldom mentioned in most mainstream histories— Western or Russian—mostly on the grounds that acknowledging anarchist polities calls into question the inevitability and desirability of the nation-state and unjust hierarchies.

With illustrations by N.O. Bonzo and Kevin Matthews, this is a fresh, humorous, and necessary look at an under examined corner of history as well as a deep exploration of the meaning—and value, if any—of heroism as history.

"A biography that reads like a great adventure story, this tale of freedom-fighting and myth-making in early-twentieth-century Eastern Europe is as entertaining as it is necessary."
—Stephanie Feldman, author of *Angel of Losses* and *Saturnalia*

"Charles Allison has turned his talents to a topic that was colorful and interesting even before recent global events gave Ukraine fresh relevance. Allison's accessible and humorous writing saturates the book with passages that are chock-full of the sort of informational nuggets that readers will enjoy passing along to friends and family."
—Matt Hongoltz-Hetling, author of *A Libertarian Walks into a Bear: The Utopian Plot to Liberate an American Town (and Some Bears)*

Fighting Times: Organizing on the Front Lines of the Class War

Jon Melrod

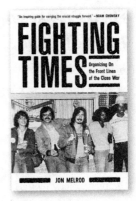

ISBN: 978-1-62963-965-9
$24.95 320 pages

Deeply personal, astutely political, *Fighting Times: Organizing on the Front Lines of the Class War* recounts the thirteen-year journey of Jon Melrod to harness working-class militancy and jump start a revolution on the shop floor of American Motors. Melrod faces termination, dodges the FBI, outwits collaborators in the UAW, and becomes a central figure in a lawsuit against the rank-and-file newsletter *Fighting Times*, as he strives to build a class-conscious workers' movement from the bottom up.

A radical to the core, Melrod was a key part of campus insurrection at the University of Wisconsin, Madison. He left campus for the factory in 1972, hired along with hundreds of youthful job seekers onto the mind-numbing assembly line. *Fighting Times* paints a portrait of these rebellious and alienated young hires, many of whom were Black Vietnam vets.

Containing dozens of archival photographs, *Fighting Times* captures the journey of a militant antiracist revolutionary who rose to the highest elected ranks of his UAW local without compromising his politics or his dedication to building a class-conscious workers' movement. The book will arm and inspire a new generation of labor organizers with the skills and attitude to challenge the odds and fight the egregious abuses of the exploitative capitalist system.

"An eloquent voice from the frontlines of the hard, bitter, exhilarating struggles for freedom and justice that have made the world a better place, and an inspiring guide for carrying the crucial struggle forward."
—Noam Chomsky

"To organize communities and workers, you have to listen to them. Jon Melrod's many stories show he did just that—and had a blast, too, as they turned their creativity and solidarity against the boss. Yes, there's a lot to be learned from Melrod's tales, but they're also a joy to read."
—Ken Paff, cofounder of Teamsters for a Democratic Union

"In Fighting Times, *Jon Melrod shares his personal experiences in historical context about his human rights battles against social injustices. Jon was an early supporter of the Black Panther Party and the struggle for black liberation. As you will read, he became a target of the FBI after landing on the Bureau's radar when he called the Chicago office to coordinate sales of* The Black Panther *community newspaper in Madison, WI. A must-read for all freedom-loving peoples."*
—Emory Douglas, social justice artist and minister of culture for the Black Panther Party, 1967–1981

Up a Creek, with a Paddle: Tales of Canoeing and Life

James W. Loewen

ISBN: 978-1-62963-827-0
$15.95   176 pages

Up a Creek, with a Paddle is an intimate and often humorous memoir by the author of *Lies My Teacher Told Me*, James W. Loewen, who holds the distinction of being the best-selling living sociologist today. Rivers are good metaphors for life, and paddling for living. In this little book, Loewen skillfully makes these connections without sermonizing, resulting in nuggets of wisdom about how to live, how to act meaningfully, and perhaps how to die. Loewen also returns to his life's work and gently addresses the origins of racism and inequality, the theory of history, confronting institutional dishonesty, but mostly, as in his life, he finds rueful humor in every canoeing fiasco—and he has had many!

Amid the laughter and often self-deprecating humility, Loewen weaves together deep and important sociological ideas that penetrate the core of our social world, revealing why and how the world is marred by injustice and inequality.

"The incomparable Jim Loewen has written a memoir like no other. I laughed at his delightful stories of canoeing fiascos that repeatedly answered his question, 'What could possibly go wrong?' In quieter intervals, I learned from his reflections on history, ethics, and race relations. About death he is funny—'I'm not dead yet but I'm working on it'—but unflinching. His spirit will live on, though, in the ways that history is told. This book's energy can sustain and inspire those who follow."
—Peggy McIntosh, author of *White Privilege: Unpacking the Invisible Knapsack*

"He is the high school history teacher we all should have had."
—Carol Kammen, author of *On Doing Local History*

"Loewen is a one-man historical truth squad. . . . He has written a devastating portrait of how American history is commemorated."
—*The Nation*

"Loewen himself is forever young at heart: energetic, curious, skeptical, irreverent, and yet deeply idealistic."
—James Goodman, professor of history at Rutgers University, Newark, and Pulitzer Prize finalist

"I'm willing to declare myself a fan of James W. Loewen. It may be difficult to uncover historical truth in some cases, but I applaud Loewen for prioritizing it and showing the importance of historical truth for all of us."
—Shomeret: The Masked Reviewer

Surviving the Future: Abolitionist Queer Strategies

Edited by Scott Branson, Raven Hudson, and Bry Reed with a Foreword by Mimi Thi Nguyen

ISBN: 978-1-62963-971-0
$22.95 328 pages

Abolish the Police
Abolish Prisons
Abolish the State
Abolish Identity
Abolish the Family
Abolish Racial Capitalism
Abolish Settler Colonialism
Abolish Society

Surviving the Future

Abolitionist Queer Strategies

Edited by Scott Branson, Raven Hudson, and Bry Reed
Foreword by Mimi Thi Nguyen

Surviving the Future is a collection of the most current ideas in radical queer movement work and revolutionary queer theory. Beset by a new pandemic, fanning the flames of global uprising, these queers cast off progressive narratives of liberal hope while building mutual networks of rebellion and care. These essays propose a militant strategy of queer survival in an ever-precarious future. Starting from a position of abolition—of prisons, police, the State, identity, and racist cisheteronormative society—this collection refuses the bribes of inclusion in a system built on our expendability. Though the mainstream media saturates us with the boring norms of queer representation (with a recent focus on trans visibility), the writers in this book ditch false hope to imagine collective visions of liberation that tell different stories, build alternate worlds, and refuse the legacies of racial capitalism, anti-Blackness, and settler colonialism. The work curated in this book spans Black queer life in the time of COVID-19 and uprising, assimilation and pinkwashing settler colonial projects, subversive and deviant forms of representation, building anarchist trans/queer infrastructures, and more. Contributors include Che Gossett, Yasmin Nair, Mattilda Bernstein Sycamore, Adrian Shanker, Kitty Stryker, Toshio Meronek, and more.

"*Surviving the Future is a testament that otherwise worlds are not only possible, our people are making them right now—and they are queering how we get there through organizing and intellectual work. Now is the perfect time to interrogate how we are with each other and the land we inhabit. This collection gives us ample room to do just that in a moment of mass uprisings led by everyday people demanding safety without policing, prisons and other forms of punishment.*"
—Charlene A. Carruthers, author of *Unapologetic: A Black, Queer, and Feminist Mandate for Radical Movements*

"*Surviving the Future is not an anthology that simply includes queer and trans minorities in mix of existing abolitionist thought. Rather, it is a transformative collection of queer/trans methods for living an abolitionist life. Anyone who dreams of dismantling the prison-industrial complex, policing, borders and the surveillance state should read this book. Frankly, everybody who doesn't share that dream should read it, too, and maybe they'll start dreaming differently.*"
—Susan Stryker, author of *Transgender History: The Roots of Today's Revolution*

Teaching Resistance: Radicals, Revolutionaries, and Cultural Subversives in the Classroom

Edited by John Mink

ISBN: 978-1-62963-709-9
$24.95   416 pages

Teaching Resistance is a collection of the voices of activist educators from around the world who engage inside and outside the classroom from pre-kindergarten to university and emphasize teaching radical practice from the field. Written in accessible language, this book is for anyone who wants to explore new ways to subvert educational systems and institutions, collectively transform educational spaces, and empower students and other teachers to fight for genuine change. Topics include community self-defense, Black Lives Matter and critical race theory, intersections between punk/DIY subculture and teaching, ESL, anarchist education, Palestinian resistance, trauma, working-class education, prison teaching, the resurgence of (and resistance to) the Far Right, special education, antifascist pedagogies, and more.

Edited by social studies teacher, author, and punk musician John Mink, the book features expanded entries from the monthly column in the politically insurgent punk magazine *Maximum Rocknroll*, plus new works and extensive interviews with subversive educators. Contributing teachers include Michelle Cruz Gonzales, Dwayne Dixon, Martín Sorrondeguy, Alice Bag, Miriam Klein Stahl, Ron Scapp, Kadijah Means, Mimi Nguyen, Murad Tamini, Yvette Felarca, Jessica Mills, and others, all of whom are unified against oppression and readily use their classrooms to fight for human liberation, social justice, systemic change, and true equality.

Royalties will be donated to Teachers 4 Social Justice: t4sj.org

"*Teaching Resistance brings us the voices of activist educators who are fighting back inside and outside of the classroom. The punk rock spirit of this collection of concise, hard-hitting essays is bound to stir up trouble.*"
—Mark Bray, historian, author of *Antifa: The Anti-Fascist Handbook* and coeditor of *Anarchist Education and the Modern School: A Francisco Ferrer Reader*

"*Where was* Teaching Resistance *when I was in school? This essay collection both makes a compelling case for why radical classrooms are necessary and lays out how they can be put into practice. A perfect guide for educators and anyone working with young people, this book vitally also speaks to the student's experience. Even for the kid-adverse activists among us,* Teaching Resistance *reminds us that kids can be our comrades if we meet them halfway. The younger generations deserve more from us— this is the primer for how to start providing it.*"
—Shawna Potter, singer for War on Women, author of *Making Spaces Safer*